The
Self-Defence Manual

David Birdsall
and Martin Dougherty

summersdale

Summersdale Publishers Ltd
46 West Street
Chichester
West Sussex
PO19 1RP
UK

www.summersdale.com

Printed and bound in Great Britain

ISBN 1 84024 227 2

Photos by Nate Zettle

About the Authors

David Birdsall (left, cheerful) is a qualified sports therapist. As the senior technical coach of Nihon Tai-jitsu GB, which is pending status as governing body for the Nihon tai-jitsu martial art, he teaches self-defence seminars across the United Kingdom. Past experience includes boxing, kick boxing, Wado Ryu karate, and he currently teaches tai-jitsu, ju-jitsu and aiki-jitsu. He has participated in security work at large public venues and conference centres throughout the world for a number of years. This work included venue security, evacuation liaison, front-of-house security, backstage security and personal VIP security at venues.

Martin J. Dougherty (right, surly) freelances in the defence and security fields and has addressed major international conferences on security issues. He trains in Nihon tai-jitsu with David and has studied judo, karate, jeet kune do and ju-jitsu. He is also a fencing instructor. Martin's other publications include novels, games, non-fiction and technical material as well as strategic reports for the defence industry.

A Note on the Photos

The people in the photos are (mostly) not martial artists as such. Most of them are members of various Nihon tai-jitsu clubs or the University of Sunderland Fencing Club who happened to be available when we were taking the photos. This was a deliberate policy on our part – most readers will not be martial artists, so we avoided a martial arts approach to the demonstrations. Only one of our demonstrators holds a black belt; some have never trained in a martial art at all. These are real, ordinary people who have learned to use the techniques mentioned in this book. If they can do it, you can too!

Some of the photos are intended to illustrate a general point. Most demonstrate a specific technique. The choice of 'aggressor' and 'defender' is not intended in any way to suggest that persons of a particular height, gender, ethnic origin, mode of dress or any other arbitrary characteristic are likely to be attackers, or to be attacked. Note also that all the techniques in this book are *universal*, i.e. they can be used by anyone of any height or build, though common sense suggests that extreme differences in size will make some options unworkable.

Disclaimer

Everything in this book is intended for the use of decent, well-intentioned people interested in preserving their own safety and that of others. The authors are strongly opposed to the use of violence except as a last resort for self-defence purposes. No liability can be accepted for the misuse of the defensive techniques presented in this book. Comments on the use of weapons are intended to facilitate understanding of how an attack might be made and how to defend against it, and should be viewed in that light. Theoretical assailants in the book are generally referred to as men. This reflects the reality that the majority of potential attackers are male. No sexism or other prejudice is implied or should be inferred from any statement in this book.

Lastly, we are not out to put anyone down or to be disrespectful to any martial art or fighting style. We recognise their merits and the long hours of hard training involved. We are well aware that the various martial arts all have a lot to offer – we have trained in many of them! However, we do sincerely believe that for the great majority of people, the methods in this book are the best option.

Dedication

We owe a great debt of thanks to the people that made this work possible:

To our families and friends, who for some reason continue to put up with us when we're difficult to live with.

To the students at the Sunderland and Billingham clubs.

To the people who taught us, trained with us, inspired us, and only occasionally hurt us.

To the people who helped out with the photos and otherwise made the production possible; especially those who came back again and again to help: Craig, Ian, Mary, Mike and Rachel, and the ones who would have been there if they could.

We made it in the end, and it's thanks to you.

Special thanks are owed to two very generous individuals:

To Geoff Thompson, for kind permission to steal his work on the fence.

To Nate Zettle, for photography, advice and the occasional bust lip.

But if we must dedicate this book, then it has to be to the person who needs it. To someone who would take charge of their life and be a little safer if they could. Someone smart enough to know that our world is a dangerous place, and courageous enough to take responsibility for their own safety. Someone who will use our humble book wisely and well, avoiding violence yet prepared to defend against it.

This is the person for whom we wrote this book, and it is to whom it is dedicated.

Who is this person?

It's you – if you want it to be.

Contents

Part V: Self-Defence Techniques

Foreword

It would be fair to say that I have spent the last thirty-odd years of my life studying different methods of self-protection, right from school where the bullies made my days very long and very sad to the present day. I thought that the bullying might end with the last bell of my schooling years; I was wrong. It continued into the work place, the pub bar, the football match, in fact, every aspect of life – hell, even life itself – seemed laced with intimidation. I blamed everyone and everything (even God, who I abandoned on more than one occasion) for my dilemma. Then one day I put my honest head on and admitted that, actually, it was nobody's fault but my own. People bullied me because I let them. Situations intimidated me because I quaked helplessly in my boots and thus encouraged my fears. Life walked over me because I lay down on the floor and let it.

Once I took responsibility for myself and for my place on this spinning planet – and listen in, unless you do take responsibility for your own safety you will always be somebody's whipping boy – things started to turn around, and my habitat and my cohorts suddenly started to take on a healthier hue. I started to get respect from people, because I demanded no less. I developed the art of invisibility; because of my confidence (developed over many years in the forging grounds of hard martial arts), people no longer saw me as a victim.

The big problem for me as a younger man was choosing the right kind of training to prepare me for an unsolicited attack, one that would likely eclipse the formulaic norms of dojo fighting. In my life-long search, I studied many arts – I would go as far as to say most. I even spent ten years working as a nightclub doorman to fine-tune what I had learned. I had hundreds of fights, I damaged a multitude of people who got in my way and at the end of it all, after the murder and mayhem, the punching and stamping, the harm and the hate I came to the same conclusion as the authors of this excellent tome: self defence at its very best does not involve a physical response, rather it is about understanding the (so-called) enemy so that we can avoid him, escape him, verbally dissuade him, loop-hole, posture – anything to avoid a physical response because violence is, and has to be, a very last resort.

An analogy: preparing people to defend themselves is a little like teaching children road safety. We don't instruct our kids in the fine art of first aid just in case a car hits them, we teach them awareness and the Green Cross Code so that they can avoid it in the first place. Because we all know that once they've been knocked over, it is too late. For most people (even many of the so-called 'trained martial artists') being attacked in the street is like being knocked over by a car: many of the victims are debilitatingly injured and mentally traumatised, most never completely recover. Some of the less fortunate die because of their injuries.

That's what I love about this book. It is not the usual gung-ho, thumb-lock and shoulder throw technique boutique of old; it is a mature, intelligent, comprehensive and life-saving manual on how to avoid becoming the next victim of an unsolicited assault.

As well as covering pre-fight strategies, everything from violent body language to attack precursors, the book also covers what to do if a physical response is called for, with the added and sensible advice that the techniques are unlikely to work unless you spend a long time practising them.

So we have the pre-fight (how to avoid an assailant), the in-fight (the stuff that will work in the street as opposed to in a James Bond movie) and a very comprehensive look at post-fight – how you stand with regard to the law if you should injure your attacker in the course of defending yourself.

There is so much in this book that I could probably write another book just telling you about it. I won't do that. It's enough to say that this is a fabulous book, very well written and researched. I highly recommend both the book and its authors.

You know what they say (whoever 'they' are): 'If you want to stay safe, be informed.' I can think of no better way of being informed that this excellent book.

Geoff Thompson
Coventry England, 2002

Introduction

This is not a book about fighting. Indeed, most of it is about finding ways of not fighting, not having to fight, and (best of all) not being in a situation where there is any threat of violence at all. True, later sections do deal with the mechanics of violent self-defence, and many readers will have already skipped there to see what's on offer. This book, however, is for those whose primary interest is in staying or getting out of trouble *without* violence.

This book is intended for the use of anyone and everyone who goes in harm's way (or who feels that harm may come to visit uninvited). In particular it will be of interest to children, students, women, the elderly and people with occupations that place them at increased risk. Increased-risk occupations include healthcare providers, members of the emergency services, taxi drivers, bar and shop staff, council employees, teachers and anyone else whose occupation takes them out alone or places them in situations where confrontations may occur.

The measures in this book will work for anyone, and everyone can benefit from increased personal security. Even people sure that they can 'handle themselves' are wise to avoid trouble if they can. The unfortunate reality is that violence of any sort can have unexpected and very unpleasant consequences, even if you 'win' the fight. It is truly better not to get involved in violence at all. Most people believe that they have no choice in the matter; either they will be attacked or they won't. Some are certain that it will never happen to them. Both of these views are wrong, as we will show. For now, two facts:

- It *can* happen to you.
- It doesn't have to.

This book asks one thing of you: that you embrace a measure of reality. Nobody is suggesting that you should become paranoid or live in constant fear, but in order to reduce the risk of attack (and you can!), you must first accept that an attack can happen, and that it will be very nasty indeed if it does. In return, this book will show you a series of simple measures that will greatly increase your personal safety.

You will learn not only how to avoid trouble altogether, but how to get out of a confrontation without coming to blows, how to escape from someone who means you harm, and what you are legally allowed to do to prevent someone from hurting you. Later sections do detail some violent defensive measures you can take, but they are a last resort; part of a package of measures that should prevent it from ever coming to that.

Think of these measures as a series of ever-finer filters. One filter will let some dirt through, but stop most of it. Another catches most of what is left. Our system has five 'layers' of filters. The first layer prevents most situations from becoming a threat. The second nullifies most of what slips through the first, and the third deals with most of what remains. Only a tiny proportion of threats actually reach the fourth and fifth layers of our defences.

By layering defences in this way, you can weed out a huge proportion of potentially dangerous situations. But what are these 'filters'? How do you create them? How do they work?

That is what the rest of the book is about.

Part I: First Things First

What is Self-Protection?

Everyone knows that self-defence is a matter of learning a few simple strikes and grappling techniques so that you can disable or escape from an attacker. Sadly, everyone who knows that is wrong. Self-defence begins with *you*; the process of protecting yourself begins long before a confrontation develops. However, the term has acquired certain connotations that can make its use misleading.

Words like 'self-defence' mean different things to different people, so we will draw a distinction between self-defence and self-protection for the sake of clarity.

- 'Self-defence' refers to the skills of fighting, evasion and fleeing that are used to thwart an attack that is imminent or already taking place.

- 'Self-protection' encompasses many layers, one of which is the act of self-defence. Self-protection also includes alertness, target hardening, confrontation management and a host of other skills used to avoid, deter or prevent attacks – or to deal with them if they do happen.

Self-protection is about acknowledging that there is a risk of attack, weighing it, and acting accordingly. That is not to say that you should be afraid. You have every right not to be. What you should be is *aware*. Aware of the dangers, aware of what you can do about them, aware that you are worth protecting and aware that you know *how* to protect yourself. There are many layers to self-protection. Defeating a physical assault is the final stage in the process of self-protection when all other measures have failed.

Self-protection begins when you take the (rather intimidating) step of admitting that there are people out there who may choose to attack you. From there it is a small step to analysing how, when and why they might do that, and taking steps to reduce the risks. Fighting (or 'self-defence') skills, and tools such as rape alarms, fall into the category of back-up plans; they are there if you need them, but it's much, *much* better not to have to use them.

Alertness Codes

The level of alertness an individual exhibits can be classified according to a colour code that is used by the armed forces and by many self-defence writers. The colour code looks like this:

- **Code White:** Oblivious of threats and totally unprepared for trouble. It is usually obvious you are Code White, and many potential assailants are more likely to attack you if you display this kind of behaviour. You won't see an attack coming, won't be able to react until too late, and your reaction will be panicky. Code White can be caused by preoccupation with other things, alcohol or complacency. Whatever the cause, it can be fatal. Code White is not the place to be, ever.

- **Code Yellow:** Alert for threats, looking around, conscious of dark shadows, lonely places, dangerous people, yet not stressed by it all. Someone who is Code Yellow will take sensible precautions to preserve their safety, and their preparedness will show; many potential assailants will look elsewhere for a softer target. If you are attacked while Code Yellow, you will react more effectively and won't be caught by surprise. Code Yellow is the state of habitual awareness we should all cultivate until it requires no effort to maintain.

- **Code Orange:** Under threat, ready to respond. Suspicious or threatening circumstances will cause alert people to move up to Code Orange; they are in balance, ready to back off, fight or run as needed. Code Orange preparations can be quite subtle and can be concealed, or they may be quite open to act as a deterrent. Either way, someone who is Code Orange is ready to react if necessary, but calmly, and without doing anything to precipitate violence in a situation that might yet be salvaged.

- **Code Red:** Violence is imminent. Someone who is Code Red is ready. Their senses are tuned for the first threatening movement or the crossing of their defence threshold, whereupon they will have no choice but to fight or run. Code Red is tiring and stressful. Many people go Code Red in response to threats that aren't very serious – often straight from White to Red. Experience and understanding allows an individual to maintain a less stressful Orange or Yellow posture until there is a real threat, yet remain just as able to respond.

The Right to Go Home Alive

You are a unique individual. You may be pretty dissatisfied with some aspects of your life, but it's yours. You have the right to go on living it; to make the best of your life that you can. Nobody has the right to intrude into that life or to take it away from you.

When someone goes out in search of a victim, they are usually looking for just that. Not a fair fight, not even a major risk. They're looking for someone they can frighten, intimidate and hurt with relative impunity. Those young men across the street may be good people, but it's equally possible that they are looking you over, trying to decide if you are a victim. And believe it or not, you do have some choice as to whether you become one. One of the key concepts in self-protection can be explained by the 'crime triangle'. For any crime to take place you need:

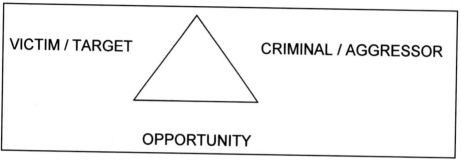

If any of the three is removed, then no crime can take place. An attacker, of course, brings himself and his willingness to attack you to the situation. You have at least some control over the other two sides of the triangle. By your actions and habits you can ensure that a potential attacker is presented with few opportunities to carry out his attack. If at all possible, you should try to ensure that the 'crime triangle' remains incomplete by implementing the avoidance, deterrence and evasion measures discussed later in this book. Simply put, this means that if you aren't there, you can't be attacked. Even if you and a potential attacker are both in the same place, there may not be an opportunity to attack you on the terms that he wants.

Depriving him of an opportunity can be as simple as making sure you can see him, not turning your back, being aware of your surroundings or determinedly maintaining your personal space.

Even if the triangle is completed, an attack is by no means a certainty. Whether you are subjected to violence or not depends upon his willingness to attack you. You do have a small measure of control over this as you can manipulate the situation or his perception of it to reduce the possibility of attack – but only if you know how to do it!

- Often the deciding factor in whether or not you get attacked is how you handle the situation.

For example, if you are facing a threatening situation and you behave like a victim – that is, you show fear and generally fit into the potential assailant's 'script' for events – then you are more likely to be attacked than someone who acts calmly and confidently and breaks the 'script'. It might seem that faced with three tough-looking thugs, you have little choice in the matter, but in fact you do.

Preparation plays an important part. Knowing that you have at least some idea of what to do when under attack can be a great help when putting on an Oscar-winning performance of confident assurance. But there are other factors too.

A large proportion of attacks occur while the victim is doing something that they know isn't very smart. Shortcuts down dark alleys are never a good idea, yet people take them. Sometimes the victim realises that a situation is sliding out of control, but is afraid that walking away would mean accepting derision and ridicule from the potential assailant. Later, they are treated in hospital for injuries that make a few harsh words seem rather trivial. (The authors have, unfortunately, both been involved in a certain amount of 'unscheduled field research' and can assure you that harsh words are *always* rather trivial when compared to physical injury!)

Most lamentable of all: someone who knows an attack is about to take place chooses not to assume a defensive posture (mental or physical) because they are embarrassed to, or because they simply cannot believe that this is happening to them. Caught flat-footed and mentally out of gear, they are an easy target. These things happen all the time, yet they are so easily avoided.

Cutting through this alley saves a whole two minutes. Is it worth it?

It is easy to become drawn into the attacker's chosen 'script' for events, or to find yourself being railroaded into going along with something that does not feel right. People sometimes place themselves in extreme danger simply because they are embarrassed to cross the road, assume a defensive stance, ask for help, or just tell a stranger that they are uncomfortable and would like to be left alone.

In order to assure your safety, you must not be embarrassed to take simple defensive measures. Most decent people will respect you for bluntly stating that you don't want to go with them – and most would be upset and apologetic at having made you nervous. Thugs might not be pleased, but they will probably decide to look for an easier victim, and if they do decide to go for you, at least your position is better than if you'd let them take you where they wanted to go.

There are less obvious alternatives to the fists-up fighting stance, which will be discussed later, but for now remember that assuming a fighting stance is *not* overreacting if you perceive a real threat to your safety. Anyone who wants to make fun of you for being ready to defend yourself is welcome to; they are either an idiot or a potential victim. Your life is too precious to be risked because of what someone else might think of what you are doing.

Rage leads to stupidity – never lose your temper. However, an edge of irritation or annoyance can give you the courage to break out of a situation or to act decisively. You are a special, unique, worthwhile person. The idea that someone might try to take that away from you should be enough to provoke some anger. A healthy annoyance at your potential assailant should give you the courage to assume a defensive stance and make it very clear that you are no victim. They may still try, of course, but the fact that an attacker will have to pay for interfering in your life might just be enough to make them back off. You have the right to go home alive and unhurt. Assert it.

Self-Defence and the Law

Many people have no real idea of what is, and what is not, legal in self-defence. Many of those who do 'know' are wrong. The law is a complex business and is subject to interpretation in a manner that sometimes defies the understanding of laypeople. However, legal cases and statements by prominent legal officials have made certain things very clear, and that is enough for our purposes.

Fighting is not legal. Exchanging blows outside a pub or a football stadium over a difference of opinion or an unkind word is against the law – nor is it acceptable conduct in a civilised society. Self-defence is a different matter. In an ideal world it would simply not be necessary, but this is not an ideal world. Sometimes violence is thrust upon us, and the only option is to meet it in kind. Therefore, the law recognises that sometimes an individual may have to resort to violent means to preserve their safety, and that within certain limits this is acceptable conduct, both legally and morally.

The authors strongly advocate that everyone should obtain at the very least some basic self-defence training; however, we do not suggest that anyone should, or needs to, 'learn to fight'.

- Self-defence is not the same thing as fighting.

Fighting is mutual combat; self-defence involves repelling an assault or protecting another individual. Winning the fight is a means to an end, not a goal in itself. Your goal is to escape the situation without being hurt, not to batter someone. Once you have an alternative to continued violence, you should take it! To put that another way, your goal is to:

- Create a window of opportunity so you can escape.

Any self-defence or martial arts training you undertake should be directed at this goal, and any self-defence actions you take should serve the same purpose. The only reason for continuing to fight is the lack of an alternative. This is not merely our opinion; it is also the gist of self-defence law in Britain.

Your Rights and Duties

Firstly, and most importantly for our purposes, you do have the right to defend yourself and the people around you, using force if necessary. You also have the right to protect property, but this is not a factor here for reasons that will become clear as we progress.

The law recognises that a person who is under attack, or honestly believes that he or she – or someone nearby – is about to be attacked, has the right to use 'reasonable force' to prevent or halt the attack. To quote Lord Griffith (1988): 'If no more force is used than is reasonable to repel the attack, such force is not unlawful and no crime is committed.'

The amount of force that is 'reasonable' will be discussed shortly. The important factor is that, subject to certain limitations:

- It is not a crime to defend yourself using reasonable force.

The law also recognises that a person under attack cannot precisely calculate the absolute minimum force required to halt the attack, nor can an ordinary civilian be expected to apply such minimum force effectively.

- There is no 'Principle of Minimum Force'.

The law recognises that it is not wise to wait for an assailant to actually attack you. As long as you have been given very clear reason to believe that an attack is imminent, and you cannot otherwise resolve the situation (say by withdrawing), then you may attack pre-emptively. Similarly, you do not need to be attacked yourself to be justified in responding with violence. If an attack is underway or is obviously imminent on any person nearby, you are legally allowed to use violence to prevent or to halt this attack.

- Striking first is not a crime.

Again, quoting Lord Griffith (1988), a person 'about to be attacked does not have to wait for his assailant to strike the first blow or fire the first shot, circumstances may justify a pre-emptive strike'.

However, if a pre-emptive strike takes place you are not allowed to strike maliciously or vindictively to get revenge after the danger has passed.

Most street attackers throw huge, slow punches. If you are alert you may be able to snap a fast jab into his face before his attack gets going.

The law even recognises that at times it may be necessary to use a weapon or instrument to protect yourself. This is, as always, governed by the concept of 'reasonable force'.

If you honestly feel that you are under sufficient threat as to warrant an armed response, the law permits you to provide yourself with some kind of weapon or instrument. However, while you may choose to obtain a weapon in response to a clear and imminent threat, it is not justifiable to arm yourself 'just in case' or to habitually go armed.

In addition, you are never justified in possessing a weapon for use in self-defence if the situation requiring its use is of your own making. That is to say, if you have been given reason to fear that someone might come to you with violent intent, then you may pick up or otherwise obtain a weapon. If, on the other hand, you go to confront someone and take a weapon along because you suspect that they may become violent, then this is very definitely not lawful. You are *creating* a situation in which you may have to use the weapon rather than attempting to avoid the possibility of violence or protect yourself from it.

- You are permitted to arm yourself if necessary, but only in response to a clear and serious threat.

Just reading the bullet points and ignoring the supporting text gives the (incorrect) picture that it is all right to go around hitting people who you think might be a threat or who are committing a crime. This is *absolutely not the case!* Vigilantism is not acceptable in law or in society.

Self-defence with Illegal Weapons

A contradiction occurs when a person obtains a weapon that is prohibited by law for use in self-defence. For example, it is illegal to own firearms or 'combat' knives in Britain, yet if the threat was sufficient then you would be justified in using one to defend yourself.

The issue is clear if the weapon is brought into the equation by your assailant, since you are likely to obtain such an instrument only by being attacked with it. If you manage to disarm someone who is trying to kill you with a weapon and he attempts to take it back or produces another lethal implement, then your use of the weapon will probably be a matter of reasonable force. This is also the situation if you are attacked in your home with a lethal weapon and grab a carving knife or a similar quite legal, but deadly, object to protect yourself.

But what of a situation where you feel that you are about to be attacked by armed individuals and that the only effective response is to obtain an illegal weapon? This is a difficult situation. Certainly under normal circumstances you could be charged with a criminal offence for possessing such a weapon. But what if you had obtained it in response to a clear and imminent threat?

A case in 1983 offers some clarification of this point. During a period of extensive rioting, fearing for his safety, a shopkeeper made a number of petrol bombs and stored them in his shop. The case went to the Court of Appeal, where it was decided that the use of petrol bombs might have constituted 'reasonable force' under the circumstances of the expected attack, and that therefore the shopkeeper possessed the weapons for 'a lawful object'.

Petrol bombs are, of course, illegal under British law. The court's view was that it was lawful to make and store such a weapon because the individual has the right to prepare to repel an attack, as long as its use is in keeping with the principle of reasonable force. However, it is important to note that the court stressed that the threat *must* be imminent.

Therefore, in the face of an imminent and serious threat, obtaining a weapon specifically prohibited under law may be considered a necessary act of self-defence. Readers are advised to be *extremely* careful however; this is the absolute outer fringe of legal self-defence, and the outcome of a court case is in no way certain.

It is obvious that a person *does* have the right to use violent means in self-defence, and to use as much force as is necessary to stop the attack. You may be called upon to justify your actions in court, especially if you used a weapon or injured someone badly. However, a wise man once said that it is better to be tried by twelve than carried by six, and if you can show that you acted in good faith and conscience, out of concern for your safety or that of others, then the law is firmly on your side.

You do have certain duties imposed by law. First, and most importantly, you are required to remain within the bounds of common law. An attack on your person is not considered in any way to be 'special circumstances'. There are laws governing what you may and may not do, and you must adhere to them.

Secondly, you are required to take reasonable steps to ensure the safety of your assailant once he is no longer a threat. This means that if you seriously injure someone or render them unconscious, you must summon medical assistance. If possible, you should render first aid, but not if this would place you in additional danger. It is perfectly acceptable to flee the scene of the attack and call for an ambulance from a safe distance a few minutes later if remaining there would place you in danger.

Finally, you are also expected to inform the police of any incident where injury occurred. You may think that this is unwise, since it draws attention to the fact that you have hurt someone, but in fact it works in your favour, *providing you remained within the law and the bounds of reasonable force.* By reporting the matter to the police you are acting as a responsible citizen, something that criminals rarely do. If, for any reason, there are legal complications and the police do become involved, your statement is already on record and your correct behaviour noted. This can be very important if your assailant becomes involved in another fight later, and is injured, or if there is an attempt to cast doubt on your character.

Some 'duties' commonly believed to exist are in fact myths. Specifically,

- You do not have a duty to warn an assailant of your skills.
- There is no 'duty to retreat'.

The first case applies to martial artists and other trained people. Many believe that they are required to warn an assailant of their capabilities before using their skills. This is simply not true. A trained person is subject to exactly the same laws and duties as everyone else – and no more. A warning may or may not be a useful deterrent. Some assailants may decide to look for trouble elsewhere if you tell them about your training. Many will not believe you, and some will attack just to prove their superiority. Issuing a warning is something that you can choose to do if it seems useful, but it is in no way a requirement.

The 'duty to retreat' is a common misconception. Many people think that you are required by law to disengage, withdraw or temporise if at all possible. You are not. If your actions are judged in court, it will do your case good to be able to show that you made every effort to avoid conflict. Of course, if it is clear that you accepted combat when an alternative resolution was available, then you will not have acted in self-defence. But you are not actually *required* to retreat.

There are times when attempting to withdraw might place you in greater danger, say, by taking you out of a public place or distancing you from the safety of your car. On other occasions withdrawal may be impossible; for example, if you are attacked suddenly or are attempting to render assistance to a person under attack. There are many circumstances where you can legally engage in violent self-defence without attempting to 'disengage, withdraw or temporise', though as a rule you should *always* seek to avoid conflict if you possibly can.

Reasonable and Necessary Force

Sometimes there is no alternative but to use violent means to defend yourself. The law in most countries is much the same in that it recognises that an individual has the right to use 'reasonable and necessary force' to protect their own safety and that of the people around them. Reasonable force is also permitted in defence of property, but common sense must be applied here. There is little in your wallet or home worth being killed – or killing someone – for, and it could be argued that by violently opposing a burglar or other criminal you are deliberately and unnecessarily creating a situation where violence will probably ensue.

In summary, reasonable force may be used to:

- Defend yourself.
- Defend others.
- Protect property.
- Make a citizen's arrest or to assist police officers in making an arrest.

Exactly what constitutes reasonable force is open to debate, and it is sadly true that there have been some horrible travesties of justice. However, in the vast majority of cases common sense wins out. Interpretation of reasonable force depends on several factors:

- The gravity of the crime you were trying to prevent.
- Whether it was possible to prevent it by non-violent means.
- Whether you were ready to try those means first.
- The relative strength of the parties involved.

It is generally recognised that an individual suddenly coming under attack cannot be expected to gauge and apply the precise minimum of force necessary to end the assault. Someone who is attacked is not responsible for bringing about that state of affairs; they are instead forced to take whatever violent measures they must in support of their recognised right to protect their own safety.

This is an important factor. In Britain (and most other places worldwide):

• a person is responsible for their own safety.

While society does its best to create a safe environment for you to live in through the exercise of law and its enforcement by the police force, it is not directly responsible for protecting you at every moment, nor are the police responsible for your personal security (though any police officer will do his or her utmost to protect members of the public).

The person responsible for your safety is *you*. You are responsible for taking sensible self-protection measures, for staying away from dangerous people and places, and for removing yourself from danger. If you find yourself under attack, you may or may not have failed in this responsibility, depending upon circumstances, but you cannot blame anyone else (except the person intent upon attacking you). The final step in taking responsibility for your safety is active self-defence. You have the right to defend yourself and the responsibility both for doing so and for the ensuing consequences.

Be aware that although a violent criminal intent upon attacking you has chosen to step outside the rules and laws governing behaviour in our society, you are still subject to them. That said, do not be concerned with thoughts like 'people would not approve if I used violence' when under attack. Our society has laws and codes in place to guide our behaviour within civilised norms. However, if you are attacked then that system has failed to protect you and you are thrown back on your own resources.

In this situation, you have been dragged into the world of the violent criminal. Trying to behave 'in a civilised manner' in these circumstances can get you hurt or killed, so you must forget about ideals like 'never strike first' or 'violence solves nothing' and do whatever you must to escape the situation.

You must match the threat with appropriate measures – however violent – and you must not hold back. If your life is in danger and the only way to preserve yourself is to cripple, blind or even kill someone, then that is what you must do. That, or choose to die – and our society has no right to expect you to do that! Violent criminals have little remorse and no honour. You must win (or at least gain enough of a victory to escape) or they will do whatever they please to you.

The law understands this. As long as you do not cease to act like a decent, reasonable citizen, then you are in the right. It is all but impossible to clearly define what level of force is 'reasonable' to fit all possible sets of circumstances, but if an attacker (or group of attackers) is clearly intent on doing something likely to result in death or permanent harm, then a considerable level of force is justifiable.

Where someone poses a relatively minor level of threat, an attempt at restraint is all that is reasonable. However, it is important to understand that restraint will rarely work against a very violent, determined individual. It sometimes takes four or more trained police officers to restrain a struggling suspect, so common sense must be applied.

In essence, you have the right to use *necessary* as well as *reasonable* force. You are not required to place yourself at unreasonable risk by remaining constrained by 'rules of engagement' forbidding, say, punches to the head, or any such thing. You may do what you honestly believe is necessary to end the assault. And no more.

If your response is judged by a court, then an attempt will be made to establish the reasonableness of your response. The reasonableness of the level of force used is judged objectively. That is, *your* opinion of how much force was necessary is not the one that counts. There is an accepted level of force associated with any given set of circumstances, and if you did not remain within those limits, then you will be found to have acted unlawfully.

However, where your opinion does matter is in the assessment of the circumstances that prevailed. A court will judge your response as reasonable or not based upon the circumstances as *you* perceived them. Thus while you are not permitted to use whatever degree of force you feel like, you *are* permitted to use a degree of force appropriate to the threat that you thought existed.

This has two important ramifications. First of all, it means that if you honestly believed that you were under, or about to come under, attack, and acted to protect yourself, then you have not committed a crime even if you were mistaken in that belief.

Secondly, it means that your assessment of the situation – probably made in a split second as violence erupted in your face – is used to judge the reasonableness of your response. The law recognises that a person under sudden and violent attack does not have complete information on the situation, nor time to determine the exact level of threat.

- The reasonableness of your response is judged based on the situation as *you* perceived it at the time.

As you can see, common sense and your judgement of the situation are highly important. Many common questions can be answered by considering the matter in this light. Is it acceptable to kick someone who's on the ground? No – NEVER – if he seems to be staying there, or is trying to protect himself, escape or is otherwise no continued threat to you. But if he's getting up to come back at you? Maybe, if you are sure he still poses a threat to you. If you'd be in serious danger when he regained his feet, then you are justified in making sure he does not, in exactly the same way as you are allowed to strike pre-emptively. But you *must* stop your attack as soon as your assailant is no longer a threat.

- If you carry on attacking someone who is no longer a threat to you, you become the aggressor, and therefore a violent criminal.

In truth, reasonable force need only be an issue for you if you are a trained martial artist or an experienced fighter of some other kind, or if you have a weapon to hand. If you have the skills to deal out a range of 'degrees of harm' then you will have to think about what is reasonable under the circumstances. For an ordinary person, the issue is in fact rather simpler.

For a start, you will instinctively estimate the threat level, based on your own capabilities and those you ascribe to your opponent(s). You will know whether you need to grab a weapon, strike out or just push someone away.

Secondly, you (as an untrained person) will have some difficulty dealing out sufficient (necessary) force, let alone excessive violence. You are almost certain to be overmatched physically or in terms of numbers or weapons.

Thirdly, you are a human being with a conscience, morals and a sense of justice. You know what is wrong; you are opposed to hurting people and wouldn't do it if there was an alternative. As long as you do not give in to outrage, panic or anger, you will not lose your humanity and thus you *will* know when to stop! Your most likely problem, as an ordinary person, is not avoiding excessive violence, but using enough force to halt the attacker.

That point is worth repeating. As long as you do not allow fear and anger to turn you into a monster, you need not worry too much about using reasonable force. Simply allow your conscience and common sense – your basic humanity – to guide you. You will know what you need to do, and you will know when to stop.

It really is this simple:

- Fight as hard as you need to.
- Stop when it's over.

This depends heavily on not allowing fear or anger to take control of your actions. We have all heard of people 'losing it' and describing the loss of self-control as 'I just saw red!' Getting the balance right takes time. Attending self-defence courses generates a certain amount of familiarity with the situation and with appropriate responses, thus reducing the fear factor. With even fairly basic training, you are more likely to remain in control.

One of the main benefits of self-defence training is that you will develop an understanding of force levels and the ability to remain calm while under attack. With suitable training, you are not only more able to deal out force to an attacker, but are actually less likely to use excessive force. Provided you do not get your training at the Headcase School of Street Thuggery, the defences you learn will be effective yet flexible enough to allow a measured response. Another hidden benefit comes to light if you ever do end up in court. You will be able to answer questions about your actions in an informed manner, and most importantly, will be able to refute allegations of excess force by saying that 'Yes, I do know restraint techniques, and I am sufficiently skilled to understand that attempting to use such an approach would, in this case, not have been appropriate.'

In short, your training will allow you to show that you chose your actions in an informed manner, calmly, and as were appropriate to the situation you perceived, in addition, of course, to rendering you capable of taking such actions.

There are, of course, several things that you simply must not do in a self-defence situation. For the sake of clarity we will spell them out. You must not:

- Habitually carry a weapon, even if only for self-defence.
- Enter into a violent situation unless you have no alternative.
- Carry on fighting when you could escape instead.
- Carry on attacking once it is clear that you are no longer in danger.
- Kick or beat a helpless person on the ground.
- Deliberately use lethal force except as a last resort.

Remember that in most cases of self-defence, there is no legal involvement and even if the police become involved, they will make a judgement as to whether legal proceedings should be undertaken. If it is clear that you acted as a reasonable, responsible citizen within the bounds of necessary force, then there has been no crime (on your part) and it is extremely unlikely that charges will be brought against you.

This is particularly true if you can demonstrate that you tried to avoid or defuse the incident, then acted only in self-defence, even going so far as to summon medical assistance for your injured assailant. Remember also that the average street thug holds the police in contempt. He is unlikely to attempt legal redress if he is hurt by his intended victim.

Thoughts of courtrooms and juries should not be foremost in your mind while defending yourself. Be aware of the need to use only necessary force, but don't hold back from doing what you must. It is better to explain to a police officer or a court why you were forced to harm someone than to be killed because you were unwilling to resist effectively or – worse – because you feared you might be punished for it. Remember you have the right to use '*all reasonable and necessary force*'.

You must also be true to your own humanity when defending yourself. You will have to live with whatever you do, and even if you think your assailant was 'just criminal scum who deserved what they got', you diminish yourself by becoming a violent animal.

- The thing that makes you better than your attacker is that you remain a decent person, doing what you must … but no more.

Pushes, Shoves and Slaps

You'd be quite justified in pushing someone away if they were very close to you and you didn't like what they were doing. But unless they were a real threat, you wouldn't be justified in hitting them. If they resist or barge back into your personal space, then they are using force and a more robust response is justified.

A slap is an assault – you have the right to press charges against someone who slaps you. But if that's all they do, then you don't have the right to hit back – that's fighting, not self-defence. If they continue to be a threat then yes, you can resist as vigorously as necessary. But the response must be appropriate to the threat you perceive. If the threat is a stinging slap then you're not justified in responding with a knockout punch.

Carrying a Weapon

The law recognises that a person who has reason to fear attack may arm him- or herself, and that this constitutes self-defence providing the weapon was obtained in response to a clear and present threat. This law does not allow you to carry weapons 'just in case' or when going out somewhere 'that seems a bit dodgy'.

The use of a weapon must also be reasonable. If attacked by superior numbers, with weapons, or by an opponent who obviously overmatches your strength, then grabbing a weapon may be nothing more than a necessary measure to ensure your survival, and thus is quite 'reasonable'. Taking a stick to someone who presents little threat or who has only offered minor violence, such as a shove or a slap, is never acceptable.

As a simple rule, if your life is in danger and you hit someone with a brick or a stick that you grabbed from the ground, you should be within the bounds of reasonable and necessary force. If you went out carrying the weapon that you used, you had better be able to show you had a reason for carrying it, because even if it was reasonable to *use* the weapon, it may not be legal to have been *carrying* it.

- The first rule of carrying a weapon for self-defence is ... don't.

If firearms or other weapons are legal for self-defence where you live, by all means get one if you feel the need. But be sure to learn how to use it effectively, or you'll just be a danger to yourself and to other innocent people. Unless a given weapon is legal in your area, don't carry it. This is especially true of knives and guns.

Knives are lethal weapons, and as such are actually very limited as self-defence tools. If you use one on someone you run a grave risk of killing them. In fact, knives are so deadly that as an untrained person, you simply do not possess the skill to avoid killing someone.

This creates an all-or-nothing situation, which can lead to hesitation on your part. Using a knife to threaten someone is pointless unless he really thinks you will use the weapon. Justifying use of a lethal implement will be difficult.

- The simplest and safest rule is *never* carry a knife.

The same comments apply to firearms of all kinds (which *are* illegally obtainable in Britain, unfortunately), with the added problem that some people will not believe that a gun is real, which again creates an all-or-nothing situation. Firearms (and imitation firearms) also tend to attract the attention of armed police, whose response is likely to be somewhat 'robust' and, assuming you do not get yourself shot, will result in criminal charges against you.

Various other implements are sold as self-defence tools or carried as weapons. Many are illegal, and in the United Kingdom carrying any implement as a weapon, even one intended purely for self-defence, is illegal. Whatever you think of that law, it is still the law and there are good reasons behind it.

There are a number of objects that can be picked up or carried quite legally that make decent weapons. These will be discussed in a later chapter. Remember, though, that if you use anything in self-defence you may have to explain why you were carrying it and why you chose to bash, stab or otherwise harm your assailant with it. Don't be caught with anything you do not have an innocent reason for carrying, and remember two vital points:

- Anything you carry as a weapon can be taken away from you and used against you.
- A weapon is no use at all unless you know how to use it – and are willing to do so.

Legal Involvement and Defence

Since criminals prefer not to operate in front of the police, most self-defence situations are over long before law enforcement officers arrive, if they ever become involved. However, let us begin with a caution – if the police do arrive in the middle of a fight, they are unlikely to be able to tell in an instant who the innocent party is. This can be important, especially if you are full of adrenaline. Police officers will try to stop more violence from happening first of all, rather than get involved in an in-depth discussion of what occurred. If you seem unwilling to stop fighting, you can expect to be restrained, and if you resist then you will have no redress if you suffer injury in the process. You will also probably face charges.

Remember that police officers are frequently assaulted in the course of their duties; far too many have been seriously injured or killed while responding to a minor incident like a fight. Officers are unlikely to take chances if your actions seem threatening to them. It is also harmful to your legal position of justifiable self-defence if you demonstrated a willingness to take on the local constabulary as well as your alleged assailant.

You must cooperate with police officers and attempt to deal with them in a calm and civilised manner. Chances are that there will be no problem here. If you are in the middle of fending off a vicious assault and help arrives, your relief and gratitude will be obvious!

What you do in front of the attending officers can be very important. You should comply with their requests and show no interest in continuing the struggle now that they are there to protect you. You may want revenge, or the attacker may have some of your property, but *it doesn't matter!* Sit on your rage and reflect on this: you could have died or been permanently injured, and that danger has now passed. Be thankful, not angry.

Attending officers will ask you questions and may caution you that what you say may be used in a court of law. Since you are likely to be in a very unbalanced state, it is possible that you may say something you later regret. It is best, therefore, to keep answers very short and to the point – and of course *truthful!* Express your willingness to make a full statement, but don't make one while you are still shocked and frightened. A statement is a matter of legal record and could land you in real trouble if not done carefully.

Remember that what you say to police officers and in any statement must be the truth. Disregarding for a moment all concerns about personal integrity and so on, it is a matter of common sense; CCTV or witnesses can show untruths for what they are, and inconsistencies in your story will probably emerge if you start to tell lies. Once you are found to have lied about what happened, your situation becomes far worse.

If you are arrested, the officers are legally obliged to tell you on what grounds. Do not resist, even if you are outraged at the injustice of it all. Provided you have acted reasonably, you will be able to prove it. You certainly have nothing to gain from creating additional charges.

If you are arrested, you are entitled to and should insist upon legal advice. The law is a complicated business and however intelligent you are, you are not qualified to conduct a satisfactory legal defence. One of the authors has actually seen someone try to do this and can attest that (in addition to the fact that the defendant was guilty and had no evidence whatsoever to the contrary) he had no chance at all in the face of an experienced and skilled prosecutor. The humiliation he received in that courtroom was probably as bad as the sentence imposed. But the simple point here is that you must take the legal advice offered, even if it is obvious that you are innocent!

Since the law *is* such a complicated business, this book will not present a detailed guide to legal defence. You will have (should the matter ever arise) a legal advisor for that purpose. There are, however, certain principles that you should be aware of ahead of time.

There are two legal defences if you hurt someone. The first is that of self-defence. This is enshrined in common law and has been explained; you exercised your right to use reasonable force in self-defence. In this case, 'self-defence' also includes protecting other people, so the common law defence can be stated as:

- A person has the right to use reasonable force to protect him- or herself or another individual from assault.

The second defence is that you were using reasonable force to prevent a crime from being committed. This is not part of the common law, but it is a statutory defence. The statutory defence can be stated as:

- A person has the right to use reasonable force to prevent the commission of a crime or to assist in the lawful arrest of a criminal.

This applies in situations where the first defence clearly does not apply, for example, where force was used to resist the theft of or damage to property, or where a bystander moved to assist police officers in making an arrest.

Note that vigilantism is not permissible in our society. The statutory defence exists primarily to protect good citizens from conviction when cooperating with the police or acting in legitimate defence of property. Readers are strongly advised not to become involved in any situation where their safety will be placed in danger unless there is an overriding need, such as to protect a vulnerable person. Property is rarely worth such a risk and is *never* worth dying for.

In any situation where you are required to account for your actions, one or both of the two defences mentioned above will apply, and your legal counsel will advise as to which is more appropriate. If you resorted to force only to protect yourself or another individual and you acted in self-defence, then it is up to the prosecution to prove beyond reasonable doubt that this was not the case. If your statement to the police was clear and to the point, and matches your observed actions, then your position is good. It may well be that the police will decide not to pursue charges, either because they agree that your actions were lawful or because they do not feel able to prove that they were not.

Even if matters still come to court, the things you said and did at the time of your arrest will stand you in good stead. Note that many people are convicted not so much on what they *did* as what they *said* to the police. So, if you are arrested and/or charged:

- Do not resist.
- Do not argue with police officers in the street.
- Do not tell friends or the media 'how it really was'.
- NEVER boast or sound like you are boasting about damaging someone, or about how he 'got what he was asking for'.
- Do not speak contemptuously of your assailant, or in any way that implies hate and rage.
- Do not be drawn into extra discussions where you might say something detrimental to your case.

But do:

- Cooperate with the police.
- Insist upon legal advice.
- LISTEN to your legal advice!
- Make a clear, short statement that spells out the facts as you perceived them.

In your statement (and in any conversation with police officers) you should not use language like 'I was terrified'; say instead, 'I was gravely concerned for my safety'. This makes it less likely that you will be accused of overreacting due to panic, and makes you sound like exactly what you are – a responsible citizen who acted in rational self-defence. Your statement should include certain critical components:

- You did not create this situation and did not react to provocation but to a real threat to your safety.
- You attempted to defuse/deter/evade the situation (if possible).
- When you resorted to physical measures, you did so with regret and as a last resort in the face of a clear and imminent threat to your safety.

- You defended yourself using only lawful and reasonable measures appropriate to the situation as you perceived it.
- You ceased your efforts as soon as you were sure the attack was over.

And provided, of course, that these things are true, then your defence should be sound.

Self-Defence Myths and Facts

There are many, many myths relating to self-defence. Many are perpetuated by action movies, others by well-meaning but uninformed or unrealistic people. A few of these myths are very dangerous, and must be dispelled.

- Violence is wrong.

Of course, hurting people is morally reprehensible. But it is *not*, and it is *never*, wrong to protect your safety and that of others in the face of attack. It is certainly wrong – not to mention rather stupid – to go out seeking trouble, but if trouble finds you then you have the right to defend yourself. If you attract comment for using violence to defend yourself, ask yourself this: in what way is it better to be raped, hospitalised or beaten to death than to respond to an attack with necessary violence?

- Martial artists and 'self-defence people' are violent thugs.

Some are, of course. Bad people can be found everywhere. But most of the people who train in the martial arts develop a deep respect for their fellow human beings. Most are decent people with jobs, homes, families and pets, just like you. Studying self-defence or a martial art is a positive activity and will no more turn a person into a thug than possessing a carving knife will make you a murderer. The discipline inherent in most martial arts is often a factor in making a person better and *less* rather than *more* violent.

- Fights happen like they do in films.

Films are staged. Those big kicks look amazing, and they can demolish the largest opponent. However, it takes a great deal of training to make them work, and even then they are simply not reliable. A kick can take you off-balance, or be so slow that you get hit before it lands. There is also the risk that you will kill your assailant with a single kick to the head. Conversely, standing in the way of big kicks or punches and blocking them with your arms works rather less well in reality than on the big screen. It is better to get out of the way of attacks and to keep your techniques simple.

Whatever you may have seen in the movies, this sort of thing is rare on the street. Even if you have trained for it, don't try it! Kick low, punch high.

- Can't happen to me.

Many people just will not believe that they might be in danger, or choose to find spurious reasons why they are perfectly safe. It requires a certain amount of moral courage to cast aside this illusion, but those who have done so and are constantly aware of the risks are far safer than those with their heads in the sand. Take this one unpleasant statistic as a challenge to the 'can't happen to me' illusion: Almost 10 per cent of reported rapes are carried out on men or boys.

- No point in resisting.

One school of thought suggests that victims should not resist in the hope that they will get off lightly. True, struggling may enrage an attacker, and in the case where there are weapons involved, you may be well advised not to resist; but always be aware that someone already engaged in hurting you is not likely to act in a humane manner. He may or may not intend to just give you a few punches or have his way and leave. It is just as likely that he will kick you on the ground or even deliberately kill you. You cannot know until it happens, and by then it may be too late to escape.

In 1989 a Home Office working group reported that people who fight back do not risk sustaining greater injury than those who don't fight. By all means judge the situation and give up property rather than risk getting hurt, but it is the opinion of the authors that if there is any chance at all that you will be successful in resisting or escaping a violent attack, then it is better to try.

- Can't hurt him.

It is hard to believe that you can do anything to harm a large, confident and violent man. However, every human being has nerve bundles and joints. It takes very little pressure to cause intense pain at a nerve point, and only 7–10 pounds of force to dislocate a joint. With very little training, even a small, weak person can apply this much force effectively enough to disable or escape from an assailant.

Gravity can also be a great ally. There are many ways to induce someone to fall, many of which involve causing him a degree of damage. Learning one or two is a worthwhile use for a few hours. And lastly, there are ways that *anyone* can be hurt. Later sections of this book will explain them in detail. For now, it is enough to say that a strike to the eyes, throat or genitals will hurt or disable the largest person. You always have a chance, but only if you are willing to act.

- He/she was asking for it.

This statement is used by rapists and people who have carried out a violent assault to justify their actions. It does not. You see, no matter how a person was dressed or what they said, he or she was *not* 'asking for it'.

The only possible justification for attacking someone is to stop them from hurting you or someone around you. No matter how insulting or offensive they are (or *you* are, but try not to be, please!), there are few words that justify attacking someone. ('I'm gonna kill you with this knife!' and similar phrases are obvious exceptions!)

As for rape, there is no possible justification. No matter what someone has done or said, the moment they say that they don't want sex, that's it. There is no middle ground here. No is no – end of discussion. Do be aware that rejection, especially rejection that seems sudden and contrary to the way you've been acting up to now, can cause hurt, resentment and anger. If someone perceives the way you are dressed or acting as a come-on, then they may be upset at being rejected. This can lead to bad places.

Be aware of this fact and ready to get out of a situation if it starts to go in a direction you don't like. Don't fuel anger and resentment by arguing, just remove yourself from danger. Protect yourself. Say no, make it clear that you mean no, and depart with as little fuss as possible.

Much the same comments apply to other assaults. Of course you have the right to walk into a pub filled with drunken fans commiserating over a 17–0 defeat wearing the shirt of the winning team, making comments about the losers' abysmal performance and to get out alive. But that doesn't mean you will.

Even if an assault is illegal, unjustifiable and morally damning, you may still be attacked if you give people what they perceive as a trigger or a reason. It doesn't matter that it shouldn't happen; it might. Be aware of this: nobody is 'asking for it', but it can still happen to you.

Self-Protection for Everyone

Everyone has the right to feel safe and to know what to do in a crisis situation. The people who are most at risk from attack are those who start out with a disadvantage. We all know who they are: lone women, children, older people. These are the ones who will be picked out as victims by an attacker who wants as little risk as possible. These are the people who start out with the greatest disadvantages. These are the people who must have the greatest awareness of danger and who should act before the situation gets out of control.

This is not to say that others should ignore the issues described in this book. Everyone is at risk; it is merely that some people are more at risk than others.

- Thugs and muggers have no sense of honour. Some people imagine that just because they are old or young, disabled or not feeling well, they will be left alone. This is a very dangerous way to think.

Increased Risk Activities

Some activities, while basically harmless and entirely normal, carry an increased risk of attack. To differentiate from high-risk behaviour, which should not be indulged in, we have grouped these activities under 'increased risk'.

It is more likely that young people will engage in these activities, rather than those with more experience, but the following comments apply to everyone.

Social gatherings, parties and dating are pretty normal activities, but these are times when the risk of attack is increased. At any good social event, you are likely to meet people you don't know very well, if at all. It is easy to assume someone is decent or harmless because they look nice or they were introduced by someone you know. It might be that the person doing the introductions has only just met this person, or doesn't know them very well, so this 'guarantee' cannot be relied upon.

In the relaxed atmosphere of a party, it is easy to get to like someone and even come to trust them, forgetting that you only know what they've told you about themselves, and you've only seen what they've shown you. This is not to say that you should never leave a party with someone you met there – you can't become a hermit, no matter how much safer you'd be. But do be aware that the persona worn in public may not be someone's real personality.

We tend to develop an impression of someone early on and do not readily change that impression, even when the signals given off by that person change quite considerably. It is thus important to watch someone's behaviour carefully the first few times you are alone with them. If it changes in a way you don't like, then you may wish to back off. As a rule, don't leave a gathering with someone unfamiliar and their friends. You might be able to deal with one person, but an ill-disposed mob will be able to overpower you easily.

Similar comments apply to dating. It's a pretty necessary part of life, but there are dangers you would be wise to avoid. Date rape is becoming increasingly common; with violence, using drugs, and the old-fashioned method of getting someone to drink too much. Currently, the most common targets for date rape in Britain are successful women in their thirties. There are several theories about why this should be, but in truth it doesn't matter. Everyone should be on their guard.

A date rapist will want you somewhere secluded and away from help if at all possible, whatever his chosen method. It is a good idea to avoid such places anyway, since there is always the danger of lurkers and the possibility that agreeing to go 'somewhere more private' might be seen as a come-on, or even as a tacit agreement to have sex. Better to go somewhere public with people around until you're sure of the person you're dating.

Also remember that a rapist may not attack you the instant you're alone. Don't ever let your guard down straight away.

- Don't trust people you've just met.
- If you do leave a gathering with someone 'new', make sure someone knows where you are going, and with whom.
- Watch for things being slipped into your drink.
- Resist attempts to get you to drink too much or take drugs.
- Be alert for changes in behaviour, especially bullying or aggressive conduct.
- Stick to public places until you're sure of the person you're dating.

Some people's jobs put them at increased risk, either by sending them to places where they may be in danger, creating confrontations, or otherwise giving people a reason to attack them. Some people (e.g. the police, security and so on) are actually employed to handle dangerous situations. They are not our primary concern here, though of course self-protection still applies to those employed to make the rest of us safer.

People such as housing officers, education welfare officers, computer engineers, plumbers, electricians, doctors and teachers who are required to make home visits are at increased risk, especially when the visit is made to address a problem. Some professions are well prepared for such situations and provide training and guidelines for people who deal with the public. Some people, however, are wholly unprepared and are sent out to deal with sensitive or confrontational situations without adequate training or back-up.

As a rule, most home visits involve a discussion, a cup of tea and an agreement on how the problem is to be dealt with. Usually the worst problem to be faced is an over-friendly dog or cat, or the unpleasant fake cream in the cake that's clearly been bought specially by people trying to be nice.

However, confrontations do sometimes develop, especially when you've gone to someone's home to tell them something they don't want to hear. It is not wise to go to a suspect location alone; most local authorities have a policy of sending officers in pairs to deal with 'difficult' individuals.

If a confrontation does develop, the important thing is to preserve your safety. If that means not delivering the information or message you came with, then so be it. Your goal is to stay safe – a summons, eviction notice or whatever can always be delivered later. Confrontation management is discussed elsewhere in this book; it should always be practised, but just as importantly you should be willing to abandon the job at hand and retreat to safety.

When out and about at work, don't focus on your job to the exclusion of your own safety. People have been attacked when leaving an amicable meeting just as often as during a confrontation. And stay on guard at all times. A female estate agent was violently raped by a man pretending to be a client. He asked to see a property she was showing, knowing that the empty building was an ideal site for his attack.

Emergency personnel – particularly A&E staff, ambulance crews and firefighters – are attacked far too often. The reasons vary, from an attempt to steal drugs from an ambulance to violent drunkenness on a Saturday night. What all these attacks have in common is their pointless stupidity. Beating up the people who are there to help others just doesn't make sense. But it happens.

If you have to place yourself in harm's way as a part of your work:

- Do not become so focused on the job at hand that you forget about your personal safety.
- Be aware that some people will deliberately set a trap. Assess the risk before you rush in.
- Be ready to summon help or to escape if a confrontation develops.
- Be willing to abandon tools or other paraphernalia if that's what it takes to stay safe.

People who work in shops, ticket offices and similar places where they have direct contact with the public are also at risk, especially if they work in an isolated location or at unusual hours.

Robbers tend to target lone cashiers at night, or managers as they open up a shop early in the morning. Other attacks are less well planned. One of the most common reasons for violence occurs when a thief is confronted. Amazingly, many shops expect their staff – entirely untrained – to confront, restrain or otherwise deal with thieves or people making a nuisance of themselves in the store. This is obviously a very bad idea, but it is hard for staff to say no when a manager informs them that it is part of their duties to do so. Of course, shops and other businesses that place staff in danger without adequate training are seriously breaching health and safety laws, but it happens.

A set of general rules for shop staff (and people employed in similar circumstances) looks like this:

- Do not confront anyone who seems dangerous, and never confront anyone alone.
- If you have to ask someone to leave the store and they won't, call security or the police. Don't argue or try to use force.
- Keep a counter between you and any customer who seems angry or otherwise dangerous. Stay back from it to prevent them reaching you.
- Don't chase thieves. Get a good description for the police.
- Don't defend the till. The money's not even yours!
- Keep the till closed and locked when not in use.
- Don't become so fixated on your job that you forget to be aware of your surroundings and potential hazards.

Employers should provide their staff with suitable training and the means to ensure their protection. Failure to do so is negligence, which can land a manager in prison. This means that you are entitled to expect procedures and measures in place to protect you from violence at work. Learn them and use them!

Relatively minor measures can reduce the risk to you greatly. For example, attacks on bus drivers, though still a problem, are less common than they used to be. Many such attacks are carried out simply because the attacker saw a lone person far from help and decided to attack for the fun of it. Screens and radio links improve protection, and thus deter many such attacks. Taxi drivers have a similar problem; they have to go out alone, often at night, and deal with groups of people who may be drunk or aggressive. People with such occupations (where the risk of violence is obvious) tend to learn to be alert for danger, but in truth everyone, whatever their occupation, should.

It's worth taking a leaf out of the US Navy's book. The world's largest navy exists to confront and deal with problems involving violence on an awesome scale. Many of its ships visit foreign ports on courtesy visits (this is called 'showing the flag' and it's an important part of the Navy's job). Imagine the embarrassment if the world's most powerful naval force was scared to enter a port! Imagine the political humiliation if a captain chose to turn around and leave because he was afraid his personnel might be in danger!

And yet that is what they do. A US Navy commander at a conference told one of the authors: 'We do a threat analysis before we enter any foreign port. If we don't like it, we don't go in. We'll take the political hit for that, but we won't put our people in danger unnecessarily. That's all there is to it.'

These people are paid to fight. They have guns, missiles *and* nuclear weapons; they have the pride of a whole nation to think of. But they won't place themselves in danger unnecessarily. If that policy is good enough for them, it'll do very nicely for us!

- Unless your job is to do something dangerous, don't place yourself in danger to do your job!

And do remember that you can also be attacked as you are leaving a difficult situation with a sense of relief at getting out intact, as you get home from work, or at any other time. Stay alert, and don't switch off.

Women

Women are often seen as easy targets. The vast majority of rapists target women, and while physical attractiveness and mode of dress *may* be a factor in the choice of *some* victims, remember that *anyone* could be a victim.

There are of course many strong, empowered women around. However, it is an observable fact that many women find it difficult to even consider using force to defend themselves (though a threat to a mother's children can prompt an entirely different response). Many women are uncomfortable with the idea of hurting someone and are very unwilling to do so.

This degree of empathy may well make the individual a better and more admirable person, but it can be counterproductive in the face of a violent attack. Overcoming the inhibition against violence is difficult for most of us. Anger is one way, or an overriding need to protect a loved one. Another way to beat the inhibition, as will be discussed later, is training. Trained responses are often carried out without a pause for thought. You are suddenly grabbed; you throw your assailant off and kick him in the ribs. Not only is such an instant response far more effective than one that requires you to think about what you are doing, but it is also far more likely to happen at all. Think for too long and you may freeze out of fear or a laudable but misguided unwillingness to hurt someone. Acting immediately and effectively is also very intimidating to an assailant, who may well wonder who he has chosen to tangle with! Sometimes a marginally effective response is enough, simply because the attacker realises that he is not dealing with a victim, but with someone who is going to make him work for whatever he wants. Criminals do not like work.

It must be acknowledged that a woman is likely to be a lot weaker than her assailant (though it should be pointed out that women do initiate violence, if less frequently than men.) While any well-trained fighter can demolish an unskilled but powerful opponent, most women should concentrate on responses intended to deter or drive off an attacker, and should seek escape rather than a protracted battle. In truth, this applies to everyone.

Children

It would be pleasant to believe that our children are safe and that no one would assault a child. Sadly, this is not the case. Children come under attack far too frequently. The perpetrators vary, but they are all dangerous in their different ways.

Many, perhaps even most, children are bullied at some point, and physical violence is frequently a part of the process. Bullying cannot be discounted as harmless. Children have killed themselves out of despair over bullying since time immemorial. We can never know how many potential suicides have saved their own lives by losing their temper and turning on the local bully. Even ignoring psychological trauma, bullying can turn very nasty and we owe it to our children to give them a fighting chance.

Children also get robbed, especially in this age of rampant consumerism. The most common form of robbery is the theft of mobile phones, often accompanied by violence. Designer coats and shoes are also common targets. Such robberies are often carried out by other children.

More sinister is the danger of abduction. Paedophiles come immediately to mind as a threat, but there are other dangers including childless people carrying out a fantasy of having a family, or the (thankfully very, very rare) situation where some twisted individual simply wants to torment and kill someone and sees a child as a soft target.

Children are at a disadvantage in any confrontation and should be thinking of escape above all else. Prevention is the key here. Children should not be frightened to go out, but they must be aware of potential dangers and capable of minimising the risks. Children should be taught to take sensible precautions that keep them away from dangerous places and also maximise the risk for an attacker. Fear of being caught is a strong deterrent.

Child abductions often begin with a seemingly innocent situation as the victim is gradually lured into danger. The most important things we can teach our children are to recognise when things are not right and how to get out of a dangerous situation before it is too late. As adults, most of us have a feel for situations and can spot when we are being manipulated. Children have not usually developed this instinct and may feel inhibited about being rude to an apparently nice stranger. They must be taught that self-preservation is an overriding concern.

But what if prevention fails? Teaching children self-defence skills must be accompanied by education and socialisation so that the child comes to understand what the skills are for. The majority of self-defence and martial arts classes provide excellent, supportive environments where personal development is encouraged and where the child will meet many new friends. A later chapter deals in detail with selecting a suitable class.

The important thing to teach children is balance – the balance between restraint and the ability to fight at need; the balance between innocence and awareness. They must learn to gauge a situation and react responsibly.

Self-defence must be approached sensitively and sensibly. Parents must not think that a child who is too sensitive and 'wouldn't hurt a fly' needs to be toughened up and hardened. On the contrary, that child must be supported and told that they are exceptional and good.

The authors have encountered parents who think that learning self-defence means allowing their children to attend violent classes where they are likely to be punched in the head repeatedly so they can 'learn to take a punch'! When offered a similar learning experience for themselves, these people quickly decided that the child needed it more than they did.

Children must not be pushed into violent heavy-contact fighting styles. For most, this serves no useful purpose as the child will not learn how to defend him- or herself; he or she will learn how to get hurt! Instead, children's self-defence must be taught in a sensitive, disciplined (but fun) environment, and should include personal safety teaching as well as measures to facilitate escape.

People with Physical Limitations or Disabilities

Every one of us has different physical capabilities. Some have far greater strength, speed, fitness or balance than is usual. Others, for whatever reason, fall below the norm in some of these areas. Age, build, lack of training and old injuries can place a person at a considerable physical disadvantage. This is not a reason to suggest that such people have any less right to self-defence, nor is there any reason to assume that a truly 'disabled' person is a helpless victim to be protected or pitied. Disability can place extreme limitations on a person's physical capabilities, yet a person whose physical abilities are somehow restricted is still a person, with all the rights and duties that entails. Why should they be barred from learning self-defence skills? The authors can find no good reason.

The proportion of people so disabled as to be helpless is actually rather small. Of the remainder, many have a specific limitation that may make some actions impossible. It is possible to work around such limitations and to achieve a considerable capability despite them.

We hear about the heroes; those who were born with, or suddenly gained, a tremendous disability yet rose above it to achieve incredible success. Yet for every blind Olympic sprinter or one-armed black belt there are dozens of ordinary people painfully struggling against the odds to achieve rather mediocre success. These people are heroes too. And so are those without any 'disability' at all, who strive to be the best they can and to push their limits. It is not in winning that heroes are made, but in *trying* to win.

This is the truth about people with disabilities wanting to learn martial arts or self-defence: they are just people like everyone else. We each have our limitations. Striving to overcome them makes us better people, and if the standard we reach for a given amount of effort differs from person to person, what of it? Unfair as it is, it remains a fact of life. Self-defence is an exercise in realism and these truths must be embraced.

One of the authors of this book is disabled. The techniques are slightly different for him, but the outcome is the same: he creates a window of opportunity to escape, and when force has to be used, he is capable of doing it right. The fact is that *everyone* has the right to learn self-defence, and what they learn may save their life.

The Elderly

Sadly, someone who is old or infirm is more likely to be seen as an easy mark than a person upon whom honour precludes an attack. Elderly people have as much right to be safe as anyone else, and the same self-protection measures work for older people as for their young counterparts. In fact, older people do have a number of factors on their side. Firstly, older people tend to be wiser and less likely to engage in dangerous behaviour. Secondly, in the event that an elderly person is attacked, people are more likely to offer assistance (though this is not always to be relied upon). Thirdly, an older person is unlikely to be asked why they were carrying the stick they beat an attacker off with.

There is no reason at all why an older person who is reasonably fit and able should not be capable of undertaking some self-defence training. This may have to be modified to fit what they can or cannot do, but any improvement in fitness or capability can make all the difference, and continued training and exercise can contribute to a longer, fitter life. One woman in her sixties whose health and mobility were quite poor even took up karate and earned her black belt despite these difficulties (and please do understand that black belts are not given lightly; this person earned the grade like anyone else, under the same criteria!).

For the rest of us mere mortals, a mild increase in health, fitness and self-defence capability might be all that is possible. But that slight improvement might be all it takes to deter or escape an attack. All elderly people (whether capable of training or not) can undertake sensible precautions such as:

- Making the home a safe place with good security.
- Being able to summon help. Get a mobile phone, even if you hate the things.
- Getting a walking stick (whether you need one or not).

- Getting a suitable dog. No mugger or burglar wants to fight your dog, and they make great companions.
- Cultivating good relationships with the people who live around you and in the places you normally go, such as the local shops.

An older person may not be quite as able to punch it out with an assailant, but hopefully will be wise enough to understand that there are better ways to be safe.

Young People

Young men and women are the least likely to take sensible self-protection measures and the most likely to engage in high-risk behaviour. It is no coincidence that the 17–24 age group is where both the most common perpetrator and victim of assaults are to be found. There are many reasons for this, many of which boil down to ego.

Ego manifests itself in many ways, including:

- A need to show off for the benefit of friends, prospective partners or the world in general.
- An unwillingness to lose face by backing down.
- An overdeveloped self-belief.
- Refusal to accept that there is danger.
- Unwillingness to be seen 'playing safe'.

Ego is highly dangerous because it fuels any confrontation. Where a wiser person might be willing to accept some abuse and withdraw, someone possessed by the demon of ego will refuse to yield an inch, and will probably decide that he needs to be seen to 'win' a confrontation. This leads inevitably to escalation, and if violence ensues this cannot be called a self-defence situation.

Many of the beliefs held by young people are also somewhat misplaced. Too many young people really do think that it 'can't happen to them' or that they are 'too hard for that to happen'. Proof to the contrary can only be provided by the most unpleasant circumstances.

Many school leavers have particularly dangerous misconceptions. School is a protected environment, staffed by professionals who are absolutely forbidden to lay hands on a pupil, and who are not in any way inclined to do so. A certain minority of young people become used to being abusive and difficult in school, since there are no consequences worth speaking of.

If this attitude is taken into the outside world, it can have disastrous consequences. A nightclub doorman or random stranger in the street may have no compunction about meeting abuse with violence. Similarly, even the schoolyard (which can be a violent place in some localities) is not the same environment as the backstreets at midnight. A fight picked in school is unlikely to be very serious. On the street, any exchange of blows could end in a stabbing or one party being kicked to death on the ground. And the involvement of authority is not a trivial matter. A criminal conviction can have life-long effects, even if the sentence is a short one.

Young people must realise that the real world is infinitely more dangerous and less controlled than the environment they inhabited in school and that their actions can have lasting and serious repercussions.

Young people are also prone to ignore good sense, wise advice and sensible conduct in favour of doing what they want. Thus they are more likely than older people to engage in high-risk behaviour. This includes going to pubs and clubs renowned for their violent clientele, hurling abuse at passers-by, and leaping into confrontations rather than withdrawing from them. In this, peer pressure is a strong factor, as no young people want to be diminished in the eyes of their 'mates'.

The term 'mates' is used here rather than friends, and in quotes, because the authors find it difficult to call a friend anyone who would encourage a person to engage in violence or to risk violence being done to them. It is important to understand that while the mob may be cheering you on, any given one of them in your place would probably want to let the matter go. It is easy to urge someone else to do something dangerous, after all.

Older people have usually developed a measure of self-confidence that enables them to assert themselves in a potentially dangerous situation. A younger, less experienced person may not even realise what is happening, and even if they do, may lack the self-confidence to act assertively.

Young people like to be accepted and to belong. Thus they are more likely than other age groups to be attracted to charismatic figures (who usually do dramatic things, many of them anti-social, to gain attention) and to very 'tribal' groups. Sometimes this simply means becoming a rabid fan of a particular star, group or sports team (these are pretty harmless and even beneficial activities for the most part), but it can also lead to more dangerous affiliations. Gangs and extremist organisations (from football hooligans to neo-Nazis) can be attractive to young people seeking to belong. It is easy to be manipulated or drawn into violence by such groups.

Young people are also prone to drinking or taking drugs. No judgement need be passed here, but it is worth mentioning that 'recreational chemicals' can seriously affect a person's judgement and also their ability to act coherently. This means that if you drink heavily or take drugs, you are not only more likely to lose your temper and be dragged into something, but are less likely to be able to deal with it. You are also less aware of danger and thus are more likely to be attacked in the first place.

Note that 'I was drunk' is not a valid defence of your actions in law, and a state of drunkenness (or other intoxication) can seriously affect your defence if you must defend yourself. The two main factors to consider are:

- A court may, upon hearing that you were drunk, become hostile towards you, losing you some of the benefit of the doubt.
- If you use excessive force to react to a situation, you normally have a defence based upon the facts as you perceived them. However, if you made a mistake or misjudged a situation because of 'voluntary intoxication' then you cannot use this defence.

Thus, overall, young people are at increased risk because they:

- Are likely to ignore danger signs.
- Lack sufficient experience to recognise many dangerous situations.
- Lack the self-confidence to break out of a dangerous situation.
- Are likely to be subject to, and give in to, peer pressure.
- Are more likely to be drawn to dangerous groups.
- Are prone to drink heavily.
- Are less likely to back down in a confrontation.
- Often do not believe or want to listen to good advice.
- Do not wish to be seen 'playing safe'.

Increasingly, young women are involved in violent encounters that are really no different from those of their male counterparts. Fights are usually between two (or more) women, rather than a woman attacking a man. However, the age of chivalry is long dead, and many men have no problems about hitting a woman.

This is one area where young women are more at risk than men. Men are not at risk from the great majority of women (there are exceptions!), but women are in danger from both sexes, though for slightly different reasons.

A dispute between two women that leads to violence will usually be more or less the same as one between two men. The same ego, pride and so forth are all at play here, and the same confrontation management measures can be used to resolve the situation.

Violence between a man and a woman is a different matter. Of course, if a man is under attack by a woman and feels that there is a real need to protect himself, he has every right to use reasonable force to do so. Gender does not enter into it – pain and injury are the same, whoever is dealing them out. But what we are concerned with here is the situation where a man is using unreasonable force against a woman. This can be very serious, and sometimes it is entirely avoidable.

Many young women feel the need to behave in a highly confrontational way. Smart or obscene put-downs, abuse and so on, are all part of the 'taking no crap' persona that some young women like to wear. They feel safe because they are female – and what man would hit them?

The truth is that behaving this way is highly dangerous. This kind of conduct causes anger and resentment, and some men will respond violently. In the authors' experience, most young women are totally sure that they are quite safe and can behave how they please, right up until someone snaps and throws a punch. The bottom line is that social convention is not adequate protection if you provoke people – someone will lose their temper sooner or later.

Some young women take this dangerous behaviour a stage further and do inflammatory things like taking a man's drink in the pub or even initiating violence with a slap or similar blow. This is dangerous for two reasons. Most obviously, someone who is angered and outraged by your actions – or who is suffering an instant of sudden shock and pain – may lash out blindly, and a man's response to a slap may be a full-blooded (if unintentional) punch. Note that we are in no way condoning this – merely pointing out that it happens.

The second danger is that once physical violence (however trivial) is allowed into a situation, the gates are opened. It's like a switch gets thrown in the mind – subconsciously, the man now feels that it is OK to use physical force. Many men, who would not normally consider hitting a woman, have resorted to violence after being struck. Again, we are not condoning this, nor is it worth trying to explain the psychology behind it. All that matters is that you should be aware of the effect.

- Once violence is brought into a situation, it will escalate.

Another situation where women are at risk is when a man feels that sexual or romantic advances are suitable, and is spurned. Whether a chance meeting in the pub, a dinner date or an encounter during the normal business of work, babysitting, going to school or whatever, any such situation is highly charged, and dangerous.

The great majority of men will deal with disappointment and remain respectful; some will be unpleasant but would not consider violence. And some may be on the borderline. The thing to do is to get out of the situation without conflict. You may feel like giving him some abuse or a slap, particularly if he has done something physically inappropriate, but this is extremely dangerous. Again, once violence is allowed into a situation, it will escalate. A great many rapes are perpetrated after the woman initiated violence in some way, and of them, the majority could have been avoided if the victim had withdrawn rather than engaged in an argument or physical violence. Again, this is not to suggest that a rape victim is to blame. It is merely advice to help you avoid becoming one.

Get out of any situation you don't like with a minimum of fuss and no 'violence triggers'. Of course, if you feel sufficiently threatened and physical action is necessary to prevent something serious from happening, then act! But don't slap or shout abuse. These are half-measures, taken in anger, and they will only lead to more violence. To summarise:

- If you can, get out of the situation quietly.
- If you need to repel a threat, do it.
- Don't hit anyone unless absolutely necessary. If you do hit them, don't take half-measures. Lay them out.

Young people, then, have some difficult challenges ahead if they are to engage in self-protective behaviour. But the rewards – a long, safe life free from violence – are worth it. Just remember that your ego isn't worth getting hurt over, and social convention will not protect you from someone who's really intent on hurting you. Try not to give anyone a reason.

Playing the Odds

Self-protection is all about stacking the odds. You've already begun to tilt them in your favour by taking steps to avoid attack. But what if it happens anyway?

More odds-stacking can help you here. You can tilt the odds in your favour in several ways. Training (actually knowing what to do!) is a big help. Being fit (fighting is incredibly tiring. Most street fighters will be out of breath in a few seconds. Stay out of trouble for that long and he'll become less effective). Alertness is vital too – your odds are better if you actually know the attack is coming!

But the biggest thing in your favour is *you*, and your determination to get out of this intact. As long as you don't give up and surrender to your fate, you have a chance.

Role Models and 'Heroes'

It is worth examining the effect of certain types of role model on common behaviour at this point, if only because understanding the influences on our conduct will assist us in rejecting certain modes of behaviour. These comments are aimed at everyone, but particularly young men and women. We don't mean any insult by this, it's just that younger people are often influenced more by their role models – and by extreme role models – than older folks who've seen more and had time to develop a more balanced viewpoint.

Many of the traits we see as 'heroic' or worthy of emulation are in fact contrary to good social conduct and enlightened self-protection. The great majority of 'heroes' admired in our society are warriors, battling devilish foes and impossible odds. Examples are as diverse as Beowulf, the Incredible Hulk and Obi-Wan Kenobi. As a culture, we are largely raised on a diet of dramatised conflict and combat. This is all very well in entertainment, but it is rather less wholesome in daily life. Real people have to live with the consequences of their actions, and a single incident can mar the rest of a person's life – or cut it short.

Similarly, the soap operas that make up much of our TV viewing seem to be an endless round of door-slamming bust-ups. Again, this is all well and good for the sake of ratings and viewer excitement, but if we behave that way in our daily lives then we are likely to run out of friends very rapidly!

The behaviour of fictional role models runs almost directly contrary to good sense, and while few people will think to themselves, 'Batman wouldn't back down!' in a dangerous situation, the things we read or see on television do exert a subliminal influence upon our behaviour. We really do identify (even subconsciously) with the characters and their conflicts. Most of us have surely, at some point, wished we could just let go and have that huge end-of-series row.

Thus a predisposition towards violence and confrontation runs subtly through our cultural psyche. It particularly affects young men, but everyone is somewhat influenced by it. The result is a set of values that are contrary to what common sense suggests are appropriate in a civilised, peaceable society.

Specifically, many people are predisposed to admire the following types of behaviour, which emulate our fictional role models:

- Feisty, 'taking no crap from anyone'.
- Smart comments and always having the last word.
- Confrontational, refusing to back down.
- Maverick, disrespectful of authority.
- Loud, opinionated.
- Brave, risk-taking.

These attitudes can lead to escalation in a confrontation. For example, a situation that would quietly simmer away to nothing can be brought to a violent boil by one or both parties involved insisting upon getting the last word.

At least one serious assault the authors have direct knowledge of occurred as a confrontation ended. Wisely trying to avoid a fight, one of the participants – we shall call him Andy – displayed submissive behaviour and placated the person who confronted him, despite clearly being in the right. After successfully managing the dangerous confrontation, Andy then felt the need to save face among his friends. Jerking his thumb over his shoulder as he walked away, he made an insulting and dismissive reference to the person he'd just gone to so much trouble to placate. Andy did not even have time to turn around before being beaten to the floor and kicked repeatedly. And this happened at the very moment when the situation was over and the danger past.

The point here is that while participating in loud confrontations, winning arguments and getting the last word in may be attractive, these things are dangerous, and all the more so because others are also predisposed to do the same. It is possible to become locked into a cycle of escalating provocation until, neither side being willing to back down, violence ensues.

Of course, in these circumstances, fighting is not self-defence. It is unnecessary conflict brought about by an unwillingness to undertake sensible self-protection measures and to act as a responsible and peaceable citizen. There really is no reason for this to happen, nor any excuse.

It can, however, be very hard to act submissively and to let someone apparently win out over you. To do so actually requires a strength of character that bullies simply do not possess. Yet this is heroism of a sort too. Just as the person who places their life on hold for months or years to look after a sick or aged relative is every bit as heroic as someone risking their life in a swollen river or blazing building, so it is also a worthy and admirable act to keep the peace in the face of provocation.

Truly, there is better karma (and a certain satisfaction) in avoiding conflict than in creating it. There is also a great deal of satisfaction to be had from 'winning' in a dangerous situation; winning in a manner that your prospective opponent cannot even understand. You got what you wanted – that is, you avoided suffering harm or all the consequences that might ensue from a fight. Therefore, you won. He may have said all kinds of things, postured for the benefit of the crowd or whatever. He may even think that he got one over on you. But that doesn't matter. You quietly got what you wanted from the situation and moved on with your life. He'll never understand, but *you* have just got one over on *him*.

Any idiot can swear or swing adrenaline-fuelled punches. These behaviours are easy and natural to many people. On the other hand it can be incredibly hard not to give in to the subliminal predisposition towards conflict; it can be a tremendous challenge to rise above the primal anger of the insulted animal. But to rise above these things, to remain true to yourself despite extreme provocation ... that requires real strength. Thus, in a very real way, it is just as 'heroic' to choose not to fight. It's also a great deal safer!

Learning How to Take a Punch

If you go in for serious training, you may find that the occasional 'ouch!' is part of the package. That's fine ... it happens when training is realistic and really, it's no big deal. But some people think that in order to learn to defend yourself, you need to 'learn how to take a punch'.

Self-defence is about learning how not to take a punch because you evaded or pre-empted it. Self-protection is about learning how not to take a punch by not having fights. Learning self-defence by being thumped is like learning the Green Cross Code by getting run over.

Times When You MUST Fight

There are some circumstances where a violent response is the only realistic option. You will have to decide for yourself whether such a situation is developing and make the awful decision to fight *now* rather than put off the inevitable for a few moments.

Fortunately, such situations are rare. A challenge to fight, issued in front of your friends, is not one. A situation where there is a grave threat to others, such as when you see a group beating up an obviously helpless individual, may or may not be such a situation. You may feel honour-bound to intervene, no matter what the odds. You may not even think about it, but just act. These are situations where you still have some options. It may be that you can best serve the victim by escaping to get help rather than in making a gallant but doomed charge to the rescue.

One of the most terrible decisions you can face is deciding whether to act in the face of overwhelming odds when there is an option that seems to offer safety or at least the postponement of violence. But there are times when you must do so. Here, we are referring to encounters in which your survival depends upon acting *now*.

You must fight whenever the consequences of not resisting are likely to be worse. You must decide for yourself whether an attacker simply means to give you a punch and steal your property (which may be acceptable to you) or whether he means to beat you to the floor and kick or rape you.

One particular example is in the event of an attempted abduction. The attacker may be armed or may threaten to hurt you or your loved ones if you do not comply. Resistance seems daunting and may be very dangerous. But you can be sure that if you allow yourself to be taken somewhere of the abductor's choosing, your position will be far worse. Resisting where you are is fraught with risks, but there are escape routes and possible assistance. This will not be the case if you allow someone else to choose the ground.

Similarly, if someone tries to tie you up, you face a tough choice. It is one thing to comply with a robbery, but if you are tied up you become completely helpless. Your last chance to save yourself will slip away if you comply. After that, you can only hope to be freed; your fate is in the hands of the gods.

Hostage situations are similar. Until quite recently, people were well advised to comply with hostage-takers and avoid drawing attention to themselves, awaiting a resolution of the situation by the proper authorities. In recent times terrorists have become more willing to cause mass casualties. It is no longer as likely that hostages will be peacefully released; they may be killed to make a statement or simply 'in passing' as part of a greater design. It seems that in at least some hostage situations, it may be best to resist, no matter what the odds.

In many ways this is similar to the decision you must make when choosing to strike pre-emptively. You must analyse the threat and the likely consequences of not acting, and decide whether or not to attack. If you do decide to act, pick your moment (perhaps pretending to comply to put the assailant off-guard) then attack – or flee if you can.

Just remember that you may have this one chance to preserve yourself. Compliance may make you a helpless victim to be toyed with and murdered at leisure. So pick your moment – and act!

Summary

- Self-protection is more than being able to fight – it's a way of living.
- Threats exist all around you, and can develop at the most unexpected times.
- It is always best to avoid fighting if at all possible.
- Sometimes resistance is your best or only option.
- Nobody 'fights fair' on the street.
- The consequences of an attack can be very severe or even fatal.
- The best time to deal with an attack is long before it happens, by being prepared or by ensuring it does not happen at all.
- Everyone has the right to obtain some form of self-defence training, and should be encouraged to do so.
- You have the right to defend yourself and the people around you.

- You may strike pre-emptively if you are sure an attack is about to occur.
- Your response must be 'reasonable', but you may use all 'necessary' measures.
- You are permitted to arm yourself in the face of a clear and imminent threat, but you may *not* carry a weapon under normal circumstances.
- If you are forced to take violent measures to defend yourself, you *must* stop when there is no longer a threat. If you do not, you become a criminal.

And more than anything:

- Do not engage in high-risk behaviour. Always act in a manner that minimises your exposure to threats, no matter what people might think of you. Your life is precious. Protect it!

Part II: Threat Avoidance and Management

Chapter 1: Self-Protection and Personal Safety

Our society is basically a safe, supportive place filled with people who mean you no harm. Many simply don't care enough to hurt you, while others are genuinely well disposed towards strangers.

There are, sadly, exceptions to this rule. You can meet one of those exceptions anywhere, and it is small comfort to the victims or their relatives that violent assaults are actually quite rare. The fact that it can happen at all is sufficient reason to assume it will, and to prepare accordingly.

It is an unfortunate fact that the people best able to take care of themselves are the least likely to be chosen as victims. This is no coincidence, but again it is little help to those of us who are not large and strong. What can the rest of us do?

What we can do is be smart and prepared. We can learn what our strengths and weaknesses are, and work to exploit or cover them. We can identify trouble and avoid it, and we can take steps to prepare for situations we cannot avoid. That means not only acknowledging the possibility of a violent confrontation, but also thinking through what might happen and being actively prepared for it.

Self-Protection Begins with the Self

Self-protection really does begin in your own mind. The defensive habits you adopt, the way you watch for danger and act to minimise it, even the clothing you wear, can all contribute to your personal safety.

There are other factors too. Preparation is vital. If you are overweight or unfit, it is worth considering putting in a little effort to correct this. Fitness has many benefits beyond being able to run from an attacker or punch him effectively, but those are a good start. It is probably not worth making a grand resolution to change your lifestyle to be ready for an assault that probably will never happen – you'll never carry it through. A few subtle changes might be useful, however. Playing a little sport or going for a walk from time to time are good places to start that won't disrupt your life too much.

However, much of your preparation can be done in your own mind. This is where the most important events take place anyway. Develop a habit of looking around you from time to time. Try to identify potentially dangerous behaviour or places and avoid them. And most of all, be aware that violence can happen to you at any time. This simple change in mindset can help you react more quickly and more assertively to a developing situation. It could save your life.

So what should you be doing as things start to go off the rails? Here's a checklist of the most important points:

- Understand that this is a threat situation, and that you could get hurt.
- Be ready to react, but don't make aggressive moves.
- Assess the threat.
- Spot additional hazards such as extra assailants or bad terrain.
- Look for escape routes or possible assistance.
- Decide what you want out of the situation.

The last point is very important. Decide what you want. Most likely this is for the assailant to leave you alone, but realistically this means escape, survival, to protect loved ones or some other clear-cut goal. Keep that goal in mind and don't be distracted from it. As soon as you get a chance to get what you want from the situation, go for it.

Having a plan like this is a big asset. If you have decided that you'll make a break *that way* as soon as you can, your actions will be subconsciously tailored to support your plan. When an opportunity arises, you'll be ready to exploit it without having to think about it, or worse, missing it because you didn't recognise the opportunity in time.

If your plan is thwarted, look for another chance but be ready to change your plan to suit the circumstances. Keep assessing the situation, and keep looking for ways out. By doing this you may be reacting to the attacker's *actions*, but you're taking control of the *situation*.

- Remember that your focus is not the attacker, but yourself.

If you have to stay, say to protect someone else, then your actions will be different. You will need to drive off or disable your assailant(s) rather than simply clearing a space to make a run for it.

Cold and Hot Attacks

Attacks can be subdivided into two types – 'cold' and 'hot'. 'Cold' attacks are premeditated by the aggressor with some gain in mind – money or property, sexual gratification, revenge or the pleasure of hurting a member (or presumed member) of a despised social, cultural or ethnic group. Cold aggressors may attack by surprise using stealth or deception or may close in overtly, enjoying intimidating the victim before striking.

Often there is no warning of a cold attack; a friendly stranger may suddenly and savagely turn on you. Cold attacks tend to come without warning unless you're alert for the signs. A cold attacker selects his victim according to his own criteria – maybe you were the only person to happen along on an otherwise quiet night.

'Hot' attacks are those where a situation flares into violence due to ego, pride, temper or some combination of causes. Alcohol is frequently a factor in such situations as it suppresses the parts of the brain that limit anti-social behaviour. The victim can be anyone, as the aggressor's rage is often self-fuelling. It is usually possible to see where a hot confrontation is going and to withdraw or at least be ready.

- Cold attacks are pre-planned and begin with deception or stealth.
- Hot attacks are made in anger, usually during a confrontation.

Both kinds of attack can be dealt with by the same measures, though they are applied somewhat differently, as we will see later.

The Self-Defence Formula: ADDER
Avoid-Deter-Defuse-Evade-Respond

Rather than rely on any one self-protection mechanism such as fighting skills or the hope that it won't happen, it is best to create a layered defence that deflects or avoids some of the potential threats. In this way the great majority of dangerous situations can be headed off or evaded long before things get really dangerous.

The steps to self-protection are summed up by the acronym ADDER. A basic overview is presented here. Each concept then receives a detailed treatment in its own chapter.

Avoid

The first stage of self-protection is to avoid danger wherever possible. This is largely a matter of common sense. Potential attackers like lone victims in dark, secluded places where they can do as they wish without witnesses. Other dangerous places include town centres at night, where considerable amounts of alcohol are consumed. It is sensible to avoid such places, but if you job or social life takes you there, then you can practise other forms of avoidance; avoid aggressive people, and avoid conduct that might spark or escalate a confrontation.

Deter

The most obvious deterrent to attack is, of course, to look like you could and will tear any aggressor into bloody strips. Failing this, deterrence is a more subtle matter. For starters, try not to look like a victim. People who walk briskly and purposefully, looking around them, seem more confident than those who amble aimlessly along staring at the ground. Smart and tidy (but not ostentatious) clothes can also make you seem confident and 'powerful'. Believe it or not, this can deter an attacker. The simple fact that you seem confident and can see the attack coming may prevent it from happening at all. Deterrence in its simplest form means not looking like a victim.

Defuse

A confrontation can sometimes be defused. In the case of an attempted robbery this can mean letting the attacker take your property rather than getting into a fight. When tempers flare, it is possible to head matters off by accepting abuse and threats without reacting. This may be difficult when you want to throttle someone, but it really is a better option than getting into a fight with someone – and all their friends too.

Evade

When other options fail, you can always evade. This may mean running, placing an obstruction such as a parked car between you and the threat, or going into a public building where there are many people around.

Respond

The absolute last resort is response. You should be ready to respond right from the beginning, just in case, but only when all else fails should it become the option of choice.

Responding means entering into a fight situation (or being ready to). Response options are varied: evading a blow, striking pre-emptively, setting off a personal alarm or simply assuming a ready stance. If matters get to the Respond stage, things are very serious indeed and you must be ready to do whatever you need to in order to survive and escape. You will have little or no time to plan or to think, so it is best to know what to do beforehand.

The ADDER formula suggests the order in which these five layers of defence apply to a situation. On most occasions the Avoid or Deter stage is as far as things get – you cannot be robbed in an alley if you do not enter it.

Threats are thinned out by the five layers of defence, so it is highly unlikely that you will need to respond. However, you should always be ready to go to the next stage – or back to the last one. Forced to respond to an attack, you see an opening and evade, placing a parked car between you and your attacker. Another time you try to evade but find your assailant catching up. Assuming a fighting stance, you look him in the eye, saying nothing but sending a clear message. He may be deterred, or you may have to progress to responding. If you do have to, then at least you'll be ready.

As a rule, the closer you are to the 'A' in ADDER, the better you are doing. There is no shame in being attacked and having to respond, but it is better to avoid, to deter, to defuse or to evade than to risk your safety in a hand-to-hand scramble.

Whatever Works

A friend of mine once drove the lens end of a torch into the face of a very determined attacker ... and screwed the broken glass into his chin. Another friend backfisted her assailant then gouged his face with her rings. Yet another swung his son's bike by the handlebars and laid out a local wannabe hard man. Highly trained martial artist that I am, I have resorted to biting someone's foot for lack of a better option.

When you are in imminent danger of serious harm, *do something!* It's better than waiting for the inevitable.

Awareness

The most important tool or weapon you have at your disposal is awareness.

- You can't do anything about what you don't see coming.

The authors still use the Green Cross Code when we want to cross the road. Why? Because we know it works, and because (although we've never tried it) we know that being hit by a car is bad. It is the same with awareness of your surroundings. You don't have to get attacked to know that being punched in the face is unpleasant, and every tool you have to prevent that from happening depends upon awareness. Practise looking around until it becomes automatic. And don't just look, see! Learn to note hazards like people loitering in narrow places or dark areas.

Even when you are in the middle of a fight, you must try to remain aware of your surroundings and seek an escape route. As a rule, awareness will serve you best before a situation develops by allowing you to either avoid it or prepare yourself to deal with it.

Many attacks come by surprise and often from behind. It is very likely that if you are attacked by surprise, you will be dazed or hurt so much by the initial onslaught that you can't respond at all. Psychological paralysis also plays a part here – the brain races to catch up with what is happening, but never quite makes it, leaving you trying to respond to the situation on instinct rather than rationally.

Being aware of your surroundings means you can (and should) turn to face potential threats. Someone who'd be happy to attack you from behind may well be unwilling to fight you face to face. And even if he does still attack you, you're better placed to respond if you can see what's coming.

Attackers of this sort could be labelled 'stealthy'. They attempt to get past your defences by either lying in wait and launching an attack from a position of concealment or by coming up from behind or on a blind side while you are distracted by, say, putting the shopping in the car. Many such 'stealthy' attacks are opportunistic; the attacker sees an opening and goes for it. If you are obviously alert, the opening may not be there, so the attack will not take place.

Awareness is far more than just having your eyes open. If you do not have the correct mindset, you will miss all but the most obvious signals. Many potential attackers – serial killers come particularly to mind here – approach their victims and try to get inside their guard either by deception or feigning innocence.

- Awareness is twofold: *seeing* threats, and *recognising* them.
- Awareness is useless if you don't act upon it!

Deceptive attackers are likely to approach openly but in an apparently friendly fashion. Some will ask for or offer assistance. Others will pretend to know you, or say that they think they do. Bogus meter-readers, date-rapists and people you know who turn out to be not what they seem also fall into this category. By chatting amiably, seeming concerned about you or simply by asking for a light, they will work their way close to you, and perhaps more importantly, inside your mental guard. When they are close and you are disarmed by their non-threatening nature, they launch their devastating attack. You are unlikely to be able to resist it.

'Innocent' attackers are those who do not actually pretend to be a friend, but instead wander into your 'threat zone' as if they have every right to be there. By seeming preoccupied and more or less oblivious to you – and engaged in some innocent activity like using their mobile phone or hurrying to their car – they encourage you to ignore them. Then, having crept in 'under the radar', they strike.

All types of attacks that do not begin with a confrontation are, by definition, 'cold'. The attacker is not the victim of alcohol and temper; he has deliberately chosen this course of action. The important thing is that he has time to think, and can quietly abort his attack if he realises that you are not such an easy target after all. This is where habitual awareness can protect you. If it is obvious that you are alert, then the typical cold attacker will probably find someone easier to pick on.

Awareness, then, is:

- The habit of looking around you.
- The rational recognition that unknown people may pose a threat.
- The willingness to act on the danger signals, whenever they occur.

Danger signals vary. Sometimes you simply get a subliminal feeling that something is wrong. This is usually a response to body language that you may not consciously recognise. Sometimes there are no real signals at all, but an alert person can be tipped off that things are going wrong by the situation rather than the actions of the person in front of them.

Situational danger signs include:

- Someone you don't know trying to get close to you.
- A feeling you're being pressured or 'railroaded' into going somewhere.
- A feeling that something about the situation is unusual.

The last point is vague, but vital. As an example, a woman in the USA saved herself from probable rape and murder by listening to her feeling that something was odd about the man offering to help her. She had come back to her car in a shopping mall car park to find a tyre flat. As she was struggling with it, a well-dressed man approached her and offered to help. He changed the tyre, then put his briefcase in the boot of her car and asked if she'd mind driving him around to the other end of the mall. He'd come out into the wrong car park, he said. The woman did not feel that she could refuse; he'd helped her out, after all. But it struck her as odd that he'd put the briefcase in the car before asking. A trivial thing, perhaps, but that and something about his manner made her uncomfortable. She told him she'd forgotten something and had to go back to get it. He said he'd wait. So she went back into the mall and approached security. The man's briefcase contained nothing except rope, rubber gloves and knives. And there was nothing wrong with the deflated tyre other than the fact that the air had been let out.

The signals in this case were not strong, but they were there, and thankfully this woman heeded them. It is easy not to; not when it means telling a helpful stranger to go away or refusing to help in return, or seeming bad-mannered. But survival can depend upon such actions. Thus awareness is more than seeing the signs of a threat (current or potential). It is also the defensive mindset that heeds the warning *and acts accordingly*.

Fear

People are afraid of all sorts of things: death, pain, wasps, disfigurement and suchlike come to mind, but other fears can be equally important; fear of 'what people would say', or even fear of being afraid. Despite the fact that we are afraid of so many things, most of us really do not understand fear. Thus we have no hope of controlling or harnessing it. Blind and confused, we can only react to it and become its slaves.

Fear is a strange and powerful thing, capable of rendering a normally competent and assertive person temporarily incapable of action or decision. And yet it is a valuable part of the survival mechanism, serving in part to prevent you from doing something stupid, and in part to trigger the 'fight or flight' reaction that frequently saved early man from becoming lunch for something bigger than he was. Fear gave him the strength to overcome his foe – or to outrun it – and it can do the same for you.

In any tense situation you will feel fear. This is not cowardice but a completely normal and pretty much unavoidable reaction to danger. (A common definition of cowardice, if it matters to you, is 'the failure to overcome fear or to maintain self-control sufficient to do what must be done'.) Thus cowardice means giving in to fear, not feeling it; if it were defined as merely feeling frightened, then there would be exactly two kinds of people in the world – cowards and hopeless psychotics.

- Fear is natural and unavoidable. The fact that you are feeling it is irrelevant – anyone would be! What is important is whether you let it overwhelm you, or let it do its job by preparing you for desperate physical activity.

The point here is that it is normal to feel fear, and it can work for you if you understand it or learn to work around it. Besides, much of what you recognise as 'fear', isn't actually that. It's the package of hormonal responses your body makes to a crisis to allow you to perform your best and get out of trouble.

We do not have space to go into much detail, so let us simply take a few examples of fear-associated symptoms and try to explain what they really are.

- Leg shake: this is due to adrenaline turbo-charging your muscles. Used right, this is *power*, not weakness.

- Heavy breathing: your body needs oxygen to generate energy from fuel stored in your tissues. Heavy breathing is the way it gets the air it needs.
- Tunnel vision: this is your body focusing on the threat. It can be dangerous, since it can mean you miss something else.
- Bladder and bowel discomfort: your body wants to stop burning energy on waste products and get rid of excess weight, like the contents of your bladder. This is an unfortunate, but natural, survival reaction.

These things are not symptoms of fear: they are reactions to it! They are how your body prepares to get you out of trouble. The problem is that while these responses can bring your body up to an incredible level of capability, they also mess with your mind. Unable to make sense of what your body is doing, it is easy to be rendered incapable by these strange sensations.

One of the worst manifestations of fear is the 'red mist' that descends upon some people when they are hurt or angered. This is how a normal, reasonable person can turn into a raging killer, driven by blind berserker rage. The line between berserk fury and total fear-induced incapacity is rather fine, and it is hard to say what will push any given individual over it.

- Fear can make you helpless, or turn you into a raging psychotic.

Fear can be a powerful ally or a terrible master. Tempered by rationality, fear can give you focus and power. Out of control, it can rob you of sanity or the ability to act. Fear cannot be banished or made not to exist – for most people anyway. It must instead be tamed and overcome.

The best tool for overcoming fear is training. Firstly, training makes the fear-inducing situation a little more familiar and thus less frightening. Secondly, even quite gentle self-defence training can help you get used to the stress of a 'live' situation. Lastly, and most importantly, you will know what to do and be used to doing it. Under stress that can be vital. Here's why:

- When you are under serious threat you may not be able to think rationally. Everything you *think* you know will be gone. What remains is what you *really do* know. This may just be ineffective, instinctive responses, but it can be trained skills, developed to the point that you can carry them out no matter what is going on. The choice is yours.

This is why soldiers spend so much time practising the same things. It is one thing to be able to clear a jammed weapon on the range, but in the field, in poor light, while desperately tired and hungry, *and with people trying to kill you*, a simple task becomes very difficult indeed. A skill must be second nature if it is to be reliable under these circumstances. The same applies to self-defence skills.

Fear can be useful to you for two reasons:

- If you feel fear, even just a hint of it, then you are perceiving a threat. LISTEN TO THAT WARNING and look for a way to withdraw from the situation.
- If you feel shaky, have butterflies and a dry mouth, then be thankful! Your body is primed and ready to go; if you have to fight or run you'll be on record-breaking form.

Fear can also confuse you and render you incapable of doing anything at all if you allow it to get out of control. The way to avoid this is *preparation*. That means get some training, mentally rehearse what you're going to do, have a plan, and above all, believe that you can get out of this situation if you can just find the courage to act!

'The only thing we have to fear is fear itself'? Well, probably not. There are plenty of things to cause us to fear. But fear itself is not something to be afraid of.

Assertiveness versus Aggression

There is a world of difference between aggression and polite assertiveness. Assertiveness can deter a potential assailant, but reacting aggressively to a situation is likely to make it far worse. For this reason it is wise to avoid sudden movements, shouting, bad language and, particularly, threats.

- Many potential assailants are bound by normal inhibitions, and are actually unwilling or unable to make the first move. However, your aggressive behaviour may trigger his 'fight!' reaction and tip him over the edge into violence.

In addition, remember that you are expected to keep the peace, not to make a threatening situation worse.

• If you respond aggressively to a situation and end up in court, your actions will be judged, and it may be decided that you are partially or even wholly responsible.

Instead of being aggressive, you should try to assert yourself calmly. This can be incredibly intimidating to someone expecting a fearful or adrenaline-filled response. By remaining calm you are less likely to make a stupid mistake, and nobody can claim you precipitated anything. It also conceals your intentions so that if you choose to strike pre-emptively it will come as a big surprise to your opponent.

Assertiveness means refusing to be intimidated by a potential assailant, but also much more. It means taking control of the situation. The importance of having a plan has already been mentioned. Such a plan is only useful if you carry it through, and this requires assertiveness. It can be hard to find the conviction to order someone out of your way or to assume a fighting stance in the face of a frightening opponent. If you can find it in yourself to behave as if you have every right not to be afraid of this bully, sometimes he will believe it too.

Assertiveness is a strange thing. You may think that you can't control a situation when you are faced with a violent person determined to do as he pleases. But humans are not rational creatures. Millennia of instincts can exert more influence than a few centuries of rationality.

• It is possible to control a situation, even when you are outnumbered and overmatched.

For most of our existence, humans were animals, living among other animals. We were smart, and we had tools. We could organise hunting parties and work cooperatively, but we were not 'above' the animals around us. We did not dominate the planet. Unwary humans could be killed and eaten by dangerous creatures.

This environment created survival instincts that exist to this day. A person facing off against you on the street is as much Cro-Magnon man facing a fearsome prey as he is today's lager lout looking for a fight outside the pub. On an instinctive level, he is not facing *you*, he is facing *potential danger.* If you give off the right signals, then you can manipulate his subconscious and thus control the situation.

To put that another way, early man did not square off all alone against sabretooth and snarl 'Come on then if you think you're hard enough!' Sabretooth was not a foe to tackle lightly. He inspired fear, and rightly so.

In the dim recesses of the mind, we face sabretooth when we confront any danger. And so, in the mind of your potential assailant, you can create a seed of doubt if you give off the right signals. The moment he realises that you pose the slightest threat, early man peeps out and starts to wonder 'Is this sabretooth? Will he kill me?' And at that point it becomes possible for you to dominate the situation. Your opponent is crippled by his own survival instincts and the doubts they create. You act. You gain control. It is possible to assert yourself over a potential assailant. But how?

As a rule, you can assert yourself over someone by:

- Telling them what you want them to do as if you expect them to do it.
- Saying little else, and nothing that sounds 'weak' or confused.
- Acting like you expect to be obeyed.

Control of a situation does not end when violence erupts. Everything you do should be aimed at controlling your attacker and the circumstances you find yourself in. How you move, and where to, should be chosen by you and not forced upon you by the assailant. Whether you strike, dodge or run is your choice. A little training will help you to decide which option to take and how to carry it out effectively.

Many people never realise that they are simply reacting and allow control to pass to the other person – who often will not realise that he has control, but simply continues acting as he pleases. It is, therefore, important to think about what is happening. Is what you are doing the best option for you? Has it happened by accident or did your assailant want this?

If you lose control of a situation, try to reassert it as quickly as possible. If you end up on the floor in a grappling match and don't want it to continue, take steps to break off and get up as soon as you can. If you are agile, move and make your attacker come after you. If he's strong, don't let him get hold of you. On the other hand, if you have some handy close-in techniques, let him close and give him a nasty surprise. Never fight on anyone else's terms.

Assertiveness is about fighting on your own terms and making the most of what you have by taking control of the situation. To even realise that you can have control, it is necessary to think about what is going on in a calm and rational manner. This is where aggression and anger fail. Neither is rational, and calm rationality is your best hope to get out of trouble. Stay calm. Take charge.

The Power of Rage and Fear

Four nice, decent young men were at a junction in a car. They went to pull away, then stopped suddenly as a car came around the corner moving fast. The driver behind (a lone man) thought they'd gone and began to pull away too. He had to brake hard, but there was no collision.

The four pulled out and drove off – no harm done. But the lone driver followed them for a quarter-mile, then rammed their car, driving it off the road. For the next 15 minutes he smashed every panel in the car, broke all the glass with rocks and his feet … and the four men inside just sat and cowered.

They all had mobile phones. None of them even called the police. They could have overpowered the attacker, but they were paralysed by terror. This is what happens when people are caught off guard by sudden fear.

Not only was the attacker stupidly, criminally violent, but he was also extremely unwise. If the four nice young men had been driven to rage by their fear, they could easily have killed him. Or they might not have been nice at all. He had no way of knowing that they weren't armed, or experienced street thugs. But such was his rage that he launched his criminal assault, and such was their fear that they were intimidated into passivity. This is the reality of street violence.

Assertiveness Issues

One common reason why people are confrontational is a lack of assertiveness. That might sound like a paradox, but it isn't. A problem can often be dealt with effectively early on with a polite (but firm) word and an obvious willingness to follow through if need be. However, most people are not very assertive (it's just not that easy!) and tend to allow situations to grow rather than deal with them. Some of these situations then explode uncontrollably.

We don't just mean confrontations with a potential for violence here. It happens all the time in daily life. We've all encountered the workplace 'Can you just ...' which causes immense problems and isn't really part of our job anyway. Or that moment when you realise that you've just been fed the thin end of a truly impressive wedge. Having agreed to (or at least not refused to) do a minor thing, it's hard to find a place to draw the line.

Many sales people exploit this fact. How often have you decided to buy the goods before the sales person mentions the 'extras package' that only costs a little more but actually doubles the amount of money you'll be parted from? Having already decided to buy, you're amenable to add-ons that would cause you to reject the deal if you were offered it in one lump. Sales people on the phone do it too. They say things that you agree with, and once you've started saying 'yes' it's hard to stop (that's one of the Ultimate Sales Truths, by the way!). Unless you draw the line at some point, you'll buy whatever they want you to.

Drawn lines are worthless unless you defend them. There's no point in saying 'No more!' and then caving in for the sake of a quiet life or the hope that the person threatening you will leave it at that. If you draw a line or take a stand, you will be challenged. Expect it, and don't give the slightest hint that you might yield. As soon as someone spots a weakness in your resolve, they'll push and push until they break through.

A recent political publication suggested an alternative approach to the 'war on terror'. It suggested that if the West stopped giving people in other nations reasons to be angry, terrorism would cease. 'The best defence is to give no offence,' it said. Rubbish. No matter how polite and considerate you are, how much you give up or give in (and this applies equally to people and nations), there will always be someone who wants something from you that you are not willing to give. Pacifists get murdered too.

No matter how much you are willing to do in order to avoid confrontation, there will be some point you are not willing to go beyond. And this is why major confrontations develop. Arriving at the point of no return will usually take the form of several small steps as the situation becomes increasingly unpleasant, and there is likely to be no single point where it feels easy and natural to put the brakes on. But suddenly, you've had enough. The pile of straws is just too big and you need a new camel. By this point, you have a certain amount of pent-up unhappiness and anger, and depending upon the situation, possibly fear. It will come pouring out, and (however hard you try) your attempt at rational assertiveness will come out as angry defiance. And, of course, someone who has got used to you giving in and doing what they want (over a timescale of seconds or years; it's the same thing) will be annoyed at your sudden refusal. Your snappish defiance will fuel that anger.

If this is a domestic situation, then a major row is the most likely result. You might do irreparable damage to your relationship with someone in the process. Far worse is the situation where someone is trying to get you to agree to sex, or a similarly volatile situation. Sudden anger and defiance can lead to violence or rape. Better to head the problem off early if you can. But that requires you to put your foot down at some point and mean it. Choosing where and when can be a problem. It's easy to say 'as soon as you become uncomfortable with what you are being asked to do', but when exactly do you hit that comfort threshold? Only you can decide. Putting your foot down quietly, politely, but in no uncertain manner, is a tough job. It requires you to develop a degree of assertiveness that most people don't have.

Drawing the Line

I worked as a teacher in some of the roughest schools in Britain for several years. Confrontation management and self-protection were high on the agenda. A paradox of the teaching profession is that if you are attacked by a 15-stone, 6-foot thug in the classroom and defend yourself in a manner allowed by British law, your career is over. And the attacker, being a 'child in your care' is unlikely to suffer anything more than a temporary exclusion from school. But that's how it is.

One thing I learned, more than anything else, was how to draw a line. My authority and control of the situation were constantly being probed; if you let one trivial thing go, pretty soon the next line has been overstepped too. Eventually there's a crisis and you can completely lose control of the situation. (I've seen it and been there. It's not pretty.)

The only way to avoid this is to draw sensible lines and defend them. No matter how tired or sick of it all you may be, you have to be consistent. If you say you'll do something, you have to do it. (This is one reason why I never make threats. I do sometimes state consequences – 'do that and I'll floor you' – but I never make threats. The only difference is that I will do what I say, regardless.)

You cannot afford to allow people to trample over your 'lines'. If you give in to threats or plea-bargaining ('just this once; I'll never ask you to do this again, promise') then your 'line' becomes worthless. The person you gave in to knows that whatever new line you draw, they can wheedle or threaten their way over, just like this one. As a wise man once said, 'As you have said, so must you do.'

In other words: 'No' means 'No! Definitely, absolutely not! No chance! Not now, not next time you ask and not ever! It is not going to happen! I don't care what I've said or done in the past, or that you manipulated me into sort of agreeing to this; I'm saying no here and now and I MEAN IT!' – and you must be willing to back that up with whatever measures are appropriate. Chances are, most people will see that you mean exactly what you say and won't bother to push it.

Developing Assertiveness

As has already been said, assertiveness is useful in gently dealing with domestic and 'life' problems before they become major issues, in fending off sales pitches, and in dealing with potential aggressors. But how do you develop it?

Some people are naturally assertive. They know what they want and are willing to try to get it, but they have good enough manners to do it politely. Others have a sort of rough, closed-minded arrogance that makes them slap down anyone who says something they don't like. This is actually not assertiveness, but a confrontational mindset that requires other people to be assertive in order not to be railroaded. But most of us, raised to be nice, gentle, self-effacing and polite (i.e. good!) people, have a problem with asserting ourselves. But we can learn to do it. It gets easier with practice.

First of all, assertiveness stems from self-worth and self-knowledge. It's not arrogant to feel that you are a worthwhile person, to respect yourself and to know what you want out of life. And it's not selfish to pursue the things you want – it's a right we all have, which is balanced against the need to interact considerately with others.

The first step to assertiveness is to accept yourself as a real, worthwhile person. You are not just somebody's partner, mum, dad, child, employee or friend, you are YOU! You exist in your own right as an individual, and you have the right to be happy. Now you know that it's OK to want certain things (to be safe, not to have to go outside in the rain, not to leave a party with this person), how do you go about getting them without causing offence?

Well, first you have to be willing to cause a little offence. Not by rude words and aggressive behaviour, of course, but you have to be willing to put your needs first and if that means that someone might choose to be offended when you say no, so be it. If you know your reasons are good for the things you say, then you need not feel guilty or give in to wheedling. Similarly, you must not worry about what your friends might think. What is important is what *you* want. If you don't want to play on the railway line, have sex with a stranger, or fight someone, even if your peers think it's a great idea, then you have to believe that your opinion is the important one. They might tease you, but what's that compared to doing something you really don't want to? Or the risk of being hurt?

It's still difficult to say the words, even now you know it's OK to do so, especially if you have developed a habit of giving in and people expect you to (or *you* expect you to!). But you have to. 'No, I'm not willing to do that' or 'That's a bit unreasonable, don't you think?' Say it quietly and politely, and without anger. But say it! The confidence to say these things comes from many places. In part, self-confidence is a habit; you get used to being assertive and confident, until you stop questioning yourself and just do it. But self-confidence can also be deliberately and consciously developed. How?

To develop your self-confidence, collect good things. Not seashells and £50 notes, but achievements, things you're proud of, reliable and good friends, happy memories, inspirational stories and similarly positive things. Keep them in mind. Let's start with appearance. It doesn't matter how attractive you are, you can bolster your self-confidence by knowing you're well dressed and you look good. (You don't have to become a fashion victim, just dress in a manner that makes you feel good.)

Now, what else have you got that's good? A nice smile? A voice people like to hear? Do you come over as honest and reliable because you make eye contact and take care to tell the truth? These things are viewed positively by others; knowing that will help develop your self-confidence. Go too far and you'll have a fat ego, but don't worry about that. You can learn humility some other time.

Turning to your inward treasures, what have you got to give you confidence? Mastery of physical skills is a great confidence-builder. Not just self-defence skills (though these are useful in so many ways), but other physical skills. Are you fit? Can you juggle? Are people impressed with your rock-climbing ability or the amazing pencil sketches you draw? Can you sing? Dance? Play an instrument? Are you good with children, or plumbing, or computers? Are you good at struggling your way through a problem or puzzle just on intuition or determination? Is there someone, anyone, who loves you? A friend or a relative that relies on you?

Once you start thinking about it, you should be able to come up with a whole list of things you can do, or things that you are, that are worth feeling good about. You don't have to be the best, or even very good; you just have to be good enough to feel good about what you do and what you are.

The train of thought that leads to self-confidence looks like this:

- What can I do? What's good about me?

- ALL THAT?

- Hey, I'm not such a loser after all!

- In fact, I'm a pretty worthwhile person.

- If I can do *all that*, then what else could I achieve if I had the confidence to try?

- Let's find out!

That's the first half of assertiveness; feeling good about yourself and being self-confident. The second half can be learned. It's hard at first, but with practice it gets easier. The telephone is a great training aid for assertiveness. Here's how it works: at some point your phone will ring, probably around teatime, and an unknown person will begin telling you how amazingly good something is in the hope of selling it to you. Most people are annoyed by this sort of cold calling, though sometimes the product is attractive enough to make them want to buy it. However, most people who do buy are manipulated into it by the caller. That's their job, you see. And while it's just someone trying to make a living, they are intruding into your life so you might as well get some benefit out of it (and you may even decide that you want to buy their product, after all!).

The pitches these people are trained to use are designed to lead you to a 'buying frame of mind'. They'll start you saying yes, offer you something fabulous, and slip the expensive part in quietly. It's all based on well-researched psychological principles, though many cold-callers don't know that. They're just doing what they've been trained to do. Normally it's a nuisance, but you can practise assertiveness in this harmless situation (just be careful not to buy a conservatory or a Pacific island).

You're probably familiar with the vague feeling of being led and not knowing what to do as the pitch unfolds. Exactly the same factors are at play here as when a situation starts to go out of control or someone starts to overstep your 'lines'.

So here you can teach yourself to break out of the situation. Interrupt the sales person with a question, and when they repeat a rehearsed textbook answer telling you some great feature of their product, don't accept that as the answer – demand that they directly answer your question rather than rattling off pat phrases. Question the details. Get answers, not standard phrases. And smirk to yourself at the manipulative ego-boosting things they say to you, since you now know them for what they are!

If you're asked for bank data, refuse to give it. Say, 'I don't give out financial information on the phone. But I am interested … please send me your literature.' Many companies that get business by cold calling like this will lose interest at this point; they want to sell you something *right now*. They'll give you all sorts of reasons to give them your bank details. Don't (that's a good idea in general, by the way).

Similarly, don't agree to have a sales person call (unless you're really interested in the product, and who knows, you might be!). Ask for literature and brochures, and say you'll talk it over with the family and decide if you want to take it further. This is a good idea in any case when dealing with cold-callers.

One of the authors has a habit of cross-examining cold-callers like this as a test of the firm's worthiness – and refuses to deal with those who treat him as a mark. Firms that treat you like a human being and are willing to accommodate your requirements are more likely to be trustworthy and do a good job or have a good product than those who just consider you a sales target and try to hustle you through a set procedure to buying, with no regard for your needs, your feelings or your humanity.

If you feel that it's a bit unkind to do this kind of thing to a sales person who's just trying to make a living, then don't do it. But these people intrude into our lives and try to manipulate us with their trained pitches. It's nothing more than an occupational hazard if you want to ask some awkward questions. And it is a good way to learn to break out of a situation where someone is leading you.

Assertiveness can be practised at all times in your daily life. When you buy something and are offered 'optional extras' that cost more; when you make arrangements with your friends ... in almost any interaction you have with other human beings. In general, to become more assertive:

- Spell out what you want from people and stick to what you agree. Expect them to do the same. (For example, 'Sure, I'll give you a lift. But I need you to meet me at 7.30 – and I won't hang around if you aren't there.')
- Don't tolerate people letting you down. You don't have to be rude, but do ask why if they don't do what they say they will. Give them one chance, but that's all.
- Be willing to compromise with people. Ask them what they want/ need from the situation and explain what you need in return. But remember where the lines you draw are, and make it clear that they're not negotiable.
- Do what you say you will, even if you don't want to.
- Defend the lines you draw. Don't be persuaded into changing your mind.

In a dangerous situation, you first have to realise that you're not happy with how things are going (awareness). Your best bet is to act early, closing the door before things can get out of hand. If you can make excuses or use humour to soften your words, then that's great, as long as your meaning remains clear and it's obvious that you aren't going to change your mind. In a threatening situation, the steps to assertiveness are:

1) You realise you don't like what's happening, or what is potentially going to happen.
2) You decide what you *do* want, or how far you are willing to compromise.
3) Once you're sure you know what you want, make it clear to everyone else.
4) Stick to what you've said and don't even show the slightest sign of changing your mind.

Assertive phrases needn't be harsh or particularly forceful. All they have to do is make it clear what you want or are going to do. Examples include:

- I don't want to do this/go there.
- Or ... (chuckle) ... we could not. Let's do this instead ...
- I have to go now.
- I'd rather not, thanks.
- I'd rather you didn't do that, if you don't mind ...
- I can't ... I promised (whoever) that I'd be back by now.
- I'd better be off ... I turn back into a pumpkin at midnight!

Sometimes it helps to offer a reason for what you say, at other times there's no need. That's something to judge according to the situation, but don't get all long-winded and apologetic. You're stating what you want and you have a right to do that. Just do it. If a light-hearted, humorous or gently polite approach doesn't work, you can try a flat statement – still polite, still non-aggressive, but no messing about any more:

- No!
- Have a little respect, will you? I said no.
- I can't/won't do that, so there's no point pushing it.
- I don't care what I said earlier ... I'm saying no now, and I mean it.
- Don't EVER try to do that again.
- I'm leaving. No, you can't come with me.

A direct stare and blunt statement cannot be mistaken. Some people will still refuse to take you seriously, and you may have to retreat or even fight your way out of a situation, but if you establish clear ground rules early on, and make it obvious that they're not flexible, then the chances are that you won't have to.

Assertiveness is difficult, yes. But if you learn to act assertively then you'll have less stress, less danger, more respect and a better chance to get what you want from your life. Don't go too far and become an arrogant, demanding person who upsets people with their abrasive attitude, but there is a happy medium where you become a confident, reliable person with whom everyone knows exactly where they stand, but who is polite, friendly and reasonable in their dealings with others. That's a pretty good person to be.

An Attacker may not be Obvious

Some potential aggressors might as well hang a sign around their neck, but others can be frighteningly subtle. This is particularly true of serial killers and the like, who have been known to use very devious methods to get their victims off guard. It is hard to tell the good from the bad, and not worth being paranoid over. You can't just shut yourself off from the world. However, it is worth remaining on guard.

A woman struggling with her broken-down car and two distraught children was approached by a seemingly friendly man who offered to help. He seemed harmless, but he wasn't! He was a skilled martial artist who could easily overpower this woman, especially with the advantage of surprise. Yet she was happy to trust this potentially dangerous, total stranger. Within minutes her guard was completely down. Relaxed, Code White, trusting, she was extremely vulnerable to anything he decided to do. People have disappeared in these circumstances.

In this case the man was one of the authors, and his intentions were good, but that might not have been the case. You can't put up walls against all of humanity, but it's wise not to trust someone you met five minutes ago, and particularly not someone who approaches you at a time when you're already vulnerable.

The Hidden Benefits of Being Prepared

There is peace of mind to be found in the knowledge that you are prepared for the worst and that at need you can protect your loved ones. But the benefits inherent in self-protection go further than this. The chief benefit is freedom from fear. Fear is debilitating, especially when it is of the long-term sort, with no relief or resolution possible. Fear increases stress and takes its toll on our health, happiness and quality of life. By confronting the reality of self-protection, you can obtain freedom from fear, and live life more fully.

This sounds like a contradiction, since acknowledging the need for self-protection also means accepting that there is a real risk of attack. However, it is better to understand the risks and to know that measures have been taken to reduce them, than to harbour dangerous illusions. Besides, the worst fear is fear of the unknown, and while it is not pleasant to think of robbers and thugs, they are at least known quantities and threats that we know how to deal with.

In being aware of and understanding both the risks and the defences available, we can achieve the best peace that can be found in our flawed world. This is just one of the many paradoxes that fill our lives.

Permanent Damage

Physical injury is not the only consequence of an attack. Sometimes the mind can take a long time to heal – and sometimes it never does. Rape or physical injury can change a person permanently, long after the scars have healed. One factor in the mental recovery process is how much a person blames him- or herself for the attack.

Someone who feels that they could have done more to resist or prevent the attack may develop this misplaced self-blame, and some go so far as to feel that they collaborated or even 'made it happen'. There doesn't have to be any basis for this; traumatic experiences do strange things to the mind.

Research has shown that people who know they did their best to prevent or resist an attack recover most quickly and fully. People who passively submit normally suffer the worst and most lasting trauma. This is, of course, assuming that the attack went ahead despite the best efforts of the victim. The purpose of resistance is to prevent that!

Confidence, Success and Health

There are benefits to be gained from the physical side of preparedness too. If you undertake some form of training (this might be for fitness or directly related to self-defence) then you will enjoy increased fitness and health. For a very modest input in terms of time and effort, general fitness can be improved considerably. This is beneficial in combating stress, increasing resistance to disease, and generally improving your quality of life. Your confidence will also improve. Knowing that you can defend yourself may seem to be of little value in the classroom or the workplace, but that confidence spills out in other ways. Other people will see it, even if you don't. Learning self-defence is learning to take charge of your life, and that does not end when you leave the gym or dojo. Learning for its own sake is a worthwhile use of your time, and along the way you will meet new friends. You will also learn to look at a problem and work out how to deal with it. This is a valuable life skill that so many of us lack.

Assertiveness

It's hard to confront a problem. (This is not the same thing as confronting a person!) Wouldn't it be easier to ignore the situation? Well, yes. But problems tend to grow if they're allowed to. Here's an example.

We moved quite recently into a nice house in a nice neighbourhood. The place we lived before was nice enough, too, but for a time it was marred by a young man who'd moved in next door. He'd party (loudly!) until one, two or even four in the morning, on average five nights a week. I'd then have to get up at 6 a.m. and drive for an hour to get to work. It was intolerable.

But nobody wanted to confront the problem. It was easier to say 'maybe it'll be quiet in a few minutes' than to confront this person and (usually) his drunken friends. Once the pattern was established, he felt that he had the right to behave as he chose. It got worse; bottles, used condoms and drugs-related refuse were left scattered about the local gardens. The noise was louder and for longer. The entire neighbourhood suffered, and when people complained, feuds started. His friends were determined to fight for their 'right' to party.

Everyone around suffered for an entire year. The gang (no other word for them) deliberately intimidated people to prevent them interfering. For a long time nobody really did anything about it. We didn't want to make things worse; we felt that we were being unreasonable (!), and we had all manner of other reasons not to deal with the problem. But eventually the lost sleep and stress became intolerable. Our lives were being run by a gang of 18-year-olds. Not hard men or even criminals (other than their drugs use and vandalism). It might have been prevented at the beginning if someone had acted, but we didn't.

Eventually, the rest of us got together and took action through the local council. They applied new anti-social laws and built a legal case with our help. Eventually the young man was evicted from his rented home – and he had no idea who made that happen. Our lives returned to normal, though the strain had told on some relationships and on the health of some residents, and there were lasting effects of other sorts too. I resolved that this would never happen to me again. As soon as it started again, I'd deal with it.

After several months in my new home I was awakened from my customary Saturday-evening doze by thunderous music from next door. The house was rocking. I fretted about it for a while. I liked my neighbour; this had never happened before. Surely it would stop any instant. I really did not want to confront him. Apathy held me back. But I had to do it. I went round, angry and ready for a row (psychological baggage from earlier incidents; loud music from next door instantly makes me dangerously angry). At the last second I grabbed the reins and spoke nicely. I apologised for bothering my neighbour, but told him that his music was disturbing me.

He was about to go out; he'd been drinking and had thoughtlessly cranked the stereo right up. He was embarrassed and apologetic, and dismissed *my* apology for bothering him, saying that I was right, he was out of line. This was the very first time he did this; it was also the last, since he knows what I think about it and that I'll act on my displeasure. A potential problem just went away. But I wonder how it would have turned out if I'd stood on his doorstep and made demands or threats?

Training and Reaction

It is a strange fact that when a crisis develops many people dither around uselessly. This is sometimes because they simply do not know what to do, but it has as much to do with an unwillingness to get involved as anything else. Those who are trained and know what to do will plunge right in and get on with dealing with the problem. Others may follow them to assist once someone makes a move, but that initial unwillingness to do anything can cost lives.

Self-defence training is primarily useful in that you will know what to do in a violent situation without having to invent something off the cuff. But the mindset that goes with the training is useful everywhere. When fire breaks out or someone is injured, you may not have the specific training to deal with the situation, but you will have one important edge; you have the habit of assessing a situation and formulating a response. That habit of getting in amongst it and dealing with the problem can save lives.

One of the habits you will develop as you study self-defence is the habit of threat analysis. This is the art of spotting danger and assessing the level of threat it poses. Very soon you will begin to apply the concept to your daily life. This can help you avoid accidents in the kitchen or on the road, and to generally go about your business in a safer manner. It is a particularly useful skill for those with small children. Things long taken for granted and considered safe can pose a deadly threat to a baby or small child. Your new habit of looking for danger could avert a tragedy.

Summary

- Be aware of your surroundings at all times.
- Fear is natural. It can make you helpless or psychotic, or it can give you the edge you need.
- Be prepared well in advance; get some training if you can.
- Most situations can be headed off by assertive but non-confrontational behaviour.
- Remember that violent self-defence is the last line of defence. Employ other measures first if you can.

Chapter 2: Avoid!

Self-protection is about more than dealing with one attack. It is a matter of protecting yourself from the attack and any consequences that might have come of it. It is a matter of staying safe. If an incident can be headed off at the cost of a few insults, aspersions on your parentage or sexuality, then this is clearly a better option.

Better Not to Fight At All

Take, for example, a situation where you're going about your normal business when someone suddenly approaches you and demands to know what you're looking at. He struts and postures a bit, acting the hard man. There is no reason that you can see for this behaviour, but it is happening right here and now, and you are the target. This is the decision point: do you try to defuse the situation, acting assertively or submissively as necessary (and accepting whatever insults the potential assailant may choose to hand out) or do you allow yourself to be sucked into a verbal exchange that gradually slides towards violence?

Let us imagine that words were exchanged, tempers became frayed and violence ensued. Let's further assume that you came off best in the ensuing scuffle – which is by no means certain. You may have successfully defended yourself, but it may be that your problems are only beginning. It is possible that the attacker will get together with his friends and come looking for you. Next time you may be attacked without warning by four or five people. Possibly with weapons. Or you may have injuries sustained in defending yourself. You may have to go to court if your assailant was seriously injured.

As a wise man once said, 'Contrary to what conventional wisdom has to say on the subject, violence really can solve a problem. Sadly, it is likely to create at least three new ones at the same time.' On the other hand, if you were able to defuse (or flee) the incident, the potential assailant may think you're a coward or a fool (do you actually care what they think of you?), but the whole can of worms remains firmly sealed shut. This is why it is better to avoid fighting altogether. But if there is no other way out … then fight hard and win.

An Offer to Fight Might be a Trap

A couple returning to their car was suddenly deluged with abuse from a man who was hanging around the car park. He threatened and abused the couple from a distance, and invited the man to fight with him, increasing the severity of his taunts as the couple warily continued on the way to their car. They left the car park and went home.

A few minutes later, a man was beaten, stabbed and robbed in the same car park. Police believe that he was offended and went over to 'sort out' the man shouting abuse, and was suckered into a trap set by a gang. He died.

Avoid!

The first 'layer' of your defences lies in avoiding trouble altogether. That may sound obvious, yet it can be seen from the actions of so many people that it is *not* at all obvious. Or perhaps it *is* obvious, yet they find reasons not to do it. It is unfortunately true that many people get hurt because they go in harm's way needlessly and are unprepared for what they find.

Unless someone has a grudge against you, an attack will be impersonal. You are a potential victim, a target of opportunity, nothing more. That may seem insulting, but it is actually to your advantage. If you do not offer a potential attacker a good opportunity to attack you (it is, of course, better not to give him any opportunity at all!) then he is unlikely to chase after you seeking a better chance; he'll let you go and wait for some other potential victim. Some attackers do select a target and follow them, seeking a good moment to strike, but the same principle applies – if there is no good opportunity, you will not be attacked.

The first stage in threat avoidance is understanding. Not of how and why attacks occur – that isn't important just yet. What we are interested in is where and when, so we can avoid those situations. Potential attackers favour certain locations and situations. Other situations have a way of throwing up random confrontations. You can reduce your vulnerability to attack by keeping exposure to these places to a minimum. Without getting into how and why attacks take place, let us imagine that there is a percentage chance of being attacked associated with any place (as long as you and a potential aggressor are both present there).

You already know what sort of places are high on the 'threat scale'. Ask yourself if you are likely to be mugged in the foyer of the local police station or to get into a fight at the Returns desk of the library? So where *are* you likely to be attacked? Think for a few seconds and you'll suddenly remember being uncomfortable the other night when you were all alone in the street, or when those young men came into the bar and started fooling around.

The point is that while many people cheerfully blank out the possibility of attack, they already know the sort of places that should be avoided. These come in two flavours. One sort is dark, secluded and removed from discovery or any possible assistance by distance or barriers such as walls and bushes. This is the domain of the gang, the mugger and the rapist, who know that they can do as they please in such places without fear of interruption.

- Dark and secluded places are potentially lethal.

The other sort of high-threat area is noisy and full of people. Normally the latter indicates a measure of safety, but with alcohol (and maybe drugs) to amplify emotions or cloud judgement, the town centre on a Saturday night is a high-risk area. No matter how many people are about, how close the police may be, or how many CCTV cameras are pointed at them, some people will become violent as a result of alcohol, a gang mentality or some random factor like a messy break-up ten minutes ago. One disturbing trend in recent years is for uninvolved passers-by to run up and kick anyone who is on the ground. Far from being a source of assistance, the boozy crowds may hide an extra threat.

- Crowds of town-centre drunks are just as dangerous as lonely places.

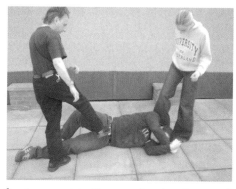

This happens far too often in our society. If you are forced to the ground, you must get back up. Passive covering will just delay the inevitable.

Why?

People who have been attacked often search for a meaning or a reason for the assault. They wonder if it was their own fault. It wasn't. It never is. No matter how unwise someone's actions are, no matter that they should not have been in that place, or doing that thing … unless you are the one who initiates violence, you're not the one to blame!

Looking for reasons is often pointless. I have been threatened and even attacked simply because I was there. On one occasion, I visited a city I'd never been to before on the same day as an important football match. Some fans of the away team decided to pick a fight because (in their beer-addled minds) I was a local, and therefore a fan of the home team, i.e. a member of 'the other side' and by inference, a perfectly legitimate target for a beating.

I didn't try to explain how and why they were mistaken. (I wasn't a local, and wasn't aware that the city *had* a football team, let alone being a supporter!) But none of that mattered. I was a target and they were going to attack me. I demonstrated a self-defence theory that I've held for some time: a sufficiently motivated sober person can run faster than several drunken ones!

I know people who have been attacked because they were students, Jewish, Muslim, gay, fans of an obscure football team, not fans of a prominent football team, wearing a tie with cartoon animals on it (!) or on the ground nearby and an easy target … It doesn't have to make sense anywhere outside the attacker's head, so don't believe that just because there is no reason, an attack won't happen.

Threat Avoidance

Threat avoidance is a matter of common sense. Stay out of areas that are high on the threat scale, or at least limit your exposure to them. Trust your instincts and think about what you are doing – and what other people might be doing. Some (hopefully all) of the following circumstances should be obvious as high-threat situations.

- Dark streets and alleys.
- Secluded areas such as parks and car parks at night.
- Areas where gangs congregate or hang around.
- 'Rough' bars and pubs.
- Town centres at night.
- Areas, and especially pubs, near a sports stadium on match day.

There is, however, more to it than this. If someone has decided to attack you, he will choose a moment when you are vulnerable and when he can gain most from the confrontation. In our daily lives, we are especially vulnerable or attractive to attackers at particular times. These include:

- When we are using an ATM or cashpoint machine.
- When we are coming out of the bank.
- In public toilets.
- While fumbling with car or house keys.
- When we have been drinking.
- When we are alone or far from help.
- When we are already distressed by other circumstances.
- When our hands are full of shopping or other objects.
- If we seem weak or helpless due to age, manner or appearance.
- When driving, wherever we are forced to stop.

The other thing that makes us particularly attractive to a potential assailant is when we are Code White – that is, not taking any real notice of the surroundings and any possible threat that might be encountered. Interviews with criminals suggest that the great majority of attacks for gain (cold attacks) are carried out on people who seemed like a good target precisely because they were not alert to the possibility. Surprise is a great ally, and criminals know this. Easy targets will be chosen in almost all cases.

You can also try to avoid people who seem to be – or are becoming – a threat. While you are out and about you should be aware of potential threats and prepared to respond if necessary as a matter of course (Code Yellow). You will be able to spot people that seem to pose a threat.

Trust your instincts – they are pretty good, despite the veneer of civilisation! It may be nothing tangible, just a feeling about the way someone is lounging half out of sight in a doorway or the attitude of a group of young men on a street corner. When the 'radar' sends you a warning like this, act on it. You are already in proximity to the threat, so complete avoidance is unlikely to be an option. A discreet U-turn is always a possibility though. Who cares if it makes you late or it's obvious you were nervous? Better that than the possible alternative! Discretion is the very best part of valour.

There are ways to minimise the danger posed by individuals. You can cross the street to put some distance between you or walk by screened by a lamp-post or other pedestrians. The majority of potential attackers don't care enough to go to any trouble – they'll act if an opportunity drops in their lap; otherwise they probably won't bother.

There is a third factor in threat avoidance, particularly in the case of a potential hot attack. Avoid confrontation and do not be drawn into an argument or a shoving match. Although it may be hard to keep your temper and to resist the temptation to get a few choice words in, just don't do it. There is a 'script' that confrontations tend to follow. The scene builds up from a seemingly minor incident into a violent confrontation that can end with you being kicked to death on the floor. If it starts, break the script and play the scene out on your terms.

Better yet, avoid being drawn into the situation in the first place. Someone looking for trouble may well be liquored up, trying to impress his mates or a girl, or he may decide to take exception to something you do, or wear, or possibly something he thinks you are. It's not important. What matters is that you may be able to avoid becoming his chosen victim.

When around potentially aggressive people follow these simple guidelines:

- Keep your distance. You can't accidentally jostle someone if you're not close. Similarly, they can't jostle you to try to get a response.
- Don't make eye contact if you can help it. Many potential aggressors see this as a challenge or a tacit agreement to a confrontation.
- If your eye is caught, break contact. Don't get drawn into a staring match. Sometimes just looking away is fine, as if you were just looking around. Alternatively you can half smile and vaguely wave, mouthing a greeting as if you think you know him but aren't sure. He may think you're an idiot, but it's a graceful way to disengage.
- Always be ready to withdraw, back down, placate someone or even leave the building. If someone starts demanding to know what you're looking at or tells you to stop eyeing his girlfriend, it's better to apologise and say you don't want any trouble than let your temper flare and get drawn in.
- Keep your temper and maintain your focus. It doesn't matter that this isn't your fault or that you weren't doing what he says you were. Just remember what *you* want out of this confrontation – to get out without a fight. You win if that happens, whatever he says.

Avoiding dangerous places and dangerous people is the first layer of your defences. Around 80 per cent of potential threats can be nullified simply by ensuring that you are not in a place where you can be easily attacked at the same time as a potential attacker.

Summary

- If you have to defend yourself, even if you win, there may be further problems. Thus the very best response to a difficult situation is to avoid it altogether.
- Avoid dark, lonely places.
- Avoid potentially dangerous people.
- Be aware of the times you are most vulnerable, and act to minimise them.
- Be willing to openly turn around and go elsewhere.
- If a situation starts to develop, look for a way out. Don't be drawn in!

Chapter 3: Deter!

It is not always possible to avoid dangerous situations or people. Sometimes you will have a reason to be in harm's way. Other times, trouble will find you – and usually when you don't expect it. So the first layer of your defences has failed. No problem; there are plenty of options left – and don't think that avoidance is useless because a threat leaked through that layer. You may never know how many threats you have successfully dealt with by being somewhere else.

Having failed to avoid the situation, we now move on to deterrence. We will assume that you and the potential attacker are in reasonable proximity. You can see one another, but nothing has happened yet. It is time to evaluate the danger.

Threat Analysis

Threat analysis is simply the skill we all have (to some degree) of spotting dangerous people or situations and weighing up the odds. Threat analysis tells us how likely we are to be attacked and how serious the threat is. That in turn leads to an informed choice about whether to withdraw, fight, run or surrender. We instinctively conduct a threat analysis whenever a situation presents itself. We become uncomfortable, even frightened, in situations where we could be in danger. This is a good thing *if* we use it effectively.

The single biggest obstacle to threat analysis is complacency. Many people wander about in a state of complete 'Code White' numbness. The brain cells charged with threat analysis may well be jumping up and down and screaming something about dark alleys, gangs of youths armed with baseball bats and the wad of money in your hand, but onward you amble, until the threat grows so big and so obvious that you can't ignore it. By then, of course, you've had it.

The other end of the spectrum is not a good place to be, either. If you are hypersensitive to threats then you'll become a nervous wreck who overreacts to the slightest threat by running away screaming or piling into everyone who comes within reach. Neither is particularly desirable.

Somewhere between hypersensitivity and total brain anaesthesia is an enlightened, balanced state of mind where you are aware of potential danger and are ready to act, but are firm enough to discount trivialities.

In this alert but confident state you can analyse the threat and act calmly and responsibly to it. That does, of course, include taking violent measures – even pre-emptively if necessary – or fleeing back the way you came, but at least you'll be doing these things in a reasoned and responsible manner.

Threat analysis is a matter of common sense (what in the self-protection field is not?). People who have violence in mind give off subtle (and often less than subtle!) signals. Your instincts know how to read them. Strong clues include:

- As you approach, an individual keeps looking in your direction, then quickly away again, and is acting excessively nonchalantly.
- Members of a group look in your direction, exchange words or a nod, and begin to move (purposefully or otherwise) in your direction.
- Individuals move to close off your path or escape route or to surround you.
- 'Twitchy' or agitated movements.
- Short words. People about to attack you tend to use short words and sentences.
- Attention fixed on you.
- Eye contact.
- Expression. Hostility is usually easy to read.
- Posture. Splayed arms or hands that seem to want to grasp something.
- Tension, sudden movements and an inability to keep still.

These are very strong clues and are certainly sufficient that you would be justified in preparing for violent self-defence or flight. You would be very foolish to ignore such clues, though many people do.

Some attackers (of the cold variety) may try to seem calm, friendly and helpful to gain your confidence. That way, they can get you into a vulnerable situation or persuade you to lower your guard before striking. Often someone who operates in this way will slip, letting you catch a glimpse of their real intentions. But by then your first impression of a nice, friendly or harmless individual will be firmly fixed, and you will probably ignore conflicting signals unless you are very alert. So be very cautious with strangers, especially when you are alone with them for the first time.

It is also possible to determine the level of threat by a quick glance. Some things about a potential attacker will quickly give you an impression of how much trouble you are in. These include:

- Weapons
- Numbers
- Physical size
- Confidence
- Obvious ferocity
- Reputation
- Appearance (tough, or rough)

However, some of these impressions can be misleading. Someone who appears rough and ferocious to the point of caricature may actually have nothing to back up their intimidating appearance. Whether or not it's worth taking the risk is an open question. But this serves to illustrate the other side of the threat analysis coin. A potential attacker will be evaluating the threat too, and you can use this to deter an attack.

Deterring Cold Attacks

Unlike in the Avoid phase, the reason for the attack or potential attack is important. A cold attacker is looking to gain something and will be careful in selecting his victim. Remember that:

- An attacker does not want a *fight*, he wants a *victim*.

The motive for a cold attack will be to get your possessions or money, to rape you or to hurt you for pleasure. The potential attacker will weigh the prospect for gain against the amount of trouble he is likely to have to go to – or the prospect of getting hurt – before making his decision. If you seem like the sort of person who will make him work for his gain, he'll probably look for a better risk-to-gain ratio.

Think of it as a see-saw. If an attacker perceives that the 'gain' end is heavier than the 'risk' end, he is likely to attack. The other way around, and unless he's desperate, he'll back off. If the see-saw is fairly balanced, then it could go either way. What actually happens is determined by how badly he needs the gain that he perceives and how you handle yourself.

How to tip the see-saw in your favour is dealt with in 'Target Hardening for Beginners', below.

Note that we project power on a subliminal level, and an assailant will pick up the signals even if they lack the brain capacity to understand why you seem powerful. A powerful or empowered person comes across as someone who is:

- Aware of what they want – and that includes not being attacked.
- Used to getting what they want. They won't surrender easily.
- Not used to backing down. They'll put up a hell of a fight.
- Assertive. They'll act with authority and effectiveness.

These are things that no potential assailant is looking for in a victim. Indeed, an empowered person is not likely to be a victim – or at least, not to act like one. They may still become a victim, be overcome by surprise or strength or cunning, but they won't give up willingly. That mental picture is quite a deterrent to the potential attacker. But how do you achieve this image? Do you need bulging biceps and a tight vest to show them off? A shotgun under your arm? Well, those would help. But for normal people, the image of empowerment is projected like this:

- Tidy appearance. It says 'I know what the world thinks of me, and I care what it thinks; I am aware of my surroundings.'
- Dark clothing. For some reason, dark clothes are seen as powerful.
- Confident, relaxed attitude. It shows that you are in control of the situation.
- Brisk, purposeful movements. They show that you know what you are doing and how to achieve your aims.

The image of empowerment is nothing to do with fighting skills. It is more a subconscious thing, whereby some people are seen to be in charge of their life and surroundings, and others are not. The image can be entirely false, yet it influences people very strongly.

Put simply, a scruffy individual ambling along, head down and apparently purposeless, is likely to come over as someone who doesn't care what happens, thus a 'victim', while a tidily dressed individual, obviously going somewhere and alert to their surroundings, is seen as a much harder target. Sufficient potential gain may make an attacker take the hard target, but the odds of your survival are better if you reduce the apparent gain while increasing the power you project. This will also increase your chances of talking your way out of trouble or forcing someone to back down by acting assertively. The psychology of this phenomenon does not concern us. It is simply useful, so we will use it for all it is worth.

Deterring Hot Attacks

Someone who is angry (at you, or in general) is still attacking for gain – he wants to release his anger by hurting someone. But his threat analysis is likely to be skewed by his anger. Other gains may be seen as peripheral advantages, but for the most part his end of the see-saw is weighted by his fury.

Passive measures as described in 'Target Hardening' do work against a hot attacker, but they are generally less effective. Even someone who is very angry at you is unlikely to launch an assault as you stroll with six other members of the Domestic Wolf Owners' Association and your pets, but for the most part you are likely to need the measures described under 'Confrontation Management'. Of course, by practising basic target hardening you make yourself less likely to be picked for a Hot confrontation in the first place …

Triggering Violence

One statistic that stands out about assaults and particularly rape is how often the victim initiates the violence in the situation. This is not to say that the victim was to blame – that is never true! But sometimes a person, feeling threatened, will strike out, usually with a push or slap that it supposed to say 'enough of that!'

Many assaults are triggered by this action. The situation is teetering on the edge of violence; it could go either way. Hitting or shoving someone may trigger a reflexive or angry response, but it has another effect. It creates a situation (in the mind of the attacker only!) that violence is acceptable in this situation. Once physical violence has entered a situation, it can only escalate.

To repeat: a rapist or violent attacker is the person to blame – not the victim. However, many such people need a trigger to open the psychological door to assault. Do not give them one. To put that another way: don't hit someone unless you fully intend to lay them out!

Target Hardening for Beginners

In general, attackers seek soft targets. You can 'harden' yourself (make it less convenient to attack you, or make yourself less attractive to attackers) with some basic measures. Of course, some targets are perceived as 'softer' than others. Many attackers will look for physical weakness, meaning that people who are most at risk are:

- Children.
- Older people.
- Women.
- Anyone who is physically small or seems unable to act in self-defence.
- Anyone who is encumbered (e.g. with children, bags and so on).

At the most basic level, a target is perceived as 'hard' if:

- An attack will have physical consequences.
- An attack will have legal consequences.
- An attack will present problems of another kind.

The first case refers to people who seem like they can defend themselves or who have sufficient numbers to make an attack problematic. An attacker is far less likely to tangle with you if you have a dog or an implement such as a walking stick with you or if you are with other people who appear to have some capability to assist you.

The second case refers to the possibility of being caught and punished. The number of people around will make a difference, especially if some of those people are obviously with you and are therefore likely to raise the alarm and give a good statement or description to the police, even if the attacker does not feel that they could stop him. Similarly, CCTV cameras can have a deterrent effect since an attacker knows he may be identified. The exception here is drunks, who tend to forget or cease to care about such things.

The third case is the target who makes it hard to attack them. Someone who habitually looks around at their surroundings and cannot be surprised or who casually uses obstacles to impede a potential attack may be seen as not worth the trouble. The following target-hardening techniques work for everyone, though some may be more appropriate than others to certain age groups.

Personal

You can make yourself less attractive to potential assailants, a harder target, or both, by these measures:

- Hide the gain. Don't display your wealth, watch, clothing, car and so on.
- Stay with others you trust.
- Book taxis rather than wandering around at night.
- Dress smartly but not ostentatiously.
- Walk confidently.
- Be continuously and obviously alert.
- Don't make yourself vulnerable by wandering around drunk.

At Home

There are a few basic security measures that you really should already be taking. Forget what people think of you. Forget about being called paranoid. Think about survival.

- Lock doors and windows. Use deadbolts if you have them and get them if you don't. A house or flat should be a safe haven, but it's no good if anyone can just walk in.
- Don't have the TV or music on so loud that you can't hear what's going on. Besides, it annoys the neighbours.
- Use the door chain or peephole. You do have one, right? And even with the chain, make sure you are balanced as you open the door so you can slam it and/or lean on it if someone tries to force entry.
- Try to get a look at callers out of a window, especially at night. You can also see if there are others lurking out of sight.
- Don't open the door at all to groups of youths. A conversation held through the letterbox is fairly undignified, but better than letting a mob into your home.
- Don't let strangers in to use the phone. By all means offer to make the call for them, but don't be talked into removing your best defence against attack – a solid obstruction.
- If you let someone in, close the door and be sure it latches so no one else can wander inside.
- Check the ID of anyone who calls claiming to be from an organisation. As a rule, even the pushiest utility company reps don't call late at night. Meter readers certainly don't.

- Keep an eye on even apparently legitimate callers. Don't leave them alone, and don't let them keep the door open.

This is all basic, obvious stuff, yet so many people don't take even the simplest precautions. Common sense is your best guide as to what is appropriate. Just remember that it's better to be embarrassingly paranoid than kicked to a pulp and robbed or raped.

Out and About
While out on your daily business, remember to follow the guidelines in this chapter. Particularly:

- Code Yellow – alert for hazards – should be your natural state. Look around you, take notice of what your instincts tell you, and don't be complacent.
- Minimise vulnerable periods. Have keys ready and make sure there is no one lurking near your car or home as you approach. Don't linger by banks or cash machines to count your dosh. Pocket it securely and depart briskly. Check that no one follows you.
- Use handy obstacles like lamp-posts and dustbins to ensure that anyone coming at you is slowed down.
- Change direction, train carriage, side of the street or bus if you sense you are moving into a dangerous situation or if you think one is developing.
- Stay away from people who seem dangerous. Trust your instincts. If someone nudges his mate, nods at you and laughs, withdraw quickly.
- Don't be drawn into a confrontation.
- Get where you are going efficiently without travelling through secluded, dark or otherwise high-threat areas.
- Carry a mobile phone. You may well feel that they are a curse on modern society, but they can be useful if you need to summon help.

Driving
Much of our travelling is done in cars these days. A car offers two excellent defensive advantages – mobility and protection. Ensure that you can use both at need.

- Close your windows (or only leave them an inch or so open) and lock the doors.

- Don't stop in risky areas if you can help it. Time your approach to traffic lights by slowing down early so that you don't have to come to a complete stop. It is sometimes better to nip through an amber light than halt beside a gang of toughs.
- If you have to stop, keep a good lookout. If someone approaches the car and seems like a threat, pull away if you possibly can. Take care to avoid collisions, of course, but if you are faced with the choice between a minor traffic violation and remaining in a dangerous position, then it is usually best to err on the side of self-protection.
- Make sure your vehicle is reliable.
- Choose your route sensibly. Major roads are a better bet than quiet back alleys.
- Consider joining a motorists' rescue service. They do not cost all that much, and if you do have problems on the road, you won't be left wandering around in the middle of the night.
- Many objects that can legitimately be carried in a car – spanners, cans of de-icer and so on can be used as improvised weapons. Never carry a weapon explicitly for that purpose, but be prepared to use whatever is to hand to deter someone from getting in the car with you.
- Drive steadily, smoothly and sensibly. Try not to get annoyed at other motorists, and don't give them a reason to be mad at you. If you are on the receiving end of road rage, remember that you can only be attacked if you stop and the attacker can get to you. If you do get stopped in traffic and someone tries to get at you, lean on the horn to attract attention.
- If you are attacked and someone tries to drag you out, your seatbelt is unlikely to stop them, but it will entangle you and prevent effective defensive measures. If you cannot simply drive off or slam and lock the door, then it is best to undo your belt and get clear of the vehicle, giving you freedom to fight or run.
- Be aware that the simplest way for an attacker to immobilise your vehicle is to grab the keys out of the ignition. Don't let that happen if you can prevent it. If someone does take your keys (and you don't have spares with you, obviously!), disregard the car as a means of escape and seek another way out of the situation. Don't try to fight for the keys or do what your assailant wants in exchange for the promise of their return.
- There are some places you simply should not drive through. So don't.

Target Hardening for Vulnerable People

Almost anyone could be considered 'vulnerable', so while these notes are aimed primarily at young mothers, older people and children, they are applicable to everyone.

Kids

Until you're almost grown up (and maybe not even then!) you can't really hope to deal with an adult attacker. Thus your best defence is the fact that your family knows where you are and when you'll be back, and if you're missing then it's full alert with search parties combing the streets!

All that shouting at you for coming home six minutes late or not being at your friend's house like you said you would be is actually wind down from DEFCON1. Your family were ready to take on all comers to get you back safe. Someone who considers attacking you will know that while they may be able to overpower *you*, they're not just tackling you – they're taking on everyone who loves you plus the local police force.

Other defences against adult attackers are to make sure you're with others who can report anything that happens (this is a deterrent, and if something happens to you then it's also your lifeline) and to only go to places that are reasonably safe; that is, places where people can see you and what's happening to you, and where you can't be quickly dragged out of sight. It might also be smart to take a dog (maybe one of your friends has one, but if not then you can score points with relatives or neighbours by offering to take theirs out with you – dogs like this sort of thing).

An attack on you by an adult is likely to be very serious, but it's also extremely unlikely to happen. You're more likely to be attacked by other kids, especially older ones or a gang. Designer shoes and cool mobiles are the prime targets; mobile phone robbery is one of the most common crimes around, and most of the victims (and the criminals!) are kids.

Maybe you can deal with another kid trying to take your shoes, but maybe not. Kids have been stabbed over a jacket or a phone, so don't rely on fighting. Your best bet is to play safe – stay away from people who seem dangerous, and get away if they approach you.

Most importantly, you should tell people where you're going and when you'll be back. That way if something happens to you, you'll know that rescue is on the way – and so will a potential attacker! It's a pain, but it really is your best defence.

Young Mothers/Young Women

If you're out with your kid(s) then you're responsible for your safety and theirs – not an easy task! And it's a sad fact that children make you vulnerable. It takes such a long time to get anywhere or do anything, and it takes all of your attention just to stop them diving under buses or eating chewing-gum off the pavement. You can't flee and leave your child (or anyone else's), and even just getting out of danger presents an almost insurmountable logistics problem.

Potential attackers know all this and will exploit it mercilessly. However, there are some measures you can take to mitigate the risk. Firstly, if your child is old enough, teach them that there are 'no messing' situations, where they *have* to do as they are told immediately. It is possible to make a kind of game of this, yet still teach your child some basic safety procedures such as what to do if there is a fire or if you have to deal with a crisis and get the older child, the new baby and yourself to safety. It is possible that even a fairly young child can actually be an asset if taught properly, but realistically the best you should hope for is minimising the difficulties.

It is wise to take another adult with you when you go out with the kids. Possibly there is another harassed parent you can team up with to do the shopping or the school run, or perhaps you have an older relative who'd enjoy the trip out (even if it does mean keeping an eye on the whirling dervish while you pay for the groceries).

Remember that even if the person you are with could not possibly protect you, they are an additional pair of eyes – many attackers will strike from behind when you are distracted, sure that you will be too stunned to get a clear look at them. It is far harder to evade two pairs of eyes than one. The other person, a potential witness, may be an effective deterrent. Besides, there is a deep-rooted reluctance in the human psyche to attack when outnumbered, even if the conscious mind says that there is no real danger.

Older People

Your chances of successfully fleeing or repelling an assault diminish as you get older, and attackers know this. They also know that the consequences of an attack are likely to be greater for you than for a younger person. But they don't care. It is therefore vital that you take steps to ensure your safety.

One particular factor affects old-age pensioners: pension day! Think about it: there is a regular time when you are sure to have money on you. This makes you an attractive target. You might want to vary the time you pick up your money or at least don't go alone. It is wise to take someone with you when you go out. Even if that person is less active than you, they are a second pair of eyes and a potential witness. You might want to consider getting a dog or carrying a walking stick too.

Do understand that a street thug has no respect whatsoever for you. He does not care that you are an old soldier or an elderly lady. All he sees is someone who is easy to hurt. You must resist the temptation to confront people and 'give them a piece of your mind'. It's just too dangerous. Instead, concentrate on your own safety.

Try to cultivate a habit of greeting people in passing; make sure the people you pass on your way to the shops recognise you. And be nice to them! Have a smile and a moment to chat (if they want), but don't pester anyone who's too busy. What you are creating by doing this is a support network; a set of people who are disposed to help you if you need it. And don't be afraid to ask for help if you need it – chances are you've earned a bit of goodwill by this stage in your life!

Strength versus Strength

You are not going to be attacked by someone weaker than you. A strong person, faced with a weaker opponent, will tend to launch big, one-shot-knockout attacks. You can't reply in kind. That means that you cannot match strength against strength and just battle your way through. So what can you do?

If you have the skill, you can pick your shots and use precise techniques to strike, or to attack the joints. It takes very little to break a bone or dislocate a joint. Anyone can do it if they know how.

And some things will hurt anyone. It doesn't matter if you are a little frail, or nine years old, or ill, or injured. There are still things you can do. Elbows and knees are powerful, no matter who uses them. Anyone can bite, scratch, poke at the eyes, kick out at the knees and shins, stamp on the instep or attack the genitals.

Target hardening is a matter of common sense. Trust your instincts, think about what might happen to you, and when, and act to minimise the potential. It's that simple.

Summary

- An attacker isn't looking for a fight, he wants a victim.
- He doesn't want consequences or comebacks.
- If an attack looks like being hard work, he won't bother.
- People alone are more likely to be attacked than people in groups.
- Don't become so wrapped up in what you're doing that you forget to be alert.
- Don't be embarrassed to take defensive measures if you're suspicious of someone or a situation.

Chapter 4: Defuse!

Once in a while, a confrontation will develop despite all your measures to prevent it. It can be very frightening to feel a situation sliding out of control towards violence. However, if you keep your head you can often defuse a dangerous confrontation and get out of it without having to resort to violent means.

Body Language, Words and Other Signals

Much of our communication is non-verbal. And just as it is possible to misinterpret a phrase, it is also possible to fail to read someone's body language correctly – or at all.

We are subconsciously able to deduce some meaning from the way a person stands, looks at us or fidgets. Most of us never realise we are doing it. However, as soon as we begin to try to consciously do it, reading body language seems to become rather difficult.

Most people's interest in non-verbal communication is related to dating and relationships; many of us deliberately study the subject (and other people) and become minor experts on the romantic signals that people send. Yet few people have any interest in body language for self-protection purposes and can miss a broad clue about violent intent when they would pick up the slightest hint of interest in a potential partner.

Some signals that a person means you harm are very, very obvious. A person who seems determined to barge into your personal space, who is talking through clenched teeth, or who keeps on advancing after the third time you back up to give him some room probably means you harm in some way. The really obvious signals that someone means to hurt you include:

- Intense, fixed stare.
- Lowered brow (head tilted down).
- Sneer or snarl.
- Eyes: very big or very small pupils.
- Pecking motion with the head and neck.
- Arms splayed.
- Inability to keep still.
- Twitchiness.

- Constant advance or invasion of your space.
- Attempts to grab you.

However, it is possible to 'read' someone at a greater distance and stay out of their way if they seem aggressive. It is always wise to avoid drunks and obviously rowdy people, but others are a little more subtle. Someone who is looking for trouble is likely to display some of the following characteristics:

- Tension in the body.
- Looks around frequently as if searching for someone.
- Sharp, angry movements.
- Frequent eye contact with anyone willing to meet his stare.
- Very direct movement if he has to go anywhere.
- Willing to push or walk into people rather than go round them.
- Meets any glance or contact with defiant, aggressive posture.
- Mutters a lot, especially one-word insults.
- Turns around quickly and aggressively if anyone comes close to him.

It is wise to stay away from anyone displaying these types of behaviour, to avoid or break eye contact and not to be drawn into a confrontation for any reason. Any encounter will be headed towards a violent conclusion from the start.

Someone who means you harm will tend to be abusive and use a lot of foul language. There are several reasons for this, from building up his own confidence by putting you down to scoring points off you with his hard-hitting insults and taunts – in effect already attacking you with his words. Words, of course, can't cause you physical harm, but allowing yourself to be goaded into a fight might have that result.

If someone is talking coherently and in longish sentences, then chances are he does not mean to launch an attack. (Although conversation can be used to disarm an opponent.) If, however, the sentences are getting shorter, then he is working up for an assault. Once someone is speaking in monosyllabic grunts, his intentions will be very apparent.

- The shorter the words and sentences, the more danger you are in!

Body language is also a useful indicator during a confrontation. Many people will give away their intentions before attacking (known as 'telegraphing' the attack) and this will give you time to evade or pre-empt. Some of the clues that give away an attack are fairly subtle:

- Narrowing of the eyes.
- Twitching of the mouth.
- An indrawn breath.
- Sudden tension around the shoulders.
- Shifting of weight.

Other signs are very obvious, such as 'chambering' a blow (cocking the fist ready to punch, then launching it). However, many 'street fighters' practise striking by surprise, often by talking to their victim while they move in close. It is therefore very important to watch for the signs of an attack developing and not to let anyone you do not trust get close to you.

Trigger

I witnessed a 'classic' assault a while ago. Two men – both had been drinking – began to argue. Neither would back down. There was no pushing or shoving, but one of the men had a point to make and the other was very aggressive and abusive in his rejection of it. Things got steadily more heated, and the less aggressive man started to shout. He wasn't ready for violence; his hands were down. He was just angry, insulted and a bit drunk. Unfortunately, he made a sudden movement and the other man lashed out in response.

It was about the worst punch I have ever witnessed: a weak, overhand downward cross hook-type thing that a sober man could have walked slowly out of the way of. Against an unprepared, flat-footed target with reflexes slowed by drink, it was all that was needed. It hit the bridge of his nose and smashed it. The victim folded up in pain and shock and – thankfully – the attacker just postured a bit and taunted him. It could have been much worse.

Confrontation Management

Human behaviour often falls into patterns; we are predisposed to act out certain roles as if there were some kind of script. Knowing that certain kinds of behaviour will trigger certain responses in other people is a useful tool, especially when you realise that most of them will not understand that it is happening. For example, two common roles that we fall into are

'Angry Parent' and 'Defiant Child'. This has nothing to do with biological relationships or who is involved. It is simply that if a person is involved in a situation and begins to act the role of 'Angry Parent' (they will probably do this subconsciously) then the person opposite them will naturally become defiant.

It is thus possible to manipulate a situation without the other person even realising it is happening. Some kinds of sales people use this technique in various ways. However, you can also trigger an argument or confrontation without meaning to and drag an unwilling person into the script by acting out a role – almost always without meaning to assume it.

You may think that once a script is underway, you are locked in to it. This is simply not true. If you change the role you are playing, the script changes with it. Thus you might choose to act as a 'Helpful Advisor' rather than an 'Angry Parent' to get the same message across, (usually) with better results.

- Change the script and take charge of the situation.

The other (rather strange) result of this script theory is very useful to us. People are comfortable when they have a script and act naturally because they know what to do. If you suddenly break the script and place them in uncertain territory, they may become confused; certainly their actions are less natural and require more thought. This is useful to us in several ways.

In a typical confrontation, one person assumes the role of 'Aggressor'. There are two natural responses. One is 'Frightened Victim', the other 'Counter-aggressor'. These are the responses that the aggressor will expect and be comfortable with. Which you fall into will dictate the remainder of the script.

Frightened Victim: He will strut and posture, threaten and push you, and generally enjoy the feeling of power. Your fear fuels his aggression and his ego; he will quickly or gradually escalate the violence he employs until he gets around to doing you some serious harm or robbing you, possibly both. Acting like a victim is unlikely to get you off lightly; it just means that he will take a little longer about harming you.

Counter-aggressor: Faced with a sudden threat, his own defensive reflexes will be triggered. As the preamble of shouting and pushing escalates, he will suddenly (and subconsciously) make the decision to 'go' and attack you all-out with extreme violence.

Neither of these scripts has a happy ending. It is not normally possible to change the script by assuming a role he will react to. Once his role is set, he will play it out. The time to change a script is before it is 'set.'

- Your best chance to change the course of a confrontation is early on.

Breaking the script, however, can and does work. If your response to his role does not make any sense – does not follow a conventional 'script' – then he will be confused. Rather than knowing what to do (i.e. being guided by the script) – he must formulate his responses; he must think. And a thought-out response takes longer than one that follows a pre-set pattern.

One way to break the script is not to react at all. Someone begins shouting abuse at you and you just pass by (at a safe distance). Your response doesn't make sense; you're supposed to react. By the time the potential aggressor has overcome his confusion, you are on your way out of the danger zone.

Another form of non-reaction is the calm readiness of a trained person. Rather than being rattled by the aggressive approach, you simply stand there, expression neutral. Without making aggressive moves, you slide into a semi-ready stance. He's now got a problem. Your reaction makes no sense to him, causing confusion and doubt, and your calm stare says that you don't consider him worth getting excited about. This can be very intimidating.

- Training will help you remain calm under stress.

The best way to break a script, however, is to say something totally unconnected to the situation. Someone snarls at you or demands to know what you're looking at and you ask him what the time is or how to get to the railway station. It is best to say something that requires an answer other than yes or no, but almost anything is better than being drawn into the script.

Once the script is broken, it is likely that a new one will begin to be created. You could attempt to set this script by assuming a role, but do understand that the person in front of you is still predisposed to violence and so any new script is more than likely to be an action film. It is better to use the confusion to withdraw if at all possible under the cover of the potential assailant's hesitation, to seek a better position or to attack pre-emptively if this seems like the only option.

It is worth noting that many attackers require a trigger before they can act. There are many reasons for this, but one is simply that many would-be fighters are such cowards that they cannot bring themselves to take someone on face to face. A surprise attack from behind is fine, but if the potential victim is aware and facing them, they are unable to just go in and attack in the face of opposition.

- Some people need an aggressive action from *you* to trigger their violent instincts. Don't give them one.

Such people will actually try to get *you* to make the first move by pushing, threatening, shouting, taunting or whatever means they think will work. Once you can be induced to shout or push back, their inhibitions are overcome by their instinctive fight or flight reaction and they can act – usually suddenly and with great violence. If you can avoid providing the trigger by remaining calm (but ready to act), then the situation will not escalate into violence.

Similarly, many people genuinely do not want to fight. Temper, ego or peer pressure makes them say something belligerent and a response in kind locks them into a confrontation. Unable to back down (through pride) but unwilling to initiate violence (either through fear of being hurt or because they don't want to fight at all), such a person will attack with words and the odd shove until something happens to break the deadlock.

If you give such a person a trigger then violence will ensue, but if you can give him a way to back off without losing face, he will often take it. This is called 'loopholing', and many people who have got into a confrontation without wanting to fight are only too glad to be given the opportunity to wriggle out of it. Some are, of course, too ignorant or too angry to take the offered loophole, and violence is a likely result unless you are willing to back off, make an apology, accept some abuse and depart the scene. Given the alternative, you really should be.

- Most of the time, if you give someone a way to get out of fighting with you without losing face, he will take it and be glad of it.

When trying to 'manage' a confrontation, it is important to remain calm and alert but to be ready to evade or attack if it becomes necessary to do so. However, a fighting stance not only gives away your intentions, it is also seen as threatening. It may be the trigger that the assailant wants. Certainly, if you have brought your fists up and gone to a ready stance, you have shown the world that you are willing to fight, and your potential assailant knows that people will have seen this. If he backs down now, he'll be seen to have retreated instead of fighting. So he won't.

• If you bring your fists up, you are going to have to fight.

Of course, if a fight seems likely anyway, then get your hands up to guard and be ready for it. But there is a better way to be ready and yet not give anything away. This is the 'fence' as discussed in the next part of this book. For now, it is enough to say that a good fence made with your hands open, coupled with a slight change in posture, places you about 90 per cent on guard without looking in any way threatening. If you also say placatory things and attempt to disengage, the gesture will look natural and non-threatening.

You get the best of both worlds with a fence ... a good guard position, deception about your state of readiness, *and* you don't cross the line and make violence inevitable. Learn how to use the fence. It is one of the most useful self-defence tools you can acquire.

Back Off and Win Later

I was involved in a long-running dispute with a neighbour who was causing trouble for the whole community. A request to desist became a confrontation. Seeing where it was going (and not liking the look of the neighbour's three mates), I backed off, accepting abuse, taunts and continued anti-social behaviour. Mr J didn't back off. Angry, he began to shout. This triggered a reflexive attack by the miscreant, who broke Mr J's nose and caused other injuries from which he still suffers.

The villain of the piece was evicted from his home shortly afterward, *and* prosecuted for his assault. I ended up in court as a witness against him. He was found guilty, but more importantly, he had absolutely no idea that I was responsible for the legal proceedings that cost him his home. There was no need to tell him, so I didn't. I just quietly won. I got what I wanted out of the situation by backing off and finding another way to win. Mr J came over all manly and confrontational, and just got hurt for his trouble.

Summary

- Learn the signals that'll tell you if someone means you harm.
- Break the script.
- If a confrontation develops, try to defuse it by giving the other person a reason not to fight with you.
- Be ready to defend, but don't make aggressive movements.
- Use the fence!

Chapter 5: Evade!

The last-but-one layer of our defences is to evade. This can be taken to mean ducking a blow, but here the term has a wider meaning. Evading is the skill of getting away from a confrontation, putting an obstacle in the way of an attacker or creating a situation where an attack is unlikely to be carried out. However, note that you cannot evade an attacker if he has hold of you. You must try not to let him get this close, and if he does, you must create a space in which to manoeuvre and begin your evasion procedures.

Personal Space

None of us like having someone move too close to us uninvited. Unless it is someone we know and trust, we are uncomfortable in this situation and rightly so. Personal space equates roughly to the distance we can punch, so it is no surprise that we are instinctively uncomfortable with a potential attacker getting that close.

This space is sometimes referred to as the 'threat zone' or 'defence threshold'. This is because someone who is inside your personal space can attack or grab you very suddenly, leaving you no time to react. Thus many people feel (with justification) that someone deliberately moving into the threat zone must be repelled, violently if necessary. This is worth emphasising:

- Your personal space must be preserved and defended if necessary.

If someone does decide to move into your personal space, don't let them stay there. Move away a little, perhaps with a smile and a joke about not being able to focus that close. Decent people will get the hint. Anyone who insists on being that close is probably up to no good and can attack without giving you any warning. This is a very bad position to be in. To keep people out of your personal space, you can move, use barriers like a table or post, or you can put up your hands to create a fence as described below. Worst case, you can attack them as they move in, but obviously there has to be a real threat before this becomes an option.

Anyone this far away is no real threat. You will have time to react to an aggressive movement – so long as your hands are not in your pockets!

Most street attacks start at 'conversation distance'. This is about as close as you want to let someone get unless you trust them. If you have any suspicions at all, don't even let them get this close!

There is no way you could react to an attack launched at this distance. No way at all. Maintain your personal space.

The Fence

Clenched fists and ready stances give away your intent to fight and can tip a confrontation over the edge into violence. Besides, it may not be considered 'reasonable' to assume a ready-to-fight stance in the face of mere posturing.

An alternative to a fighting stance, which also helps preserve your personal space, is the 'fence'. There are many ways to create a fence around your personal space: a glare (non-verbal fence), a request to give you some room or a sharp warning to stay clear (verbal fences of two very different kinds), or interposition of an object (physical fence). We are concerned with the most useful form of fence, one made with your hands, which places them to act as a barrier, but in a non-threatening way that should prevent escalation.

The fence serves the purpose of preserving your personal space *and* positioning you to defend or pre-empt, yet it does not look threatening. Assuming this stance cannot possibly be construed as an aggressive action, yet it offers nearly 100 per cent of the benefits of a good fighting stance – and one other. It hides your readiness to respond to the threat, a fact that may be decisive. A basic fence will serve you in many situations. It is very much like a fighting stance (as you'll see in a later section), but it's non-confrontational and does not give your intentions away. To assume a fence:

- Move your right foot back a little and turn the foot to your right about 45 degrees. Let your front (left) foot turn a little too.
- Flex your knees slightly. Your torso will turn a little so that your left arm and shoulder are slightly more forward than your right. This body position is very much like a boxer's guard, but is less pronounced.
- As you're doing this, bring your hands up with your palms out in an open and non-threatening way. Your left hand will be slightly higher than and forward of the right, in a position similar to a guard, but lower, as if you're making a placating gesture or an apology.

Your hands are now positioned ready to deal with attacks, and more importantly they form a barrier between you and the opponent (a fence!) which he subconsciously knows he must remove or get around to get at you.

If you do all of this surreptitiously without obvious, 'fighting' movements, then your opponent will not realise you are preparing to fight, giving you a surprise advantage if you do have to resort to force. Hopefully, however, you won't, since you're both fencing him out of your personal space and talking him down. One other important advantage is that if you end up in court, nobody can say you provoked the fight by acting aggressively – putting your open hands up and moving back a little is hardly an aggressive action!

- A good fence preserves your personal space, but doesn't look threatening.

If you raise your hands while speaking (not snarling threats but just as if you are in the habit of 'talking' with your hands) then the person you are fencing out may not even realise how close you are to a ready stance.

Moving smoothly and evenly (not necessarily slowly), you will get ready to defend yourself without triggering a response from the opponent.

What if he insists on moving in anyway? He may bully or weasel his way in, act pally or just keep advancing as if oblivious of your fence. This is proof that he means no good, and therefore must be kept out.

You can try moving back a little (keeping the hands up) and ask him to give you a little space. Your fencing hands make a slight pushing gesture as you say this, making the whole thing seem more natural. He might back off at this point. If not, you can assume that he means you real harm. He's been asked to stay out of your personal space and even given a barrier to contend with. If he chooses to barge in anyway, then it's obvious that he cares nothing for what you want. You don't want someone like that close to you, so you're going to have to stop him.

- If someone tries to barge through your fence, you *know* he means you harm!

Here, the fence serves another useful purpose. Your left hand, which is forward, is ideally placed for a straight-fingered eye jab if necessary. And when his chest touches your left hand, the range is about right for a right cross or hook. If you've been subtle about setting up your fence, he will not even know that you're ready. You'll have a single clear shot at him if you choose to take it.

A good fence is little different to a defensive or fighting stance, other than the open hands. However, it might not be identified as a fighting posture, which can allow you to talk your way out of trouble or launch a surprise pre-emptive attack.

Deterrence

A friend of mine stopped for a bite to eat on the way home from a sporting event. As he waited at the fast-food counter, he spotted a couple of young men nudging one another, nodding at him and talking conspiratorially. Sure enough, one of them started to purposefully approach. My friend did nothing overt, just shifted his feet slightly and started scratching his chin (his hand close to a guard position without seeming to be). He looked steadily at the approaching would-be attacker.

At the last second, the attacker bottled out. His purposeful strut evaporated and he veered off to head for the toilets. My friend isn't a big guy, but the attacker realised that he wasn't going to be the easy target that he'd seemed at first. The young man was quite willing to shove around or even assault a random stranger, but at the first sign that there might be resistance, he changed his mind about the matter.

If you know what to do and are clearly ready to do it, you give off signals that many (but sadly not all) potential attackers will pick up. Knowing how to defend yourself actually makes it less likely that you will have to.

Obstacles

Obstacles can be vitally important in keeping an assailant from harming you. The most obvious obstacles that come to mind are large physical objects like cars, pillars and doors, but a creative person can find something to place in the way of a potential assailant. Obstacles need not be large, nor are they always a physical obstruction.

For example, bad footing, broken ground and so on can obstruct an attacker. He may not want to step into a patch of deep mud or come at you through a nettle patch, and if he does he will be slowed down. In this way, some obstacles can become traps for an attacker. Positioning yourself so that if he does rush you, he will have to come through an area of loose and uneven footing may not stop him from doing so, but he may turn an ankle, be suddenly slowed or even made vulnerable to your counter-attack by your choice of battleground.

Barriers can help you in many ways. Here, the defender has backed up until she's got a post between her and the aggressor. As she turns to flee, the obstacle delays him.

People make good obstacles too. Not only are they solid and difficult to move out of the way, but they often take exception to being manhandled in this manner. People who may be quite unwilling to protect you from assault could still be allies if you can entangle the attacker with them. This should give you time to escape.

In a fight situation, obstacles can be used to temporarily neutralise one or more assailant while you concentrate on another. When you are attempting an escape, visual cover provided by disappearing behind an obstacle can give you the chance to change direction and elude pursuit, to find a hiding place or to ambush a pursuer.

In summary, obstacles:

- Can provide physical protection from attack.
- Can provide respite or simply make you hard to get at.
- Can be used to cover your escape and/or slow pursuit.
- Can limit an attacker's mobility.
- Can thin out an attacking group's numerical advantage.
- Can be used to conceal you.
- Can be almost anything.

Assistance

Assistance for threatened individuals is, sadly, far too thin on the ground in modern society. You cannot passively rely on assistance being rendered, but must instead base your response to a threat around the assumptions that:

- Help will not present itself unasked.
- Even asking for help may not get a result.
- Help, if it arrives at all, may well be too late.

Thus you should assume that you have only your own resources to rely upon, though at the same time you should take active measures to ensure that help *does* come. You might think that a crowd of potential witnesses should be a reasonable deterrent. This is not the case. Some attackers simply do not care or become so blind with rage that they forget about witnesses and CCTV cameras. Other factors are at play too.

- Some attackers are too drunk or enraged to care who sees what they do.

For some reason, attackers are generally not deterred by the presence of people who were there when the attack began. There is a feeling that these people have tacitly agreed to the confrontation, and therefore are no threat to the attacker. This is not always the case, but it happens with surprising frequency, especially in town centres at night. It appears that for far too many people, witnessing a fight is simply part of an evening's entertainment.

If you can take the situation into new surroundings, the attacker's perception often changes; he begins to feel the threat posed by witnesses and may back off. He also has the feeling that he does not 'know' this crowd; the perceived risk of intervention is greater. The psychology at work here is complex and irrelevant to us; it is enough to know that the phenomenon occurs and to use it.

The police and other services are bound to assist you if you can make your plight known to them. However, unless you call them yourself, you cannot be sure that they will be called at all. Many people will dial 999 the instant they see someone in trouble; it is a trained social reflex and an important part of our society. Yet others will simply shrug and get on with their business, so it is something of a lottery as to whether someone will place that vital call or not. And, of course, responding to an emergency call takes time, especially on a busy night.

- You can't always rely on the police to get there in time. They may not even be called at all.

Some people are predisposed to offer assistance wherever it is necessary. This includes well-intentioned passers-by as well as that curious creature, the 'white hat' street fighter. The latter is a rough individual who is quite possibly out looking for trouble, but whose personal code requires him to 'keep it in the family' – that is, only fight with people who also want to fight. Such people often use the laudable ideal of protecting the weak as an excuse to indulge their darker instincts and yet maintain a feeling of moral rectitude. As long as you don't pick fights with these people, you're in no danger from them, and anyway, it really doesn't matter where help comes from, as long as it comes. The problem is that most of the time – it doesn't!

There are some steps you can take to ensure that help is summoned or given. Many people can be more or less forced into becoming assets in your struggle for survival. This is because one of the strongest motivating factors for humans is fear of the consequences of action (or inaction). Someone who is willing to ignore the sounds of a struggle or even cries of 'rape!' from outside their home will probably respond to the word 'fire!' – because fire might have consequences for them!

Similarly, someone witnessing an attack may sidle off out of the (probably valid) fear of becoming a victim and will probably not head for a phone or even use their mobile. If you grab them and tell them to make the call, you create a moral imperative that may break through their apathy. You have also created a new consequence for them – the possibility that they may have to explain to the police or their peers why they ignored your request for help.

- Apathy, fear and selfishness may stop people from helping you.

This is an important factor. People will pretend they have not seen anything or that they did not recognise a dangerous situation unless you give them no excuse. That means you must make a noise, hammer on doors or if necessary, break something to get attention. It is strange how the sound of a car window breaking can bring the owner tearing out of his home when he failed to hear your cries for help a moment before. Do not be concerned with property damage if your life is in danger.

If you are being followed or pursued, it is sometimes possible to 'wipe off' the pursuer on other people; that is, to lead him into a situation where he becomes entangled (not necessarily literally) with other people and thus slowed down. If he is barging through a crowd, it is possible that he may end up in a confrontation with someone else, allowing you to escape. This can also work when you are under attack. Leading your assailant in amongst other people may or may not prompt them to assist you, but if he starts forcing his way past them, the likelihood of intervention increases greatly.

- Active measures are often required to obtain assistance from the people around you.

Try to ensure that the people around have no excuse not to help you. Thrust your problem in their collective face; demand help, and if possible, use them as entanglements to slow or get rid of your attacker. Criminals and thugs do not want an audience. The more fuss and noise there is, the more people will look. That correlates directly to an increased chance that some of them will actually try to help you.

Not Everyone is What They Seem

A friend of the authors, a student unfamiliar with the city, was walking home from a party past a park that was notorious for assaults, rapes and even a murder. It was three in the morning and he was dressed as a clown. Spotting a bunch of skinheads up ahead, he changed direction and headed into the park. The skinheads saw him and shouted something. He hurried on, so they started to follow him, still calling out to him. Thinking he was about to be attacked, he fled.

The skinheads gave chase. He fled, but a clown outfit isn't the best attire for jogging. Despairingly, he turned to face the six breathless skinheads. To his surprise, their leader said, 'Here mate, you mustn't go in here at night. Don't you know? People die in here.' He gestured towards the park and went on, 'Come on, we'll see you get home safe.' And they did.

Summary

- Maintain your personal space.
- 'Fence out' anyone trying to get close to you.
- If you must escape, run towards safety rather than just away from the threat.
- Have an escape plan in your mind.
- Use obstacles and other people to slow a pursuer.
- Don't rely on intervention by 'white hat' passers-by. Make people help you.
- Remember that your personal safety is worth a little inconvenience or embarrassment.

Part III: Under Attack

Chapter 1: The Attack

Much of self-protection has nothing to do with being under attack, and your attention should be on avoiding any situation where you may have to use violence to defeat an attacker. However, the worst-case scenario can happen at any time, and if it does you must be ready to react without hesitation, to carry through your actions and to do whatever you must to escape intact.

What is an Attack?

An attack is a physical assault on your person intended to cause you harm. That is fairly obvious. The trick is to detect when a situation is deteriorating to the point where an attack becomes likely and to gauge how and when it will come. Understanding the nature of a potential attack will enable you to formulate an effective defence or escape.

As has already been said, nothing is certain in a self-defence situation, and unusual and downright bizarre things can happen. It is impossible to predict with absolute certainty what will occur in a 'live' situation. However, certain common factors emerge again and again from studies of physical assaults. In the vast majority of attack situations:

- The attacker is full of alcohol and/or adrenaline.
- The attack is made in an untrained but highly aggressive manner.
- The attacker is strongly right-handed and employs this hand as their main striking tool.
- The attacker does not employ sophisticated martial arts techniques.
- The attacker grabs or wades in swinging.

Something like 80 per cent of attacks begin with a grab of some kind. The usual follow-up is a right hook – *but this is not certain*. Often someone who is full of adrenaline will grab his target in such a way that his favourite swings are awkward, so he'll do something else, like headbutt or wrestle. If you can elude or break the grab you will often spoil the attack – but don't be so mesmerised by your efforts to break a wrist grab that you get punched in the face with his other hand.

Perceived Threat

One of the dumbest things I've ever seen took place while I was at university. I was standing around in a metalwork shop, waiting to start work on my latest engineering masterpiece. One of my fellow students said something. I didn't hear him properly, so I turned … straight into a right hook!

It was a big, slow punch, but I was flat-footed and had nowhere to go. I can't begin to explain what was going on in my head at that moment, because there was nothing … I just saw the threat and reacted. I threw a fast jab into the shoulder joint with as much weight behind it as I could manage. The shoulder stopped moving forward and the hook never reached me. I backed up and assumed a defensive stance, but my attacker just went grey and walked slowly away.

Demolishing fellow students was frowned on by the university, but my colleague realised he'd been stupid and didn't make a fuss about it (he wasn't seriously hurt, though his arm didn't work properly for a few hours). But even if he had, I was legally justified in what I did – I perceived a sudden attack, and dealt with it. I did nothing more than I had to. The fact that my colleague wasn't really attacking me didn't matter – I thought he was, and that's what matters in court.

And why did this happen? Well, apparently my colleague was bored, and had suddenly remembered my interest in martial arts. 'Hey, you do kung fu, right?' he said (which is what I half-heard) and threw a huge punch at me to see what I'd do! Well, he found out.

The Top Five Physical Assaults

The five most common physical attacks, which occur far more often than all the others put together, are:

1. The big right hook: the classic bar-brawl punch is actually a very inefficient way to hit someone. Almost always aimed at the head, this wide, swinging punch takes time to reach its target but connects with massive force. If in fairly close, the assailant will often try to grab you with his left hand to pin you for the strike. His weight may well shift onto the back foot and he will lean back to wind up for the punch. Further away, he will usually step forward with his left foot as he launches the

punch. Unless you are caught off-guard or flat-footed, you should have time to evade. Blocking such a big punch with an arm is unlikely to succeed. If you have fast punches, you can usually land a good tight blow while the attacker is wasting time and effort with his big wind-up and swing. Hit him hard enough and he'll be driven back and his attack will evaporate.

2. Body punch: either as an initial attack (usually without a grab) or after grabbing and dragging you in close, the attacker swings a large uppercut (a 'shovel hook') into your stomach region. If he has a good grip on you, he will usually keep hold and hit again and again. Breaking his hold will allow you to move out of reach. The only viable alternative is to smother the blow, get in close, then hurt him and drive him back so that he's too busy to hit you.

A body punch or 'shovel hook' like this one can demolish you if it lands.

3. Grab and headbutt: a favourite in tight spaces, the assailant will usually grab you with both hands and attempt to butt you in the face. Worst case, you can lower your head and let his brow meet yours, hurting both of you rather than just you, but it is better to evade the grab or at least get a hand to his forehead, pushing his head away or cushioning the blow.

4. Choke: standing or on the ground, from behind or in front, chokes are very dangerous. Methods of breaking them are discussed in Part III, but again it is better not to allow your assailant to get that close. If someone gets a choke on you, do whatever is necessary to make him release it. Don't counter-strangle or pull at his hands; it won't work. Instead you must hurt him and make him recoil from you in shock or pain. If you are being choked, your life is in danger and you have seconds to deal with it before you lose consciousness. Do whatever you must.

A grab around the throat like this can be used to immobilise you, drag you off, or choke you to death. You must react immediately if you are to escape!

5. Grab and drag: an assailant may try to drag you into a vehicle or a secluded place, or perhaps hold you for someone else to attack. Even if he is much stronger than you, you must make him let go. That means causing him pain and possibly injury by any means possible. Make a noise while you're struggling to escape. In about 50 per cent of cases of attempted rape, women who struggle escape unharmed. That figure rises to nearly 90 per cent for those who struggle violently or flee while making life difficult for the assailant and drawing attention to the situation, you affect his risk assessment. Are you really worth all this trouble? He may decide that you are not.

Once someone has a good hold on you or your clothing, you are very vulnerable. Try to keep your distance to prevent this from happening.

Attacks with glasses, bottles or knives are very dangerous, but are not quite as common as any of the previous attacks. Most assaults with such weapons take the form of a sudden threat or attack, usually with a thrusting action. Any such weapon must be treated with the utmost respect as a mere touch can cause serious injury. Evasion is vital.

- Armed attacks are extremely dangerous, no matter who is using the weapon.

These are the most likely forms that a sudden attack will take. Often, if a fight develops, the combatants will end up on the ground, and there you are exposed to the risk of being kicked by your assailant, his friends or sometimes a passing stranger. Measures for dealing with these scenarios are presented later, but it is really much, *much* better not to end up wrestling on the floor.

Recognising the Signs

Most assaults do not happen without any warning. You may not see the assailant sneaking up behind you but you might have, with a little more vigilance. Any attack from the front is usually preceded by a period of confrontation. The assailant will often engage in pushing or insults before actually attacking you. He may actually need to provoke you into responding to trigger his own 'defensive' reflexes. It is best to say little or nothing to a potential assailant, simply watch him from a position of readiness. If you must speak, try to restrict yourself to telling him what you want from him in a calm and assertive manner.

If he cannot provoke you into doing something stupid, your assailant must come to you to make his attack. There will usually be signs that this is about to happen:

- A sudden indrawn breath.
- Narrowing or widening of the eyes.
- Shifting of balance.
- Enraged or hateful expression.
- A 'twitch' or other movement as he gathers himself to make his move.

He may also have to close with you, entering your personal space in an aggressive manner. This is a very broad hint that something is happening. Most assailants, being untrained thugs, will come in with big, powerful but fairly clumsy grabs and swings. If you are ready to move and have read the signs correctly, you should have time to pre-empt, evade and/or counter the attack.

Most importantly, accept that an attack is likely and watch for it. Don't be mesmerised by fear or try to kid yourself that it won't happen. It might not, but it is better to be ready in case it does.

Justification and Response

There is a fine line between what is justified and what is not. It's never acceptable to hit someone just because they offend or annoy you. Likewise, a non-violent sexual approach (hetero- or homosexual) is not grounds for a physical response, even if you are offended or a bit scared. So how do you know when you are justified in using force and when you aren't? Most of the time it's really, really obvious. However, there are some situations that are just on the borderline, and this is where your judgement is vital.

If someone makes a sudden movement that alarms you, and you respond thinking it is a punch, *and your response is appropriate to a punch*, then you are justified. If a large, strong man has his hands all over you and won't back off when warned, and you fear that he is going to try to overpower you, then you are justified in striking – the consequences if you don't make him stop might be dire. In a situation that's right on the borderline, it all comes down to the level of threat *that you perceive*. Trust your instincts. Don't worry about being wrong. Protect yourself.

What Actually Happens in Fights

Most people have no idea what to expect from a fight situation. Indeed, many martial arts give a somewhat false picture as a result of an overstylised approach. There are, however, several things that come out again and again from studies of real-world conflict.

The great majority of combatants have no training (though they may be experienced street fighters). Of those who do have training, the majority do not use it for a variety of reasons. Usually the situation escalates through threats, pushing and shouting before any actual blows are struck. The most common exception to this occurs when the attack is 'cold'. In this case, the attacker has already decided that he is going to make his assault and either piles straight in or uses stealth or deception to sneak up for a surprise attack.

The most common opening attack from behind is a grab. From the front it is a badly executed but powerful right hook. If it lands, such a blow can end the matter there and then. However, it is relatively easy to avoid if you are alert. Most attackers will not use sophisticated combinations. They will instead launch a series of large one-shot attacks. If any of these land, they can be very serious, but they do not flow; there are momentary pauses between them. At some point the matter usually becomes one of grabbing and wrestling. Most fights that last more than ten seconds go to the ground, and this must be avoided wherever possible.

- Most attackers will hurl a series of powerful one-shot attacks.

Where a fight does not immediately go to the ground, it often becomes an unscientific grabbing match interspersed with powerful but relatively clumsy blows. Few brawlers make any real attempt to evade or manoeuvre. Most simply keep moving forward, getting closer and closer while swinging punch after punch. Some people attempt to kick a standing opponent. This is rare, and when it happens it is usually a clumsy (but still dangerous) untrained blow, attempted instinctively. Knees and shins are the most likely targets.

Street encounters usually degenerate into scruffy grappling matches where the odds are in favour of the biggest and strongest. Training and good tactics are required to end the matter before it starts to look like this!

When brawlers do succeed in getting close in, things get really vicious. Many attackers bite, grab hair or jewellery, or knee their victim. More raw strength than skill is used here, so the combatants tend to lurch about crashing into obstructions. This usually leads to one or both parties falling to the ground as much by accident as design.

- Most fights that last longer than ten seconds end up on the ground.

If an attacker gets his victim to the ground, he will almost certainly kick, even if the victim is helpless and no longer resisting. This threat does not just come from the initial attacker. Anything on the ground seems to be considered a fair target by certain kinds of people, some of whom will run in and kick even if they are uninvolved in the incident. Being kicked on the ground can be fatal.

- If you end up on the floor, you will get kicked.

Being hit – or hitting your attacker – is not necessarily the end of the matter. A single blow rarely ends a fight, but it can be the deciding factor. A quick and painful, but not damaging, jab to the face or kick at the knee sometimes gives an attacker second thoughts, though this is not usually the case. More often, a single, relatively light blow simply causes pain and anger in someone who is full of adrenaline. However, a sharp blow can open the door for a more powerful strike or gain you time to do something else. This is why trained fighters never strike once and wait to see what happens. They use combinations, opening the door with a quick strike and exploiting the opportunity that follows. That initial quick jab is the decisive blow, making an opportunity for a more powerful follow-up that *will* end the fight.

In summary, the usual course of a street fight looks like this:

- Some preamble involving threats and shouting.
- A large right hook.
- A grab and close-in wrestling.
- The fight goes to the floor.
- Close-in strikes and other vicious combat.
- Kicks to the helpless victim's body and head.

This course of events *must* be avoided. Fortunately, there are several ways to break out of the cycle or to turn each stage to your advantage. Later sections of this book demonstrate how this can be done, but there is one idea you can consider right now: you cannot be dragged to the ground if your attacker cannot get hold of you. Evade. Whatever else you do, keep him from getting hold of you.

The Battle of the First Salvo

Most fights are pretty much over the first time someone lands a decent blow, particularly if that blow is to the head. This is most likely to happen when someone attacks by surprise or uses deception and distraction to slip in close while disarming the victim with non-threatening dialogue. A sudden attack from this position almost always lands exactly as planned.

Similarly, a strike from behind or the side is usually extremely effective. Since the attacker can set up a perfect strike, the victim is stunned or rendered insensible. It is likely that the victim is wholly unable to respond, even if still conscious. Think of it as a naval battle where one side detects the other and is able to launch a salvo of missiles before the other is even aware of their presence. This catastrophic first salvo shatters the defenders, who can be finished off at leisure – if anything remains of them.

- A first strike, launched by surprise, is likely to render the target helpless.

However, this 'first salvo' may be pre-emptively launched by the defender, and may take an overconfident attacker by surprise. If this first salvo fails for whatever reason (alertness, evasion or countermeasures on the part of the victim), then a fight or scuffle situation commences.

- If the matter is not decided by the first strike, it will inevitably become a scruffy mess of shoving, grappling and random punches.

In a scuffle where attacker and defender are moving around, throwing punches, grabbing and shoving at one another, it becomes very difficult to get that clean, perfect shot in. With all those arms and legs flailing about, distance opening or closing, and the risk of being struck while you are attacking, opportunities for a precise, fight-winning strike are distinctly thin on the ground. What tends to happen is that most of the blows that land, while painful and frightening, are survivable.

Amid all that frantic scuffling, punches tend to be weakened by being thrown while off-balance. Often they only glance off. Some miss entirely. Most people naturally react by trying to get close and start grappling (this is a strong instinct in human beings), and once that happens the fight almost always goes to the ground. If it does not, then both participants in the scuffle will probably take a few painful knocks but, if they are full of adrenaline or trained to remain in control under such an attack, they will manage to keep fighting.

- Strikes launched in a scuffle are less effective than blows struck by surprise or in a sparring situation.

At some point, however, someone will either land a lucky blow or their opponent will make a mistake and walk into a punch. A really skilled fighter will find or make an opportunity for a good, solid strike. At that point, the 'first salvo' situation is restored. The opponent may not go down to the blow, but for a brief moment the door is open. This is an opportunity to get as many good, powerful blows in as possible or to close for a takedown and end the matter.

Obviously, if your assailant is on the floor and appears to have taken up residence there, you can leave it at that. But if he shows the slightest interest in resuming hostilities or is dazed but still upright, then you should escape immediately if you have the opportunity. If that is not possible for any reason then it will be necessary to finish him off. This does not mean delivering a brutal kicking or attempting to kill him. It means lining up and making a fight-winning attack while you have a clear shot; in effect, launching a new 'first salvo'.

- If you get the opportunity to land one or more clean blows, take it! The moment will be fleeting, and this may be your only chance to get out of the situation intact.

Note that this is a last resort. If you have done enough to win your escape, then escape! You should only 'finish' someone if you have no alternative, say if you cannot escape or are trying to protect someone. Remember:

- Most fights end with the first salvo.

- Those that do not usually go to the ground.

If it turns into an extended scuffle, you will need stamina to keep moving and punching until you get a chance to escape or you land that door-opening strike. Once the door is open, take the opportunity for all it's worth.

Keep in mind that the first salvo in naval warfare is usually launched with cruise missiles capable of blasting a ship into small pieces of blazing wreckage. If you get a chance to launch such a salvo, that's the effect you want to have on your opponent. Don't mess around when your life is in danger.

Sudden Grabs

A sudden grab is a major threat. Many attacks begin by immobilising you, and chokes only take a few seconds to render you unconscious. As soon as you feel a grab, break it! Move away, turn to face the grabber (if they're not in front of you) and be ready to defend yourself with the utmost vigour. If you wait to see what's going to happen or who's got hold of you, you place yourself in mortal danger.

Summary

- Learn to recognise an attacker's intent from his body language.
- Treat weapons with the utmost respect, whoever is holding them.
- Most street attacks start with a grab.
- The street fighter's favourite strike is a big right hook.
- Most protracted fights go to the ground.
- Most fights are decided by the first solid blow to the head.

Chapter 2: Respond!

When all else (Avoid, Deter, Defuse, Evade) fails, you may have to respond to a developing threat. If things get this far, then you are in a dangerous situation – a self-defence situation. However, this does not necessarily mean that you will have to get physical. There are still a couple of options available.

Successful self-defence does not have to involve violence. You may still manage to defend your safety by withdrawal or deterrence in the form of an obvious willingness to protect yourself. If things do get physical, self-defence may mean creating an opportunity for a record-breaking sprint to safety. Or it may, if there is no alternative, mean battling it out with your attacker. Just remember your objective: dealing with an assault does *not* mean winning a fight!

- An effective response means getting out of the situation with minimal damage to yourself or the people you were protecting. 'Winning a fight' is irrelevant except as a means to this end.

That is your goal. Remember it, and *stick to it*. Only carry on fighting if you have to. Escape if you can, as soon as you can. If you can't then you must fight and win!

The Big Secret

We make assumptions all the time in our lives. Most are based on our experience and are reasonably valid. In deciding to attack you, your assailant has made the assumption that he can get what he wants out of the situation without suffering much harm. It may look that way to you too. If you give in to the assumption that you can't escape or deal with this problem, then it becomes true and you'll get badly hurt.

Fortunately, assumptions can be incorrect, and here we discover the big secret about self-defence; the thing that most people, even skilled martial artists, never consciously understand. It is simply this:

- Nothing is certain or clear-cut in a self-defence situation.

In practical terms, this means that the unexpected can, and often does, happen. You may beat the odds. Your assailant may have all the advantages; numbers, skill, weapons, size or strength, but you may still manage to escape or even defeat him. Or you may actually have aces up your sleeve that are not apparent at first.

Whatever other factors may apply, you have one advantage that an assailant does not. Desperation. He can withdraw from this situation at any time; you cannot. You must *make* the opportunity to escape. You need to win more badly than he does. That, and the fact that you understand that nothing is carved in stone, can be enough to turn a situation around. But only if you possess the will to try.

- If you are willing to try, you have a chance. Give up and you're finished.

The odds against you may be huge, but that's all they are – odds, not certainty. Knowing that, you can set out to even up those odds or even stack them in your favour. You might get lucky by sheer fluke – anyone can trip up, become distracted or otherwise mess up when they have all the advantages – but there are things you can do to manipulate the odds and give you a far better chance of escape. Later chapters will discuss some of them. For now, remember that fighting hard is good, but fighting smart is better.

Perversely, there is an advantage to be had from seeming defenceless. An attacker who thinks he is going up against someone who could really hurt him will usually come in hard and fast, if he attacks at all. Against someone he holds in contempt, he will rely on dominance and his overpowering presence. He is more likely to grab or strike to hurt rather than damage you. He will not be expecting his weak, terrified victim to be able to do anything useful about it. You can use this to your advantage if you react in a determined manner and don't hold back. As long as you keep trying to win, you have a chance.

You Really Can Defend Yourself

However bad things are getting, you must always believe one thing:

- You *can* successfully defend yourself against attack!

You may be wondering what use it is to know that or indeed if it means anything at all. In fact, this is the most important thing to know, since without it you are helpless.

As you will see, self-protection is as much a state of mind as a set of physical skills. Many martial artists and confident people never even consider whether or not they have the ability to resist an assault, but if you are a physically small or weak person, it may seem that you would have no chance and should just give up. This is not the case at all; *you always have a chance.*

If you are convinced in your own mind that you are beaten, you may not even try to resist. Your responses will be half-hearted and easily brushed aside. Your assailant may well be encouraged by your feeble struggles.

- If you are defeated in your own mind, you are truly beaten before any blows are struck.

If, on the other hand, your assailant can see that he's going to have to pay for whatever he wants to do to you, he may decide to back off and seek an easier victim. If you do still have to fight, a response made with the intent of winning, in the knowledge that you *can* win the fight, will be more determined than one made with defeat in mind. It will be fast, hard and committed – and you are 500 per cent more likely to succeed.

One simple statistic bears this out. It has been found that victims of attempted rape who flee, struggle violently and/or make a noise are 50–90 per cent more likely to escape unhurt than those who surrender. In almost all cases, a rapist possesses advantages of size and/or strength, yet 'active' victims are far more likely to avoid harm.

Two examples from our own experience occurred during a 'free form' self-defence session in our dojo. One of the high-grade men was assigned to grab and 'attack' one of the women. He should have known better than to be complacent; she was wearing a blue belt (and we don't give those away with breakfast cereal), but, encouraged by her apparent dithering and lack of response, he marched straight in. She didn't bother with techniques, just waited until he overconfidently reached for her and kneed him between the legs. Game over.

Another of the women, who is very small and light and a relative beginner, was 'attacked' by one of the big lads during the same session. She'd just fended off one of the women in a calm and 'very dojo' manner.

As this new assailant reached for her, her reaction was totally different. *No way* was she letting this large man (who she didn't really know and wasn't inclined to trust) get hold of her! Her response was single-minded and vigorous to the point of viciousness. Even though this was a controlled dojo situation, he backed off dismayed. He didn't even *try* to use his strength; he *knew* she'd hurt him if he tried. Her obvious willingness and ability to defend herself was enough – she scared him off.

These are two very different approaches, but in both cases a much stronger assailant (one of whom was a skilled martial artist) was defeated by a determined defence put up by a small, light but resolute person. It can be done.

Non-Physical Responses

We can divide the possible responses to a 'live' situation into two categories: those that involve the direct use of force against an attacker, and those which do not. We will begin by discussing the non-physical responses you might make.

Withdrawal and Flight

Sometimes it's possible to simply walk (or run!) out of a dangerous situation. Forget any thoughts about cowardice; this is an effective response! After all, what do you want out of this situation? To escape without getting hurt! And you cannot be hurt in a fight that you don't have …

If it seems safe enough, you can simply change course to avoid the person shouting insults at you from the pathway ahead. Pride and ego might want you to keep on and walk right past to show you're not intimidated or even to stride up and give him a clout. But this is not wise. Muggers sometimes use verbal abuse to draw in their victims, and anyway, who cares what street trash think of you? Play safe instead.

- Life is more precious than ego.

If the person threatening or insulting you is already close, you will have to be careful about turning away. If you are within reach when you turn your back, you risk a sudden assault when you become vulnerable. Better to back off a little first and remain highly alert for a sudden movement or attack from behind. Basically it should be obvious when not to turn your back. Trust your instincts on the matter – they preserved Cro-Magnon man against sabretoothed tigers, and they'll work for you against the descendants of either that you may encounter on the street.

- If the only way to get clear of a situation is to run, then run!

You may find the thought of flight undignified or embarrassing, but really, who cares if that's what it takes to come home safe? Taking a beating or getting killed because you were too proud to flee might also be considered somewhat undignified.

Many times, a potential assailant will not bother to pursue you for more than a few steps or may give half-hearted chase for the fun of it without any real intent of catching up. If, however, you have a determined attacker behind you, your options begin to narrow. If you are fit you should be in good shape to escape and may be able to outrun him, especially if you are desperate.

If you are not fit enough to escape, then you still have some options. If you can run a short distance then you can use flight tactically to string out a group of attackers and even the odds somewhat or to tire them a little. Remember that when they get tired, they have the option to withdraw. You do not. Going for a little jog before the boxing match begins may be too much like hard work for lazy thugs. You, propped up by desperation, will fight until you drop. They are more likely to sidle off and find something less exhausting to do.

It is best to have an aim in mind when you choose to flee. Running can take you into more dangerous situations or locations, or cause you to trip or otherwise injure yourself, reducing the chances of successful self-defence. Better to choose an escape route or goal and make for it at your best speed.

- Flight should be directed towards an escape route or assistance.

Sometimes you'll just have to run randomly until they give up. Other times you'll be able to reach a public place, your car or some other means of ending the chase on favourable terms. But never run yourself to exhaustion. Better to turn a corner and stop, then vigorously attack the nearest pursuer as he comes racing around after you than to run till you drop and get attacked as you choke and wheeze for breath.

Verbal Resistance

By verbal resistance, we mean using your voice against an attacker. There are many ways this can be done. The authors have heard the same stories as everyone else about martial artists who can stun a grown man or kill a rabbit with a single shout. Handy as this talent may be (air is certainly cheaper than buckshot!), most people are not likely to be able to do much damage to an assailant this way. Shouting and screaming does have certain uses, however.

A sudden (LOUD!) shout or shriek can startle someone, creating an opening for a strike or a swift departure. The flinch reflex can cause someone to lose their grip on your lapel. A sufficiently loud noise can actually cause pain, and who wants to get close to a shrieking lunatic? Shouting also attracts attention. No assailant wants that.

The martial artist's *kiai* (shout while striking or kicking) is more than a dramatic flourish that says 'Look! I have punched stylishly!' The *kiai* tightens up the stomach muscles, creating extra power for a blow and ensuring that any return blow does not hit you while you are full of air. In this way, it serves the same purpose as a boxer's grunt or nasal exhalation. However, a loud *kiai* also distracts the opponent as you strike, while remaining less likely than a snort to dump the contents of your nasal passages down your shirt front.

Shouting while you fight wastes air but can be worth it for several reasons. Yelling as you thump someone may startle or distract your target while it adds power to your blows. It also makes you look like a 'complete nutter', which may put off others from tangling with you.

Verbal resistance also extends to the things you say. It is best not to snarl and make threats or, indeed, to speak much at all. Speak in a firm but calm and even tone. By all means give orders; telling people what you want from them implies that you have the power to make them comply. But say little else unless you have a good reason to (see 'Deception and Surprise').

Calm assertiveness can be intimidating to an assailant who expects fear and submission or adrenaline-fuelled rage. It helps if you have some succinct phrases to use. But whatever you say, make sure it comes out as a polite instruction or a firm order, never a plea. Good places to start are:

- Just stay there!
- Get out of my way!
- Don't!
- Keep away from me!
- I am armed!

The latter is a warning and obviously requires that you do have a weapon within easy reach. It can apply equally to the pool cue, kitchen knife or large spanner that you grab upon sensing the need for a weapon.

If you need to state a warning, make sure that what you say comes out as a statement of the natural consequences of a given action rather than as a threat. Especially avoid lame threats that are vague or obviously badly thought out.

- Stay there or I'll put you down!

This is far better than, 'If you come any closer, I swear, I'll tear your arms off … I really will …'

Sometimes after a situation has gone out of control, speaking calmly simply will not get through. This is the one and only time when snarling something like 'Fucking back off or I'll fucking kill you!' serves any useful purpose. The rest of the time, foul language is a waste of breath and may cause witnesses to wonder if you were just as bad as the attacker. Better to speak calmly and with authority than to yell obscenities.

Note that while you may find it intimidating when some thug starts screaming obscenities and threats, this does not mean that it will work for you. Such behaviour offends and frightens decent, civilised people but to the average street thug it's normal conversation. All you'll succeed in doing is giving him a trigger for his attack.

- You can't intimidate street thugs by trying to seem 'rougher' than them. So don't try.

There is one occasion when you might want to try acting the part of a complete psychopath. If you are attacked and manage to beat off one assailant only to find that his friends are starting to close in, it may be worth capitalising on the fact you've defeated one of their number. At this point, sounding and looking like a real animal is sometimes the only way to drive the message home. However, as a rule, an air of calm assurance is the best option. It is intimidating, gives nothing away and will not usually provoke a response. It is also useful if you end up in court defending your actions.

Above all, remember:

- Speak little, use short sentences and act like you're in charge.

Physical Responses

Once an attack has begun, you *must* deal with it. There was a time when a sense of fair play prevailed in fights; it was common for an assailant's friends to drag him off if he went overboard or for strangers to intervene to protect a victim. This is no longer the case. Giving in and 'taking it' is not an option since the great likelihood is that the attacker or even random passers-by will run up and kick you once you're knocked to the ground. Whatever this situation may say about our society, it is fact. Your only chance to escape without serious harm is to deal with the assault. That means making an effective physical response.

Appropriate and Effective Responses

What response you make to an assault must be governed by your judgement of the situation and it must be within the bounds of reasonable force. If you are sure that your life is in danger or your assailant means to do you serious harm, you should use whatever measures are necessary to defeat him. If you can avoid danger by, for example, allowing a burglar to escape unhindered, then this is the best course of action.

Whatever you do must be *effective*. Hitting someone in an ineffective manner is likely to anger them and may provoke them to hurt you more than they would have otherwise. Obviously, in some situations you have nothing to lose on that score, but you will need to weigh the risks for yourself on a case-by-case basis. If you must respond to violence, follow the ten basic rules listed below, always remembering the law as regards self-defence.

Ten Basic Rules for Self-Defence

Let us assume that all your preventative measures have failed and you are being attacked. You can assume that the assailant has some advantage. Only very occasionally is someone stupid enough to attack a superior 'victim'. Your attacker(s) probably has superior numbers, size, fighting ability or weapons. He also has the advantage that he is actually seeking a fight and you are not. This being the case, you must obey the most basic rule – survive!

You must do whatever is necessary to get out of this situation with your hide – and that of your companions – intact. That may mean running, fighting, biting, scratching or handing over your wallet. There's nothing in it worth dying for anyway. If you are forced to fight, then do so as effectively as possible. This is where your training, if any, comes into its own. Even if you have no training, there are certain rules that it makes sense to follow in a street fight or self-defence situation.

1. Don't go to the ground!

Anything on the ground seems to be considered a target by certain kinds of people. Even if your assailant has no accomplices with him, it is possible that someone will run up and kick you. *Never* go to the ground by choice.

2. If you do go to the ground, get up fast!

Many fights do go to the ground – most that get past the first-punch stage in fact. Sometimes it can't be helped. But if it happens, get up as soon as you possibly can. Don't pin an opponent and wait for him to submit; hurt him and get up.

3. Move!

Do *not* stand still, especially if outnumbered. It is surprisingly difficult to hit a moving target. If you can think clearly enough, you can manoeuvre tactically to make multiple assailants get in one another's way. At the very least you can make yourself far harder to hit or grab by moving about and be ready to make a break for it. This can be very tiring, but once you are static, you are an easy target – so keep on moving!

4. Don't overcommit!

Use simple, quick techniques to hurt or disable your attacker, but try not to get into a wrestling match or use overcommitted techniques that leave you vulnerable to counter-attack. Strike, shove or throw, and move on.

5. Stay alert!

Try to remain aware of your surroundings, of potential escape routes, new assailants and improvised weapons if such measures become necessary.

6. Remember, this isn't a kung fu movie!

There is no script, and your enemies will not line up to be knocked down one by one. Big, flash techniques will get you into trouble more often than they help. Never, ever try massive spinning kicks and other impressive techniques. Real experts know how to make them work – but they also know how risky such techniques can be. Keep it simple.

7. Don't fight strength!

Don't try to oppose physical strength or numbers. Move to make attackers get in each other's way. Push or throw them into one another. Evade attacks rather than meeting them head on. *Do not get involved in a wrestling match with someone bigger and stronger than you.*

8. Finish it!

Hit hard, throw attackers onto the ground, apply locks and, if necessary, use sufficient force to break or dislocate a joint. You did not start this; you didn't want it. But you had better finish it if you want to walk away. It is never acceptable to kick someone who's helpless on the ground, but if you get an attacker down and think he's about to get up and carry on attacking you, exploit your advantage. Kick him while he's trying to get up and keep doing it until he changes his mind about fighting you. Then stop!

9. Move on!

Unless you have a profoundly good reason for remaining at the scene, move on after the incident. Don't stick around to taunt your attackers or go back for a sly kick while they're down. Just get away from there and get on with your business. If you disable someone, you have a legal obligation to summon medical assistance for them, but this can be done from a phone a safe distance away.

10. Cooperate with law enforcement officers!

If the police become involved, you can help your case in any investigation by behaving in a calm and reasonable manner. If the attending officers find you enraged, swearing and kicking at a bloody pulp on the floor, you're in trouble. A rather better profile to present is this: you were attacked while going about legitimate business in a manner that threatened no one. You feared for your life or safety, and defended yourself in a calm and restrained manner, doing only what was necessary to ensure the attack ended. You stopped when it was obvious you were no longer in danger. You cooperated immediately and fully with the police and seemed pleased or relieved to see them (they are, after all, there to protect innocent citizens like you!). If you are arrested, comply politely with instructions but insist upon a lawyer. The police are not draconian fascists looking to stitch you up, but it's better to have the benefit of legal advice.

You Can Hurt Him!

I'm not a big guy, but I'm much, much bigger and stronger than the young woman who was my training partner for a while. I should have been able to demolish her. I moved in overconfidently, meaning to grab and drag her … and met the Mother of All Punches coming the other way. It went in under the breastbone and felt like it was coming out the back. I was on the floor before I knew I'd been hit. The woman who laid me out wasn't really trying – this was training, after all. And she weighs 6 stone less than me. She hit the right spot, not even very hard, and that was it – job done.

During an Assault

Coming suddenly under attack is a terrifying experience. An escalating confrontation with threats and shouting can actually be worse. If you find yourself dealing with an assault, these are the cardinal points to remember:

- Preparation: know the law and get some training *before* it happens! This will free you from doubt and give you effective responses to use.

- Assumption of threat: be ready in case a situation starts to become dangerous. Don't leave it until you are sure it's happening. That will be too late.

- Withdrawal: back off if you possibly can.

- Evasion: keep your assailant from getting hold of you or striking you.

- Escape: as soon as you can, find or make an opportunity and flee.

- Effective response: fight as hard as you have to until you can escape or there is no longer a threat.

As you realise a situation is sliding out of control towards violence, there is a strange, panicky numbness that can paralyse your brain. Don't give in to it! This is the time you need to think most clearly. Decide what you want out of the situation and set definite goals.

It is vital that you are ready if someone initiates an attack on you. Fighting stances are discussed elsewhere, but essentially you should be balanced and ready to move or resist an attempt to push or drag you. Your hands should be up. You can react more quickly that way. You must also stay alert – a second attacker could sneak up and attack you from behind. You should be doing these things and be ready for a physical response even while you try to withdraw or talk your way out of trouble.

Before an attack (during a confrontation):

- Say little.
- Give orders.
- Don't make threats; state consequences.
- Assume a ready position.
- Be ready to move.
- Withdraw if possible.
- Prepare a plan of action.
- Prepare an escape plan.

Once under attack:

- Make a noise.
- Escape as soon as you can.
- Only stay to fight if you *must*.
- Stay alert for other threats.
- Follow your plan.
- Escape towards help or safety.
- Finish what you start if you cannot escape.

After an Assault

The aftermath of an attack can be as bad as the attack itself. Even if you aren't seriously hurt, the trauma can cause lasting mental anguish. However, the effects can be mitigated by sensible actions at the time.

Medical Assistance
First of all, if there is any physical injury (to yourself or someone else, even the attacker) then it must be dealt with. If you fight someone off and he leaves under his own power, you are safe in assuming that he'll

see to his own medical needs. If he's unconscious or helpless, then you have a legal responsibility to see he receives medical attention.

Anyone with a serious injury should be taken to a hospital. (It may be quicker to use private transport or a taxi than an ambulance, depending upon where you are and what time of the week it is!) Even relatively trivial injuries should be looked at by your doctor, just in case.

While you wait for medical attention, there are a few simple things that you can do – and that may save your life. We will borrow a mantra from the British Army to help us. This procedure is designed for battlefield self-help by wounded soldiers. It'll serve us nicely on the street:

- Check the breathing!
- Stop the bleeding!
- Treat for shock!

The aim of battlefield medicine is to keep casualties alive until they can be properly treated. This is our aim too.

First, ensure that the casualty is breathing. Obviously, if someone is standing up and able to talk, they can breathe well enough. If the casualty is not breathing, you may have to perform CPR or assisted breathing. If you don't know how to do this, you may want to consider taking a first-aid course. We are not going to try to explain the procedure here for legal reasons. We will give a warning though: if there is any pulse at all, do *not* attempt to use chest compressions. You could stop the heart!

If someone is bleeding, then this must be controlled. If the blood is thick and dark, this is very serious, since it means that an artery has been severed. Thin, runny blood is less critical, but should be controlled quickly anyway.

Bleeding can be controlled by direct pressure (using a makeshift dressing or just your hand to close the wound). For very large wounds, push the edges of the wound as close together as you can and use a pad to cover the area where bleeding is worst, trying to hold the wound closed. If there is a knife or other implement in the wound, leave it there and pack around it.

Elevating a damaged area can also reduce bleeding, and very serious blood loss can be reduced by pressure on arterial pressure points. A first-aid course will teach you how to find these reliably. Note that stress is a factor in bleeding. If the casualty can be calmed and reassured, their heart rate and blood pressure will fall, reducing blood loss.

Other injuries, such as fractures, are unlikely to be fatal. The casualty should be kept still and treated for shock, and medical assistance should be summoned. If it is necessary to move a casualty (say to escape further danger) then try to immobilise the fracture. Someone with a suspected back or neck injury should not be moved.

Shock is caused by blood loss, extreme pain or a sudden, traumatic injury. It can kill even as a result of relatively minor injuries. A person going into shock may behave strangely. Symptoms are:

- Cold, clammy skin and possible cold sweat.
- Shallow breathing.
- Weak pulse.
- Low blood pressure.
- Thirst.
- Feeling sick or vomiting.
- Confusion, dizziness or feeling faint.
- Unconsciousness.

It is possible to 'fight' wound shock and carry on with whatever you are doing, but it is very unwise. Unconsciousness can be sudden, causing further injury. An unconscious person in shock may die.

Shock is best treated by the following measures:

- Lie the casualty down and raise their legs slightly (unless they have injuries that prevent this).
- Stop bleeding and immobilise fractures.
- Keep the casualty warm.
- Allow only small amounts to drink.

Shock requires expert medical attention, which should be sought immediately. The casualty may not want to cooperate, may be incoherent, confused or just incredibly stubborn, but they should be treated. If not, they may suddenly collapse or die.

Dealing with the Aftermath of an Attack

Not all injures are physical. To a gentle person, the memory of an attack can be very traumatic. Even if you acted perfectly correctly and escaped with no harm to yourself (and little to the assailant), you may suffer mental trauma for some time. It is possible to mitigate this, however.

Firstly, you should report incidents to the police as soon as possible. There are many reasons for doing this. A strong one is the fact that you've just been the victim of a crime! You may feel that the police cannot do anything, but one of the reasons they have trouble is lack of help from the public. Your report may become part of a bigger picture and lead to a successful arrest.

- You are expected to report crimes to the police. They can't act on what they don't know.

Other reasons for informing the police have to do with your own protection. If the details of the incident are on record and there are future complications, then you will be shown to have acted correctly. This is important if the attacker goes away with seemingly trivial injuries which turn out to be more serious than was apparent, or if they are later hurt by someone else. Also, if there are threats or some sort of comeback, a timely report of the original incident will help you build a case against the person harassing you.

There are two final reasons to inform the police. When you do so, your statement will be taken and the matter discussed with you. If it is obvious that you are an innocent person and were forced to defend yourself, the officers you deal with will be sympathetic and may offer you advice (police personnel tend to be less sympathetic towards people who go out fighting for the fun of it!).

One important factor here is reassurance. After your statement has been looked over at the local police station (this will probably take a few days) you will be told whether any action against you will be taken. More likely, you will be informed that action will *not* be taken against you. If you don't inform the police, there will be a slight doubt hanging over you about this. Making a statement clears the air.

- Being 'sure' that there will be no legal difficulties over what happened isn't nearly as good as knowing (because the police told you so) that there will not.

You may also be struggling with your conscience, especially if you hurt someone. The things said to you by police officers, coupled with the fact that you'll be informed that no action is being taken, should help you to put it behind you. Knowing that individuals and the organisation best placed to understand these things think that you have done nothing wrong can help *you* come to understand that too. The police can also advise you on local victim support groups.

If you find that you are still traumatised by the incident, you may be able to get some support from a local victim support group (the police can put you in touch or you can try the phone book), or from a more general support group such as the Samaritans. Talking to your friends and relatives can help too. Not, obviously, rehashing the gory details, but just 'talking it out' with people who care can help you get everything in perspective.

- Talk to someone – professionals, friends or family – about what happened. Don't let it stew.

Some people are contemptuous of counsellors. Don't fall into this trap. The human mind is an amazing, but delicate, thing. It can be damaged in an incident and need some help to heal, just like your body.

This is not to say you should wallow in self-pity – quite the opposite. One of the best ways to beat mental trauma is to be busy and active, allowing fewer moments for your mental injuries to sneak up and beat you about the head. In time, the scars will fade and you'll come to terms with what happened. But at first, that can be hard, so don't be afraid to ask for a little help. You'd ask a friend to help you stop your arm from bleeding or would go to a hospital with a knife wound, wouldn't you? What's so different about mental injuries?

Summary

- If you must respond to a situation, you must do so effectively.
- Be ready for physical self-defence, but try to withdraw or escape.
- Speak calmly and with authority. Say little.
- If a situation gets 'physical' remember that your goal is escape or survival, not 'winning'!
- Make a noise.
- Take any opportunity to escape.
- Remember, you *can* defend yourself if you try hard enough.
- You're not beaten until you give up or are rendered unconscious.

- Afterwards, report the matter to the police.
- Ensure any injuries receive medical attention.
- Talk to someone about the incident.
- Don't blame yourself.

Chapter 3: Tactics for Successful Self-Defence

Once a situation has gone so badly wrong that you have to fight, then it is imperative that you put up enough resistance to drive off the attacker or win an opportunity to escape. There are a few little tricks that you can use to greatly increase your effectiveness, plus a few things that you should *never* do.

What You Should Always Do

- Have a plan of action.
- Remain aware of your surroundings; watch for opportunities to escape or new threats.
- Keep moving – it makes you harder to hit.
- Escape as soon as you can.
- Use combinations rather than single strikes.
- Use terrain and obstructions to slow or hamper attackers.
- Remember the law!

What You Should Never Do

- Don't go to the ground.
- Don't wrestle or grapple with someone bigger or stronger than you.
- Don't wrestle or grapple with *anyone!*
- Don't stay to fight if you can escape.
- Don't lose control and become an animal.
- Don't fight unless you have no alternative!
- Don't let someone take you to a more secluded place.

Distractions and Deceptions

It is possible to use tricks and distractions to create an opening to escape or give you a chance to land a pre-emptive strike. There is absolutely nothing wrong with using such tricks – after all, you are using them against someone who is attacking you!

One simple distraction that really works is to throw something in your attacker's face. The object thrown can be almost anything. A handful of loose change is good, but anything you have in your bag or pockets will do as long as it is heavy enough to fly straight. You can distract an attacker with a comb, a handful of sweets, your half-eaten sandwich … almost anything! But *never* throw your car keys or mobile phone. These are tools you might need to escape or summon help later.

If you throw something at someone (it need not be hurled; an underhand toss is fine) then they will naturally react. The usual reaction is to recoil, throw up the hands to protect the face or try to catch the object. This creates a momentary distraction for you to attack or turn and flee. Be aware that some people will not flinch and that any distraction lasts for a second or two at best, so you must exploit the opportunity immediately. Even if you have more things to throw, this trick is unlikely to be effective more than once.

- Distract and act!
- Deception will probably work only once.

Spitting in someone's face, uncouth as it may be, can be an effective distraction. Similarly, kissing or licking someone's face as you grapple with him, or (if you are suitably unshaven) scraping him with your stubble may cause him to flinch away.

Other distractions include suddenly glancing off to the side of your opponent as if someone is approaching him from behind or making a sudden noise. Noise can be a powerful ally. A sudden scream or yell in the attacker's face may make him hesitate, and of course there are other benefits of making a noise as discussed earlier.

- Distraction takes many forms. Anything that breaks an attacker's concentration is useful to you.

Deception can be used to hide your real intentions. For example, if you have decided that your only option is to launch a pre-emptive attack, then speaking to your attacker can be a good cover for your preparations. Don't make threats – that gives too much away. Say something that makes him think for a second, something totally irrelevant like suddenly asking the time or how his brother is (even though you don't know him or his hypothetical brother from Adam!), or something disarming, like saying you don't want to fight.

Sometimes it is useful to attack while you or the attacker is still talking. Gunfighters in the Old West found that not only do people tend to concentrate on your words and not on the preparations to attack them, but they are also mentally disarmed while a conversation is going on. This can let you gain time on your opponent, which can be vital. If you intend to use deceptive speech:

- Ask a question or say something that gets his attention, and act immediately afterwards, or
- Start talking, and act in the middle of a sentence.

Another way to conceal your intentions is to use movement and timing. If you stand very still, it is easy for an attacker to spot you starting to move. This is especially true for poorly trained or untrained people who visibly gather themselves before acting. If you are already moving a little – moving your hands, changing the distance between you – then it is harder for him to spot when you start an attack. Again, this lets you gain a little time. Moving also makes you harder to hit.

- It is easier to spot a stationary object or person that starts moving than to identify a threatening movement among constant non-threatening and fake-threatening ones.

You can also suddenly change direction and speed to confuse an opponent, backing away slowly then suddenly closing in for a strike. Unless he is very skilled he will have trouble adjusting to the change in speed, and since he is probably following you as you retreat, you will suddenly be in range for an attack. This may make him reluctant to follow you afterwards, allowing you to gain some space or even enough room to turn and flee.

You can also deceive an opponent by feigning an inability to react, perhaps through fear or extreme tiredness. This ploy can be somewhat risky, since your opponent may see it as an opportunity to launch a devastating strike and come in hard and fast. Thus it is best to do this when you have a little space. In most cases, an attacker who sees his opponent fold up out of fear or exhaustion will not be able to help himself. This is when he is most vulnerable to an all-out counter-attack. He will be physically off-guard and, more importantly, mentally unprepared for his 'helpless' victim's sudden attack. This ploy (feigned fear or helplessness rather than tiredness) is also useful at the beginning of a confrontation if you plan to launch a pre-emptive attack.

- Faking exhaustion or panicked surrender can create a window for a fight-winning attack.

More complex deceptions, such as 'foot feints', where you shift your weight as if doing one thing, then do something entirely different, rely upon your opponent 'reading' them and reacting. This only works on experienced or well-trained fighters (*very* experienced ones learn *not* to fall for this sort of thing) and can be difficult to execute if you are not highly skilled. In short, complex feints and deceptions are not something you should worry about on the street. Most thugs will just come in swinging and your deception probably won't even be noticed.

Balance

It's a fact that everyone has an aversion to falling. The moment they lose their balance, people will stop worrying about whatever they were trying to do, and concentrate on regaining equilibrium. This can be turned to an advantage. If a big, strong person has hold of you, it's difficult to break free. Wrestling isn't going to work. But if you get him off-balance, you can twist away (or hit him) as his attention shifts to not falling over.

There are many ways to break someone's balance. One of the best is to shove up and back against his face and nose (or throat, but this is dangerous). He'll flinch and lose his balance. Follow up with a strong, sharp push, then twist away. It doesn't need much force, and it works.

Pre-Emptive Techniques

Contrary to popular belief, it is perfectly legal to strike someone pre-emptively if you have reason to believe that there is a real threat. 'He was about to punch me' is good enough. 'He's a skinhead' is not. Pre-empting an attack with a powerful strike is a good option if you're sure things are about to go out of control. This can prevent a situation reaching the point where you cannot win. However, there are other options if you are unable or unwilling to strike first.

If you are confident of your grappling abilities, you can close in, smother any attempt to hit you and use a takedown or restraint technique to gain physical control of the opponent. This is unwise if he is obviously stronger than you, and even if he is not, it's always fraught with risks.

Another option is to use a strike that causes pain and moves the attacker away from you. A double palm-heel strike to the shoulders will send most people reeling away in pain. Hopefully, the shock and pain of the strike will cause the attacker (who is now out of reach and able to withdraw if he chooses) to lose interest in you. There is always the chance that he will charge back in full of rage and endorphins, however.

The level of violence you employ must always be judged according to the situation. You will get no second chances; it is better to be sure than to be kicked to death for trying to use minimum force on someone bigger and stronger than you who was looking for trouble in the first place. Remember that you are the person responsible for your own safety. Do what you must to survive, and if that means striking first … then do it.

Pre-Empting

I once had a fight with a local bully. He planned to have a fight with me but I beat him to it. He'd spotted me and decided to 'give me some'. He came over to where I was standing, shoved me around, called me various names, invited me to hit him … the usual routine. He'd beaten up several people I knew who tried to fight him, and several more who didn't even try because they were so scared of him. This guy was *huge!*

I tried to wriggle out of the situation, looked around for help, but the only people around were six of the bully's mates – and one of mine who was edging nervously away. Not much help there. So, realising that it was going to happen anyway, I let fly a powerful body punch into the solar plexus that started moving about a second before I decided to hit him.

By the time he realised the fight had started, he was on the ground groaning and I was departing the scene at a rate of knots. His six mates just looked puzzled – they hadn't even seen the punch. I got well clear before the penny dropped and they decided to come after me.

Had I tried to slug it out with this colossus of a man and all his mates, I'd most likely have been hospitalised at best. As it was, I got out unhurt, and I owe that escape to a hard-nosed decision that since things were about to get as bad as they possibly could, I might as well chance all on a pre-emptive strike.

Improvised Weapons

All manner of things can be used as a weapon in self-defence. Any heavy object can add weight to a blow, anything sharp can cut and anything that looks remotely like a weapon vastly increases your chances of deterring an attack. Someone who does not believe you can hurt him with your fists may not be so sure about a table lamp or a kitchen knife.

- Remember that the use of weapons is governed by the law, and their use must constitute 'reasonable force' in the circumstances.

Many martial artists train with strange and interesting weapons of a sort that you are unlikely to find lying around. However, it is worth understanding that most of these weapons are derived from things that a Chinese peasant (or whoever was developing the art) might have had lying around. Skills learned in the dojo with a five-foot staff or a rice flail may or may not be useful on the street where these things are not available, but (with the exception of some of the really esoteric devices), many everyday objects behave remarkably like the traditional martial arts weapons.

Whether or not you want to get some weapons training is up to you. It's only really worth it if you intend to pursue a martial art. But it is worth understanding how some of the skills transfer across and how to use certain objects as weapons.

One important factor about improvised weapons is that they have an innocent purpose, so if you do have to use them, explaining why you had the weapon handy is not a problem. As an example, if you use a rice flail to disable an attacker, then even if the act of using it was lawful, you are going to have to present a good reason why you were carrying it. On the other hand, if you are attacked while driving and your hand falls on a can of de-icer or a steering wheel lock, then you are justified in having these weapons to hand. However, your use of them must still constitute reasonable force.

Knives and Similar Objects

Your home (and possibly place of work) has a number of objects that can be used to slash or stab in desperate self-defence. Scissors, kitchen knives, chisels and screwdrivers can all serve to deter an armed attacker … and they can kill very easily. It is actually harder *not* to kill someone with sharp objects, particularly impaling weapons like carving knives, than to inflict a mortal wound. Use a sharp implement for defence *only* where your survival is at stake.

Blunt Instruments

Lamps, pans, odd sticks found lying around, hammers, stools, the plug end of a power cord (the end with the vacuum cleaner or TV on it is just too unwieldy!) or even an unopened drink can add weight to the impact of a strike and can serve as a deterrent in a way that fists cannot. Blunt objects can be also used to jab with; even a rolled-up newspaper can be effective if used in this way. Blunt instruments can be used to inflict non-lethal injury. Blows to anywhere but the head are unlikely to be fatal, though they may well break bones. It is relatively easy to kill by hitting someone over the head with a hard object, so again, this is a matter for extreme circumstances. Otherwise, a blunt instrument makes a fine defensive tool.

Small, blunt (but hard) instruments such as keys or pens can be used to apply force. If you poke a hard object like a pen or key against the side of the head, the ribs, collarbone or the neck, someone who has hold of you will let go and recoil in pain. This can be vital if you are borne to the ground where there is little leverage. A bunch of keys held in the hand with a few sticking out of the bottom of your fist could also be used in this way, and the sharp edges of keys can be used to gouge at an attacker's face, which will usually make him back off or give you a chance to get up from the ground. Hairbrushes and combs also cause a remarkable amount of pain if used this way.

Bottles and Glasses

A large bottle makes a fine club, and even a small one can be held by the body and used to jab with, which can cause real pain to an attacker. Note that bottles do not break like in the movies, and slamming them against a kitchen bench is likely to leave you holding just the neck – if you don't cut your hand to ribbons!

Glasses, on the other hand, do break easily and become capable of inflicting nasty, jagged wounds. Obviously, only fairly solid glasses are any use here – champagne flutes are stylish but not very effective. When breaking a glass (even breaking one by ramming it into someone!), you run the risk of cutting yourself too. Broken glass is best saved for desperate situations.

Hot Liquids and Other Hot Weapons

Coffee, tea, soup or even a pan full of sauce can cause severe injury. Faced with an armed attacker, you are justified in threatening him with a pan off the stove or in throwing the contents of your coffee cup over him. This does not simply apply in the obvious location – the kitchen – but wherever you happen to be. Many people buy coffee and drink it while going somewhere. Some people make a point of having a nice hot cup of coffee in their hand while waiting for a late night train, and while this could hardly be described in court as 'being armed', it does provide a defensive weapon should you need it. Anything else that is hot can be used to cause pain to an attacker and distract, deter or disable him. Potential weapons range from a domestic iron to soldering irons and even hot food. Shoving a slice of hot pizza in someone's face will distract him while you escape or attack if necessary!

Note that hot fat is so damaging that it might be viewed as 'lethal force'. If you have nothing else in reach and your life is in danger, then perhaps a pan full of hot fat might be an option as a defensive weapon, but do be aware that it would be considered a very extreme response.

Flames

A cigarette lighter can be shoved into an assailant's face (while lit, naturally). Similarly, if you work with one, a hand-held blowtorch is a powerful deterrent. Don't bother trying to make a flame-thrower out of an aerosol can, though. The spray will work well on its own, without the risk of setting fire to your home, yourself or even causing an explosion.

Clothing

Several handy weapons can be improvised from clothing, whether grabbed from the laundry pile or taken off for the purpose. Heavy shoes can make a decent blunt instrument, while stilettos can be swung overhand to strike with the heel. A sock stuffed with anything heavy makes a good club, while a belt with a heavy buckle makes a weapon somewhat similar to the martial artist's rice flail. Odd items of clothing (or towels, rugs and so on) can be thrown at or over an attacker to entangle or blind him for a moment. More substantial clothing such as a heavy coat can be wrapped around an arm as a shield against a weapon, while anything heavy with metal zips can be swung as a flail.

Sprays

Many things come in spray cans or trigger-operated sprayers. Oil, de-icer, oven cleaner, deodorant, hairspray or almost anything else can be sprayed in an attacker's face to distract or disable him. Note that some things – such as oven cleaner – are highly caustic and may cause permanent damage. Such weapons must only be used where there is a very serious threat. Fire extinguishers also make excellent weapons since you can spray an attacker and/or bash him with the metal body of the extinguisher.

Improvised Shields

Chairs, bicycles, the kitchen bin (or an old-style dustbin lid if available) can be used as a shield and a (rather clumsy) club to defend against an attack. Jabbing the legs of a chair or stool at an opponent while keeping the seat in front of your body can be very effective. One of the authors once stopped a kick and demolished the kicker with – of all things – a large plastic laundry basket!

Other Improvised Weapons

Taking a lead from old Westerns, you can throw a handful of loose material like sand or gravel in an attacker's face to distract him or hopefully irritate his eyes. Irritants such as pepper, salt or chilli powder can be very effective.

   Almost anything striking the face causes a flinch reaction (especially if it is wet), so you can gain a moment to escape or find a better weapon by throwing the first thing that comes to hand. Random examples include:

- Potato peelings.
- A CD box.
- The cat (!)
- Rocks.
- A handful of soil.
- A bottle.
- A shoe.
- School books.
- Absolutely anything else that is to hand.

If you look around you, you will spot many objects that can be used to deter, distract or disable an attacker. It may seem silly to consider throwing a household pet in the face of an armed assailant, but if this gains you the time to run into the kitchen and find a suitable weapon, then it could save your life.

On To the End!

It is vitally important to finish what you start. A single strike may create an opening for another blow or give you time to escape, but if you freeze, horrified at what you have just done or wait to see what effect it has, you will have an enraged assailant to deal with.

- If you must use force, do not stop until you are sure the assailant cannot continue to attack you or you have a good chance to escape.

Don't worry about the legality of this. Refer again to the section on self-defence law, but in simple terms:

- If your assailant is still a threat, then you are justified in continuing to use force.

- If he isn't then you're not.

Body Armour

Contrary to popular opinion, it is quite legal for private citizens in this country to own body armour and to wear it while going about their business. The overt flak jacket type is probably not appropriate for ordinary people, but concealable body armour that can be worn under other clothing is available. At present, vests are normally slash and stab-proof or are designed to stop bullets. Combination vests are more expensive and bulkier.

There is really no point in most people obtaining body armour, but for some high-risk occupations, such as ambulance crews, doormen, taxi drivers and journalists, the investment may be deemed worth it. A stab vest is the best choice for most people. The basic type costs around £200, or £250 for a vest offering protection from the increasing 'syringe threat'.

Body armour, even the best available, is somewhat hot and bulky, and it does not make the wearer invulnerable. But if you feel the need is great enough, a stab vest may be an appropriate investment.

Dealing with Multiple Attackers

The truth of trying to fight multiple attackers is summed up in two words:

• You can't.

This does not mean it's all over if you're outnumbered. It just means that you cannot possibly hope to fight two, three or more people all at once. It is just about possible to shove, punch and generally battle your way through a small mob of attackers to gain an escape route, but as a rule if two or more people grab you at once or get into a position where one of them can attack you from behind, things look bleak. It's even worse if you end up on the ground wrestling with one of them. The others will take their time lining up the kicks and you won't have a chance.

• If two or more people grab you, you're in serious trouble.

If you manage to remain upright, you need to manoeuvre so that they can only attack you one at a time. This is incredibly physically exhausting, but you need to keep it up. Situational awareness is vital here. If you can use obstacles to slow or block some of the attackers, then the odds are better for you. Not good, but better.

If you get a chance to flee, then take it. If not, then you may be able to deter the group by dealing with the leader (he's the one with the big mouth who struts and postures for the benefit of the rest). You may be able to face him down or 'manage' the confrontation before it gets physical – it's unlikely but possible.

Once matters do become physical, if you can't escape then you are going to have to fight your way out. It may be possible to take the fight out of the whole group by demolishing one of their number (the leader is best) with a pre-emptive or highly skilled attack, followed by an obvious readiness to do the same to all the others.

If that doesn't work, then you're going to be involved in a desperate scramble with attacks coming in from all quarters, people trying to grab you – and sometimes getting in one another's way. Your only real chance is to attack everything that comes near you. Strike hard, fast blows intended to keep anyone from getting hold of you and (hopefully) cause sufficient pain and injury to make that individual drop out of the fight.

- Keep moving so they can only get at you one at a time.

You may actually have to attack one of them rather than let them all attack you at once. As always, your goal must be to create an escape route. If you can do this, then you aren't fighting several people at once, you're fighting them one at a time. This truly is your best chance, but it's not a good one.

If you find yourself grappling, you will end up on the ground where you'll get kicked. One option to defend against this is to get one of the attackers on top of you (that should present little problem, given how you got to be on the ground in the first place) and use him as a shield while you choke him out (if you know how). You can also make him recoil suddenly by attacking the face or throat, creating a space so you can get to your feet.

That's the crux of the matter – you have to get back up! A good grappler can defeat one person on the ground – indeed, many people train for ground fighting to the point where it's their preferred arena – but you can't deal with several attackers from the floor. If you can't get up and escape, at least start moving around to keep them from ganging up on you, otherwise you're in big trouble.

- If you are taken to the ground by multiple attackers, you must get up again!

If your attackers' goal is rape, then things may work out slightly differently. Rapists will want to subdue you or hold you down; they may hit you to take the fight out of you, but their main goal will be to get you down and helpless.

If you are upright, then your tactic is the same as before – you should keep moving and try to keep anyone from getting a good hold on you; cause pain or (better) injury and try to gain an opportunity to escape.

If grabbed or forced down, you still have some options. Your clothing and theirs will be in the way and will distract them. Or you could more or less stop struggling for a moment. (Only do this if you're well and truly held; if there is a reasonable chance you can get free then keep fighting!) Rapists are not focussed on hurting you; they want to get on with the act. That means that if you are not fighting back, they will keep hold of you, but they are unlikely to hit you. Their attention will quickly turn to savouring what they're about to do. While they are distracted, do something unbelievably violent and break free.

What you want is to not only disable whoever's got hold of you, but to get his accomplices to turn their attention to him rather than you. Biting, eye jabs and throat strikes are good options. You don't want to struggle free – you want the nearest one to recoil in agony and horror and his mates to look to see what he's screaming about – thus creating an escape route.

- Do not try to wrestle with one or several rapists.
- Cause pain or, better yet, damage and break away as they recoil.

As long as you keep on trying to get up and get away, you still have a chance. Anyone who has tried to administer a pill to a cat will be familiar with the sensation of trying to keep hold of a small hurricane with fur and claws. Take your cue from our furry friends and struggle like crazy. Bite, scratch and kick out at anything that comes within reach. Grab an attacker around the knees and pull him over. If you can create enough confusion you'll get a chance to surge to your feet and run for it. Or the attackers may decide that battling a wild-eyed dervish is just too much effort and back off.

Summary

- Prepare! Learn to look for improvised weapons and for potential escape routes.
- Make use of deception and distraction.
- Strike first if you are sure you are about to be attacked.
- Move, and KEEP MOVING!
- Use only simple, reliable techniques.
- Make use of improvised weapons.
- Break off and escape if you can.
- Finish what you start.

Part IV: Training

Chapter 1: Martial Arts and Self-Defence Classes

Even a small amount of training can be hugely beneficial to your chances of successfully defending yourself. Training not only gives you useful things to do, but makes the close-in, physical confrontation situation more familiar and thus less frightening. In some people this can be counter-productive because they start to think they're invincible after a few sessions, but for most the training experience is a positive one.

Anyone, of any age, has the right to some form of self-defence training, and a good club or course will make whatever special arrangements are necessary to allow students to learn what they can. Some martial arts clubs cater almost exclusively for young people; however, many instructors tailor their courses to older or less active people. The ones who really do not want to know are mostly into 'hard man' styles that are not appropriate for any but a small group of – let's say 'special' – people, anyway.

If a suitable course cannot be found, it may be possible to get together with a few other people and contact a local martial arts school and ask for one. If enough people are interested, such a course might be arranged and – one would expect – tailored specifically to the recipients.

Why Take a Class?

In a crisis situation, people react according to their training. That's why it's better to have some! Most people can figure out a fairly effective solution to a crisis, given time. But with the clock ticking and the stress piling up, panic can paralyse even the smartest of people. Any solution invented spontaneously will be sloppy and hurried, and so will its execution. This is still better than nothing, but a prepared, calm response is far superior.

- Fear and adrenaline will cloud your thinking. But if you know what to do ahead of time and you've practised it, you'll be all right.

Training has two benefits in this area. First, self-defence training gives you trained-reflex responses to carry out. This can be vital if someone tries to choke you or drag you off; such attacks can be dealt with if you know how. If you don't, your chances are slim. Usually you will have only a few seconds to respond … do the wrong thing and it's all over. There is simply no time for trial and error, and brute force rarely works.

The second benefit of training is hidden, but just as real. The knowledge that you know what to do helps you think more clearly and respond more assertively. This can deter an assailant who is not totally committed to attacking you. Even if a situation is beyond your experience, your familiarity with self-defence situations may help you come up with a response that would not have occurred to an inexperienced person.

- If you know what to do, it'll show. This means you may not need to do anything at all!

There are other reasons for going along to martial arts or self-defence classes, of course. Learning something new is a worthy act in itself. The achievement looks good on a CV and there are real fitness benefits. You get to meet interesting people … and throw them around the room, try to choke them, stamp on their fingers … Seriously, martial arts require rather more effort than most people are prepared to put in, but a couple of one-off self-defence classes cost little in terms of time or money, and they could make all the difference.

It takes regular and effective training to develop 'muscle memory' and the fitness required to be really effective in a self-defence situation, and this benefit is gradually lost over time. However, most people experience a huge jump in capability after attending a class or two. This is for two reasons.

Firstly, a decent class will teach you some basic things to do, and you'll go from having absolutely no idea what to do or how to do it, to at least having a general idea. As an example, many people really don't know how to throw a punch. A basic class will teach you, along with simple ways to break a grab or strangle.

Secondly, and most importantly, having some idea of what to do means that you are more likely to do *something*. What you actually do when under attack may be sloppy, unplanned, incoherent and not terribly effective, but that is still a thousand times better than rolling into a ball and waiting for the inevitable! Remember that most attackers don't want a fight, they want a victim. The instant you start doing something about the attack, you stand a chance of deterring the attacker.

- A few good classes will give you a quantum leap in capability.
- After that, progress is slower, but steady.

The primary benefit of taking the occasional self-defence class is psychological. Your attitude will change from 'Help!' to 'Hey, get away from me! I'm not helpless you know!' And what a difference that makes!

Be advised, though, that some people go along to a class, bash the pads and break a couple of wrist grabs, and strut out feeling invincible. This kind of psychological change isn't beneficial. All you'll have is an attitude and nothing to back it up. That's not much short of suicide, so don't let it happen.

Do take a class. A quantum leap in capability can be made in a couple of hours. Your chances of repelling an assault will be greatly increased and your chances of having to will be correspondingly diminished.

Finding a Suitable Art or Style

The first question is: self-defence or martial art? The issue is quite complicated, since some 'martial arts' are actually sports, and some are so stylised that they have no real self-defence value. On the other hand, self-defence courses are often quite superficial and while they can instil a basic capacity to defend yourself, there is usually little depth. Worse, some self-defence courses are little more than placebos. Students are shown some amazing techniques, spend some time punching a bag and are allowed to go on their way feeling better about their ability to repel an attack, when in reality they have learned little. The available courses and styles can be categorised as follows:

Stylised Martial Arts

Some arts are so concerned with aesthetics, forms and kata (solo displays of technique) that they have little value on the street. Some martial arts are very much bound up in tradition and do not take account of the real threat on our streets today. The situation is complicated by the fact that one instructor in a given art may be committed to practical applications of the techniques, while another may be concerned only with the correct performance of kata and forms.

Fitness Martial Arts

A current fad, this is actually a form of aerobics that uses kick-boxing-type movements. Fitness benefits aside, it has little combat value.

'Inner' Martial Arts

Some arts, such as t'ai chi, are a form of moving meditation using slow and graceful versions of fighting techniques. They are a great way to relax and learn balance (physical and psychological) and are beautiful to watch or participate in, but have very limited applications on the street. Some martial artists use 'inner' arts as part of their training package, usually as a warm-down at the end of a session.

Sport Martial Arts

Some martial arts are aimed primarily at competition. These arts are limited by their rules, which prohibit some techniques from being used in competition (so they are not learned), but there is still a lot to be gained from training within those rules. To give an example of drawbacks, take judo. Both the authors have trained in judo and have a great deal of respect for the art and its practitioners, so no insult is intended when we say that some aspects of the art are not well suited to self-defence. Judo practitioners train for competitions in which punching and kicking are not allowed. A defensive move when downed on the judo mat is to go into a ball or lie flat, face down. This is ideal for judo competitions, but on the street it will get you killed. Sport martial arts represent an excellent way to learn certain techniques – throwing and grappling skills in the case of judo – but you must remember to leave the competition techniques in the dojo.

Submission Fighting Training

This is aimed at the specialist arena of full-contact submission fighting. Practitioners are excellent fighters and are certainly able to take their formidable skills out of the arena (which has only a few more rules than a bar brawl!). Submission fighting training is very, very violent and not for most people. Also, ground fighting is a big part of submission fighting training, and as has been mentioned, the ground is the last place you want to be. That said, submission fighters are very capable of defending themselves if knocked to the ground on the street.

The two styles that are of most interest to us are:

Self-Defence Training

A good self-defence course will cover critical issues such as threat awareness and self-defence law, in addition to teaching simple and effective counters to likely street attacks. Such courses tend to stick to 'boring', 'vanilla-flavour' techniques with a heavy dose of reality thrown in. While a one-off course cannot create the muscle memory and high state of readiness that regular training does, such a course is a good option if time is limited.

Self-Defence-Based Martial Arts

These arts offer much the same as a self-defence course, but are structured as a traditional martial art, with grades signified by belts or sashes. A practical martial art of this kind must evolve to meet new threats, teach techniques that work for everyone (not just large, strong young men!) and must involve cross-training so that practitioners can do something effective if they are knocked to the ground, are caught in a tight space or find themselves facing more than one opponent. In other words, a self-defence-based martial art must, more than anything else, be practical!

These classifications are not intended to denigrate any of the groups listed. Each has its merits and within its own field is highly effective. We have a particular set of requirements, and it is worth understanding that many martial arts are simply not appropriate to that need. However, the lines are somewhat blurred. Boxing, for example, is technically a sport, but boxers are extremely effective fighters outside the ring. So are muay Thai practitioners (Thai boxers) and kick boxers. A judoka (judo student) can be deadly if someone is foolish enough to grab them. You can thus find the skills you need in a variety of places. What is most important is to find a style and an instructor that suits you. In fact, the single thing that matters more than any consideration of art or style is the instructor.

Choosing a Class or Course

If you can only spare a little time, a one-off self-defence course may be the best option. Indeed, unless you intend to train regularly, a self-defence course is probably best for you. Such courses tend not to be very in-depth, but they offer a few simple, practical techniques for dealing with an attacker or at least gaining enough time to escape. Self-defence courses tend to be relaxed, accessible and fun, which is good for people not wishing to get involved in the formal martial arts.

If you do decide to take it further and study a martial art, be aware there are many on offer and some will simply not suit you. It may be necessary to try a few before you find a style and an instructor that you are happy with. Some arts require a long time to become proficient at, or are aimed more at sport than serious self-defence. Some are so deadly that use outside a controlled environment is fraught with risks. It is the opinion of the authors that a martial art taken up for self-defence should be practical, not stylised, and should include both striking and grappling work.

When searching for a suitable class or style, the following rules are good guidelines:

- Shop around. Have a look at a few different classes before you decide on one.
- Ask to sit in on a class, or take a 'taster' session if one is available.
- Talk to the instructor. Do you feel this person can be trusted to give you what you need?
- Talk to some of the students (*not* during a class!) without their instructor present.
- Evaluate the teaching. Could you learn this way?
- Evaluate the techniques. Would they work for you?

If you get the impression that the class would not suit you, then you are almost certainly right! There are certain concrete signs that a class is not appropriate:

- Arrogant, abusive or offhand teaching styles.
- Overcrowding or other safety issues.
- Emphasis on 'flash' techniques.
- Emphasis on power to defeat an opponent.
- Attitude of 'Harder! Stronger! Faster!' rather than good technique.
- Racism, sexism or similar unacceptable conduct.
- Insistence that you do not train elsewhere.
- Attempts to pressure you into a contract, sell you T-shirts and equipment, and generally make money from you before you've had a fair chance to find out if the course is for you.
- Expensive gradings and other high costs.

Overall, you are looking for a class that will help you learn and will motivate you to make the most of your abilities while making allowance for any limitations you may have. (This is not the same thing as letting you get away with laziness!) You should also get a fair return for your money. Quality is not always expensive, and cheap is not always good!

And if you find yourself thinking 'these people are headcases!' then you really should look elsewhere for your training. Remember that if the training is more likely to get you hurt than going out on the street untrained, then you're really much better off without it!

The most important factor is the instructor. A good instructor has some or all of the following characteristics:

- Competence. The instructor can do it as well as show it.
- Patience with struggling students as long as they're genuinely trying to learn.
- Firm but polite and respectful control of the training environment.
- Approachability. The instructor is willing to answer questions and help with problems rather than just 'teach and go'.
- Sensible and realistic attitude to the reality of street self-defence.
- Insistence upon safety in the training environment.
- Respect for students as human beings.
- Refusal to accept sexism or racism.

Summary

Do take a course. Even a one-off session will make a huge difference.
It does, however, take regular training to become skilled.
Choose your course wisely. The instructor is the most important factor.
Choose someone you can respect and trust who'll show you the same conduct.

Chapter 2: The Martial Arts

There are many, many arts out there, and the situation is further complicated by the fact that many instructors offer several styles depending upon the needs of the students, but advertise their club under a general title. What follows is a rough guide to some of the more common arts on offer. Within each, there are often different sub-styles.

Summaries of Martial Arts Styles

Aikido

Aikido is a self-defence art based on the concept of 'blending' with an opponent and using his momentum against him. One very strong plus is the emphasis on evasion (tai sabaki), which teaches a fundamental self-defence skill – that of not being in the path of an attack. However, aikido does surrender the initiative to the attacker and relies on fine motor skills that may be heavily degraded by stress and adrenaline.

Aiki-jitsu

Aiki-jitsu is basically a stripped-down version of aikido optimised for street self-defence. Aiki-jitsu places less emphasis on flowing with techniques and more on 'persuading' an attacker to be thrown by the use of joint locks and similar coercive measures.

Boxing

Not considered a martial art by most, boxing is all about punching, with no kicks or grappling at all. Boxers are excellent punchers and also learn a lot about timing, distance and evasion. However, boxing tends to involve contact when training and is perhaps most useful as a side-study to develop striking skills rather than as a main self-defence art.

Hapkido

A Korean art that draws on many traditional arts for its techniques and fuses them into a coherent and versatile whole that has been adopted by some law enforcement agencies. Hapkido uses high kicks similar to those of tae kwon do as well as close-in combat techniques.

Jeet Kune Do

Primarily a striking art, jeet kune do was developed by the late Bruce Lee and incorporates concepts from Wing Chung kung fu and other arts. Different styles of jeet kune do exist, leading to considerable variation in teaching. As a hard striking style, jeet kune do is practical and effective. However, association with the Lee name makes jeet kune do highly attractive. Some instructors are not true jeet kune do teachers, but are merely trying to cash in on the popularity of the art's founder.

Ju-jitsu

A mixed striking/grappling art, ju-jitsu is highly effective for self-defence in most situations. Ju-jitsu eschews high kicks for the most part in favour of close-in work ideally suited to the 'pavement arena'. Various styles of ju-jitsu exist, including Brazilian (or Gracie) ju-jitsu, which is primarily focused on ground fighting.

Judo

Judo is a 'combat sport' spun out of ju-jitsu. It is limited by competition rules to grappling and throwing techniques, but practitioners tend to be very skilled at those. Judo is thus an excellent training ground for grappling skills but is not the first choice for self-defence.

Kali/Escrima

Both of these arts are primarily weapons styles, though they deal with basic, practical weapons such as sticks and knives rather than the more esoteric weapons often associated with the martial arts. Probably not a good option for beginners, these arts are highly pragmatic and very powerful in armed self-defence.

Karate

There are several styles of karate. What they have in common is an emphasis on hard striking techniques. Shotokan karate in particular is very stylised, while Wado Ryu is more 'natural' in its stances. Karate, if well taught, is extremely effective as a striking art. However, some instructors place more emphasis on display than self-defence and concentrate on kata rather than on practical applications.

Kick Boxing

Like boxing, kick boxing is a sport and is constrained by competition rules that prohibit certain strikes and all forms of grappling. Kick boxing is an excellent way to practise striking and kicking techniques and also teaches concepts like timing and distance, but it is not primarily focused on self-defence.

Kung Fu

Several styles of kung fu exist, of which Wing Chun is probably the most famous. Developed for the tight spaces of the Hong Kong alleyways, Wing Chun is excellent at close quarters. Other kung fu styles are more 'open'. Kung fu is mainly about striking an opponent and can be tricky to learn (though well worth the effort).

Muay Thai

Muay Thai, or Thai boxing, is a sport similar to kick boxing, but all strikes are permitted and grappling can also take place. Training is tough and painful as body conditioning needs to be developed, but muay Thai remains (for those who become skilled at it) a fearsome striking art.

Nihon Tai-jitsu

Nihon tai-jitsu is the favoured style of the authors. Very similar to ju-jitsu, it places strong emphasis on close-combat techniques, short-range striking and throwing, and tai sabaki (evasion). It is designed as a street self-defence art and discards many stylised movements in favour of simplicity and effectiveness.

Ninjutsu

Ninjutsu is usually billed as the 'fighting art of the Ninja', though in fact 'ninjutsu' refers to the whole range of stealth and assassination skills used by the Ninja of feudal Japan. Exactly what is taught under the banner of ninjutsu depends upon the instructor. Usually it looks like a variant of karate or ju-jitsu with some extras thrown in. The mythos associated with the Ninja name is a powerful selling point, though whether it lives up to expectations depends on the instructor.

Pencak Silat

Originating in the Philippines, pencak silat is gaining acceptance in the West. There are actually many, many versions of silat. Silat instructors are quite uncommon and very selective about their students, so the art is probably not for beginners, though it is highly practical and powerful in self-defence applications.

Savate
Savate is 'French kick boxing' that includes some wrestling moves too. Savate practitioners often participate in full-contact matches, making the art highly practical for self-defence.

Sombo
Similar in some ways to judo, sombo is a jacketed wrestling sport originating in Russia. It has self-defence applications but is primarily a sport.

Tae Kwon Do
Tae kwon do is a Korean striking art similar to karate. Like judo, it has been altered to become a sport, and this limits its usefulness in the self-defence arena. Tae kwon do requires great flexibility and makes use of many high kicks that, while devastating if they land, are difficult to use effectively on the street.

Personal Styles/Cross-training
Many martial arts instructors are cross-trained in several arts and teach a mix of techniques drawn from their various styles. Cross-training allows practitioners of, say, a style emphasising striking techniques to 'cover the gaps' by learning some grappling and ground fighting moves. This mixing of arts means that it is not always possible to simply categorise a martial arts school. Many instructors run a school under their own name or a general title like 'North-East Fighting Arts'. Observing a class and talking to students or instructors will give you a good indication of whether a particular instructor or school is suitable for you.

Grades, Belts and 'Licences'

Many (but not all) martial arts have a grade system, which shows how advanced students are. Others have a system whereby you're an instructor, assistant instructor or a student, and 'grades' are subjective – the student standing up is 'better' than the one getting up from the floor!

In the majority of arts, grade is shown by a coloured belt, though some use sashes, gloves or have no outward indication of grade but award certificates to show achievement. Typically, a student starts as a white belt (martial arts uniforms come with a white belt) and progresses through steadily darker colours to black. Different arts have their own system, but typically you can expect to progress through yellow, orange, green, blue, purple and brown belts before taking your black belt.

- Most arts have a grading system shown by coloured belts or sashes.

Black belt is not the end – nor should it be a goal! Black belt status is simply something that happens when you are very skilled. A belt is, after all, just a piece of cloth. It is you, and what you can do, that is important. This is really, really important. Don't look at the people in the dojo and say 'Of course she's good – she's a blue belt!' or worse 'I'll be that good when I'm a blue belt' because you won't be.

This is because you don't get good when you earn the grades – you train hard and get good, and you earn your grades as you do it. A belt or grade system is helpful in measuring your progress (which might improve your motivation) but it's not an absolute necessity. You can become just as skilled without ever taking a grading.

- Your grade is an indication of your proficiency, but it is what you can do that's important, not the colour of your belt!

Gradings are done in various ways. Many arts run formal gradings every three months or so, with students aiming to be at their peak at this time. Depending on the art being studied, you may also have to attend a certain number of courses or fulfil other requirements to reach a certain grade. Those who pass are awarded their new belt; those who fail try again next time. Senior grades usually have to wait longer periods between gradings.

The authors use a different grading system, which some arts have now adopted. It is based on assessment during normal training. This is less stressful for students and more flexible regarding when a new belt can be attained. Some students (and this is exceptional) do it in one month. Others take six months or more. As with any other grading system, it really doesn't matter how long it takes you; you only 'fail' when you give up. Otherwise, the worst that can happen is that you don't pass today and have to do it again some other time. This is a better, more positive, way to view it than 'I might fail' – which means you have a better chance of passing!

As has been mentioned, black belt is not the end. At black belt (or its equivalent) you may choose to become an instructor and can go on collecting grades (first Dan, second Dan and so on) as you continue to develop. It's a strange fact about graded martial arts that 90 per cent of students never make it to black belt (hardly surprising – it's not easy and life can send you in other directions rather suddenly) but of those who make it, about 90 per cent then give up martial arts. It's as if they've reached their goal and have nowhere to go.

- Black belt isn't a goal. It's something that happens when you get really, really good at what you're doing. But don't aim at black belt – aim at being as good as you can possibly be!

The truth is that black belt (or any other grade) is just another landmark on the road. What is important is how good you are at self-defence (or your chosen art). And you can go on getting better forever!

Many martial artists possess a small book that is usually referred to as a 'licence'. This book is used to record grades earned in various arts, courses attended, katas learned and all manner of other pertinent information. It's a sort of logbook of your martial arts career. However, it's not really a licence in the same way as a TV or driving licence is. You don't have to be licensed to be a martial artist, and you don't get any real benefit from a licence outside the martial arts community.

- You don't need a special licence to learn martial arts.

There are two exceptions to this. Firstly, some competitions and events will want proof that you're skilled and safe enough to enter or attend. A licence is a convenient (and the standard) way of providing such proof.

Secondly, some shops will want to see your licence before selling you certain weapons. This is basically to assure them as far as possible that you've trained with these weapons and will use them responsibly. People who just want to stab someone are unlikely to go to the trouble of training in a martial art and diligently recording their grades – they'll just buy a knife! Other than this, a licence is just a convenient way of recording your achievements. You don't *need* one, though many organisations require you to have one.

Clothing and Equipment for Training

Most training is undertaken on mats, which means bare feet or specialist footwear. If you train off the mats, you will need trainers. Indoor-type trainers (e.g. squash shoes) are a good choice. They're light and designed for indoors. Most fashionable trainers are thick-soled running types. It's not that critical, but if you have to buy trainers specially, squash shoes are much cheaper and are actually better suited to martial arts training.

The typical training uniform is a white gi (suit) consisting of loose trousers and a long jacket fastened with a white or coloured belt to display your grade. Some organisations use black or coloured gis, especially those that compete and want a distinctive appearance, while others have traditional or specialist clothing. While a specified training uniform does result in a nice appearance for a class, it isn't really necessary. It does, however, avoid the problem of 'fashion war' and wear on students' clothing.

Some styles simply use track pants and a T-shirt for training. Most self-defence courses allow you to wear what you like, though common sense suggests that sports clothing is a good choice. T-shirts bearing the logo of the art, school or organisation are popular, and a class wearing uniform pants and a T-shirt looks just as good as one in pristine white gis. More importantly, clothing has nothing to do with the quality of training.

- Suits and uniform clothing look good and have practical advantages, but they don't make you better – that you get through training!

If you are going to get involved in sparring, you may find that you need to get some gloves or other equipment such as shin pads and groin protectors, though only if you are going to study a martial art in depth for some time. You will not be expected to have a gi or other uniform for your first session, and requirements will be explained to you if you decide to stay.

If you do decide to buy a gi, there are two basic types. Light karate-type gis are ideal for training that doesn't involve being dragged around by your clothing. A typical starter gi will last quite a while. The alternative is a heavy judo-type gi, favoured by people who do aikido and … yes, judo. Much heavier and more robust (people tend to swing on your clothing when grappling), a heavy gi has the disadvantage of being a little bulky and a lot hotter to wear. One of the authors uses one and compares it to wearing a thick towel.

- Unless you're studying something with a lot of grappling involved, a light gi should be fine.

Ask an experienced student or your instructor about clothing. They'll be glad to advise, and many clubs can get you clothing at a discount.

Street fighting

Street fighting is listed here rather than in the main text because it is not a martial art. You cannot go to a gym and learn street fighting, though you can learn fighting skills and take them out 'on the street'. There is exactly one way to become a street fighter – go out and get into fights. 'Street fighter' is a more glamorous way of saying 'thug' or 'bully'.

Some martial arts teach 'street applications', and even describe their style as things like 'scientific street fighting'. This is a different thing entirely. While anyone can get some training and take it out on the street, many martial arts teach techniques specific to street self-defence. There is nothing wrong with this – indeed, it is a very good thing provided the students' intentions are honourable. Given the discipline inherent in learning a martial art and the excellent role model offered by the majority of instructors, most people who train in 'street defence' methods will be reluctant to use their skills except in dire need.

The difference, then, between a street fighter and a person who is skilled in street self-defence is in the character of the person and their intentions. One is a violent thug who goes out looking for fights. The other is a good citizen who has sensibly obtained a means of self-defence. Street fighters are the reason we train, not what we try to become.

Summary

- There are many martial arts available. Not all are suitable for self-defence use, and not all are suitable for you.
- The same comments apply to choosing an art as to picking a self-defence course. Take a good look before you commit to anything.
- Remember that you're not there to learn to fight, but to learn how to defend yourself. There *is* a difference.
- Don't be mesmerised by gradings and belt systems. Your goal is to be as good as you can be, not to get another belt.

Chapter 3: Learning and Training

Sensible Training

If you are going to train, then you must train sensibly. Many people want to dive right in and get involved in sparring, groundwork and other 'fun' activities, when in fact this may not be the best approach at all.

Sparring and groundwork serve a useful purpose, but they are primarily about learning to apply your skills in a fluid environment. First, you must *have* those skills. Just piling into sparring is a good way to have your morale dented and to develop some bad habits that'll take a long time to train out.

- Training must be appropriate to your level of ability and fitness.

You will gain fitness through training. However, if you frequently suffer strains and exhaustion in training then your ability to train effectively on a regular basis will be reduced. Overall, this is counterproductive. It is better to train at a pace that gently pushes your limits rather than suddenly exceeds them. In the long run, you'll improve more and better this way. Note that 'gently pushing your limits' is not the same as slacking!

Some factors are critically important. A good (as opposed to 'hard') warm-up is vital to avoid straining yourself during training, and a warm-up should include some light stretching to improve mobility and flexibility. Note that flexibility is a long-term project and hard, painful stretching sessions will achieve little while exposing you to the risk of strain. Better to stretch gently each day and gradually improve your flexibility than risk injury by doing too much too soon. In truth, everyone should stretch a little every day, just for the sake of health and fitness for life.

- If you do a little flexibility and fitness exercise every day, you'll be fitter and healthier whether you train in self-defence or not.

A really hard workout at the beginning of a session may be good for fitness, but it means that you will begin training tired and out of breath. This is not conducive to learning skilful techniques. It is better to pace yourself and get warmed up beforehand, then put some effort into the training itself. This will help you develop the actual skills you need and will promote fitness too.

If you want better fitness (this is good for so many reasons, of which self-defence is only one) then this is best done by using a gym or running, cycling or playing intense sports like squash, away from your self-defence training. The change of pace will help you avoid becoming bored too.

- Fitness is good. It's worth a little effort to maintain.

While training, it is vital to listen to your body. Awkward movements are ineffective; let your body guide you and find a natural way to perform each technique. This is not a licence to ignore your instructor, of course. It is merely the suggestion that if something is awkward or feels wrong, then it probably is, even if it looks exactly like what you were shown!

You should be diligent about training. This has two meanings. First, you should practise *what the instructor teaches you*, rather than *something vaguely similar*. This tends to happen when you are taught a technique that is similar to something you already know or when you return to something you haven't practised for a while. It is better to ask for another demonstration and get it right than to muddle along doing something similar only to find that when you need it, the technique doesn't work.

- Don't practise something that you think looks about right. Practise what you *know* is right!

Secondly, diligent training means taking responsibility for your own learning and not waiting to be chivvied by the instructor. Practise techniques lots of times, even if you're a bit tired or demotivated. If you think you're doing something wrong, ask about it rather than waiting to be corrected.

If you have limitations (including injuries, extreme unfitness or illness as well as things normally defined as 'disabilities') then work around them – but be sensible. There is a fine line between not wanting to injure yourself and using your limitations as an excuse to slack off. Be honest with yourself and find a path between laziness and over-zealousness. Similarly, if you are not as apt or as fit as someone you train with, don't try to compete. Try to do *your* best, not *theirs*. Any decent instructor will respect you for making your best effort, even if there are people in the dojo who are far 'better' than you.

- Train to be as good as *you* can be – not as good as everyone else.

Finally, remember the ultimate test you should apply to anything you learn. No matter what belts, badges, sashes, pins or gloves you may earn, the real test – the one that matters – is 'Can I use this technique to defend myself from attack?' If the answer is no, then you need to do some more work.

The skills you learn in a self-defence or martial arts class are very, very important. You owe it to yourself to learn as efficiently as possible and to stick at it even if it takes a long time to learn. We've all been in a situation where everyone else in the room has 'got it' and you still have no idea what you're even *trying* to do. It happens to everyone at some point, but if you are diligent and stick at it, you'll get there.

- It can be hard sometimes, especially at the beginning when you don't know what you're doing. Actually, it's always like that, but you get better at dealing with it! There will always be something you'll struggle with – it's just that the things that make you struggle will be more impressive as you get better.

To quote an unknown but wise martial arts instructor: 'The thing about this art is, the techniques work … unless the students don't!'

Train sensibly: well rather than hard, diligently rather than aggressively. Push yourself, but don't hurt yourself. And if you get fed up and wonder if it's worth it … remember that your training may be the only thing between you and death or serious injury. So train, and train well.

Reliable Techniques

Many of the techniques taught in martial arts schools are archaic, dating from a time when samurai fought in armour with swords and bows. Others are overstylised, excessively complex or intended for competition use. And some are just plain useless. Nevertheless, every martial art has a range of highly effective moves that can be useful in protecting yourself from attack if you take the trouble to learn how to use them properly. Take a good look at what's on offer before you make any decisions as to the utility of any given technique, style or art. First impressions, gained without any real understanding of the hows and whys involved, can make an art seem awesome or useless when in fact the truth is very different.

When learning a martial art for self-defence (as opposed to competitive, aesthetic or fitness purposes) you would be well advised to discard borderline-useful techniques along with any obvious rubbish, then sort through the genuinely useful techniques for the ones that work best for *you*. Each and every one of us is different, so some otherwise really fabulous techniques won't be much use to you. That's fine. It's *you* that you're selecting tools for, not everyone else.

What you'll end up with is a small selection of moves that you can use reliably and without thinking about them. These are the tools that you will instinctively select when the tactical centre in your brain says 'Got a clear shot' or 'Incoming right hook!'. Learn to perform them to maximum efficiency.

- Choose a small selection of techniques you find effective and hone them.

Eventually, you will find that you have a toolbox containing two or three favourite techniques at close and striking range, plus a larger number of backup options that are there if you need them. Make sure your chosen techniques are both simple to use and highly effective, but flexible enough to be employed in many situations. You're better off with an adjustable spanner than a pair of surgical tweezers, however finely made they are.

Everyone is different, so exactly which techniques you choose as your favourite tools is a matter for your own judgement. As a general rule, don't bother with more than one kick or any high kicks at all. Leave out light techniques such as backfists, except possibly as a 'door-opener' for a combination. Make sure that at least some of your techniques are good for when someone has hold of you.

Chances are there will be nothing complex or sophisticated in your toolbox because it's better to have a limited repertoire of techniques that you can do reliably under stress than a boatload of flashy stuff that needs cue cards!

- Find out what works for you, practise it, polish it and make it second nature. Then, and only then, add a range of extra stuff that you might find a use for.

Chuck away the kung fu movie stunts and you're left with a bunch of vanilla-flavour, boring, prosaic and above all *simple* techniques. If you've got any sense, that should be exactly what you want!

Fitness

Fitness is an important part of self-defence. If you are fit you can fight better and longer, you can run away more quickly (and further), and if you seem to be in good shape, you're more likely to be seen as a hard target and thus probably won't be attacked at all.

If you are reasonably fit and plan to become good at an art, then some form of additional training is a good idea. An unfit person wanting to get into slightly better shape before taking a class – or just because it's a good idea to be a bit fitter – may also want to do some basic exercise. Mostly, this will be general stuff: flexibility and cardiovascular (CV) fitness.

Many people are worried by terms like 'stretching' and 'CV fitness'. They have connotations of Lycra-clad people with bodies you could use for an anatomy lesson, pumping dumb-bells the size of a bungalow. But it needn't be like that. Fitness training works at any level, and everyone can benefit. Only people who are already quite fit need to do really strenuous exercise.

If you don't ask your body to do much, it gets lazy. Ever found yourself suddenly doing something physical (like playing frisbee with the kids or an impromptu football game) and discovered that you're too out of breath to enjoy it? That's your lazy body protesting.

- If you don't maintain your fitness level, you'll lose it.

If you don't make your body work, you will lose muscle and, if you eat more than you need to (pretty much everybody does), you'll put on some fat. You'll stiffen up as your joints become less flexible; you'll get out of breath more easily. Older people will lose mobility and become older than they are.

You can fix this, though. Older people can turn the clock back a decade or more. Younger people can build some impressive physical capabilities. Everyone can halt or even reverse their body's decline and be more active, fitter, 'younger' and healthier. And as a spin off, you'll be more attractive. We're not necessarily talking toned abs and bulging biceps here; just the natural improvements that come with feeling good about yourself and being active and healthy.

- Fitter people are more resistant to disease and recover better from injury.
- They can do more and get more out of life.
- They feel good, which is a prize in its own right.
- And it shows, making them more attractive.

The question is, how? It's not so hard. In fact, it's best if you ease into it gently. Many people make their decision to get fit and rush to the gym. There, they lift weights until they're so exhausted they can't even get their shirt back on, think 'aargh!' and never do it again. Instead, start gently with a minimal amount of effort, but stick at it and gradually work up to whatever level you think is appropriate. For some, this means three to five heavy gym sessions a week and long road runs. For others it's ten minutes of gentle stretching every day and a walk in the park on Sundays. Whatever you do will be better than nothing. Do what you feel you want to; make exercise a part of your life and you'll live longer and more fully. You'll also be better able to defend yourself. There are three component parts to fitness: CV fitness, flexibility and muscle tone.

CV Fitness

Cardiovascular fitness refers to your heart and lungs – everybody needs those! If you are of fairly advanced age or are very unfit, then your CV fitness will be very low. Note that it is possible to be heavily overweight and still have good CV fitness or to be whip-lean and terribly unfit.

CV fitness is an important part of stamina – the ability to keep going when things are tough. It also has to do with muscle conditioning and will, but since a good level of CV fitness means that your body is able to make good use of air and energy, it's pretty vital if you want to do anything lasting more than twenty seconds.

Flexibility

Flexibility isn't just for gymnasts and people who want to kick high. It's a vital part of a healthy life. While recovering from a chronic and serious back injury, one of the authors discovered what a simple joy it is to be able to tie your own shoes or pick the cat up – and how frustrating it can be when you can't.

There is no need to dive into harsh stretching routines (please don't!), and your goal should not be to get your foot behind your head or do the splits. Your goal should simply be to improve the range of movement available to you and to maintain that improvement.

If you join a class or take up any organised sport, you'll be taught some appropriate stretching exercises, or you can get advice from a fitness coach, say at the local gym. Just remember to take it gently and don't 'bounce' on stretches or do them violently. Don't stretch when cold. Listen to your body, find its limits and gently push them.

Muscle Tone

The third component of fitness is muscle tone. Big, bulging muscles may or may not impress people, but they're not really necessary to self-defence. You don't need massive strength to defend yourself. Your natural strength is enough as long as you act effectively and decisively. What you do need is good tone. That is, your muscles need to be used to working hard and efficiently.

Muscle tone is developed by working your muscles. You can do this by using weights (though if you do, it is best to seek advice from a coach rather than just plunging in and pumping away) or by engaging in toning activity such as playing sport, gardening or other work. What you do need not be amazingly strenuous at first; any activity will tone you up a little.

Getting Fit

If you take up a class or martial art, then getting fit will be a part of your training, though as has already been remarked, it's worth your while to do some extra work. You can get fit independently of a class, however. We will discuss some general things you can do to improve your overall fitness level. Any or all of them may work for you – pick those that suit you best.

General

If you are fairly (or very!) unfit, then start very gently. Walk somewhere every day. Use the stairs instead of the lift. Play fetch with the dog. Take it easy and build up a little every time. You can also 'con' yourself into doing healthy exercise. Take up some sport or other – it doesn't matter, just something you like. Squash, five-a-side football or whatever. While you're having fun, you'll keep going longer than you would have if you'd been doing exercise. Don't overdo it though, or you'll be stiff and sore for days! Even if you are pretty fit, you can maintain your level by working exercise into your daily routine.

Jogging or Running

As your fitness improves (or you are more able to handle exercise) then you might start jogging a little. This does not necessarily mean 'road work' or putting on a hooded sweatshirt and going out for a run; it can just mean walking down to the petrol station in the morning to get a paper and jogging some of the way.

- If you're going to jog outdoors, plan your route with safety in mind, and consider wearing a decent pair of running shoes. Running can be quite hard on your body, but it can be substituted with cycling or riding an exercise bike. Bikes and running machines can be found in most gyms, which have the advantage of less motor traffic too!

At first, jogging a short distance will really take it out of you. Actually it can be rather frightening to discover that running one hundred metres at no great speed can leave you feeling sick and breathing like a bellows. Don't push it; walk gently until you feel better (it's better to keep going a little than to stop completely). Maybe you will feel up to another little run, but don't give yourself a heart attack. The purpose is to get fitter, not kill yourself. If you feel bad, call it a day and have another go tomorrow.

Other CV Exercise

Various alternatives exist to running. These include rowing machines, exercise bikes and so on. Start gently and gradually push your limits. If you do this regularly, you'll see a steady improvement over time. There will come a point where you have to do something really quite strenuous to get yourself hot and tired. You won't really notice at first, but suddenly you're fit!

Weights and Machines

By all means join a gym and use the weights or the machines. Free weights are best, since you have to balance them as well as pulling or lifting them. Just be sure not to drop them on yourself (or anyone else!). Weights work your muscles effectively, but they can also damage you. Don't use the heaviest thing you can lift; use a sensible weight and gradually increase the number of repetitions (reps) of your exercise.

You should be able to do 3 sets of 12–15 reps with any given weight (and it should be an effort!). Once this becomes fairly easy, it's time for the next weight up. When using weights, you get far more out of the exercise if you go *slowly* than if you pump away like some colossal engine component.

Weights are good, but don't be mesmerised by them. The myth of the slow, muscle-bound fighter is just that – a myth. You can be hugely muscled and still fast, as long as your tone is good. But you really don't need to be.

Press-ups and Ab Crunches

Some exercises need no equipment, so you can do a few in any spare minute. Again, these exercises are more beneficial when done slowly than at speed. It's better to do crunches than sit-ups.

Press-ups work the arms and upper body. Lie face down with your feet together and your body more or less straight. Put your hands palm down on the floor and push yourself up (keeping your back straight) until your arms are straight. From there, lower yourself (fairly slowly) until your nose is close to the floor, then push yourself back up. That's one! Do as many as you can, in sets of ten. If you can't manage it full-length (most people can't), then put your knees on the floor. It's easiest when you're more or less on all fours and hardest when you're almost full-length. Work up to it.

Crunches work the abdominal muscles. Lie on your back with your legs straight out and your feet comfortably apart. Bring your feet towards your body by bending and raising your knees. Cross your hands lightly on your chest. Sit up as far as you can (slowly) and go slowly back down. You'll be able to feel the abs working.

Swimming

Swimming is great exercise for toning your body in general. It's ideal for people with back trouble. If you're going to swim, do proper lengths of the pool rather than just splashing about in the water.

Punchbags

Punchbags are the best form of exercise for self-defence. They not only let you develop very specific muscle tone for hitting, but also stamina too. You can also work on your technique, ironing out mistakes and getting the most out of your strikes. Most gyms have a punchbag or two. You'd be well advised to use bag gloves though as repeatedly hitting a bag can rip your hands to pieces!

Other Exercise

Almost any sport or exercise is good for you and is useful in developing your self-defence capability. Forget anything you've seen in movies though. Leave ideas like training under waterfalls or kicking down trees where they belong – in the realms of fiction. Stick to simple exercises that a fitness coach would approve of, work at it regularly and push your limits gently but consistently. Before you know it, you'll be fitter and healthier and will probably lose some weight into the bargain.

Training

We have tremendous fun training. Really! There's a great joy to be found in the application of physical skills; there's the stress-busting release of chemicals that takes place when you undertake intense physical activity. There are the benefits of fitness, flexibility and health to consider too. And there are those moments when something goes horribly wrong and everyone dissolves into laughter, to be rehashed in the bar afterwards. And – in one of the clubs where we train, anyway – there is also a tremendous feeling of closeness, of 'family', that comes from sharing intense experiences (and what is more intense than trying to take someone's head off with a punch?). Training can be a chore; a necessary task determinedly undertaken. We're lucky to be able to make it a fun part of our lives.

But we're also pretty serious about it – after all, we're training for an event in which the first prize is not waking up in a hospital bed (and third place means not waking up at all). We hurl punches with every intention of knocking each other out (you have to train realistically, after all) and apply painful joint locks, or slam one another into the deck. But it's all done in conditions of courtesy and respect, with no malice or anger, even when we fail to evade and get soundly clobbered round the head.

Is this a paradox? Light-hearted diligence and violent respect? Maybe. But life isn't clear-cut or simple, so who says you have to be grim and silent when training? Be effective; that's what matters. But also be aware that if you train, then training is part of your life. Live it to the full, and wring everything you can out of it.

Summary

- Improve your fitness gradually but consistently.
- Develop a few techniques you can use well rather than a whole collection that you get muddled up with.
- Train sensibly but diligently. Push your limits gradually; don't try to do too much at first or you'll hurt yourself.
- Stick at it and work towards your goals. You'll get there in time.

Part V: Self-Defence Techniques

This part of the book deals with the act of physical self-defence. If you use the measures you've already read about, it is unlikely that you will need to use these techniques. All the same, it's wise to be prepared.

The techniques discussed here are universal; they can be used by unfit, small, light people as well as hulking martial arts monsters. There are, of course, many other highly effective techniques, but these provide a basic core of useful moves. If you want more, the place to get them is on a course or in a martial arts class.

Chapter 1: The Basics

Before plunging into the mechanics of dealing out damage, it is worth understanding what you are trying to achieve. What exactly is your aim in a self-defence situation? Remember that self-defence is not the same thing as fighting. In a fight, the goal is to hurt someone and win. In a self-defence situation, the emphasis is on keeping yourself intact and safe.

Your aim when defending yourself will always be to get out of the situation unhurt, or with as little damage as possible. Early on in a situation you have time to make some choices. This is the best time to begin protecting yourself against all the dangers of the encounter.

At this stage it must be reiterated: violent self-defence is a last-resort option! If it does become necessary, then this chapter explains some of the basics of how to go about it. Note that this is in no way a comprehensive guide to combative techniques. There are many, many ways to strike, to throw and to otherwise disable an assailant. If you want to know more, then you should take a class. What we are showing you here are the basics; simple things that you can do without extensive training.

Ready Stance

A good ready stance is a must for successful self-defence. A good stance is a stable platform to throw hard, accurate punches from; it allows you to manoeuvre out of the way of an attacker's rush and it creates some space for you to work in.

A good stance is balanced and comfortable – and nothing at all like you see in the movies! Feet are about shoulder width apart, turned in about 45 degrees or as much as is comfortable. Hand positions vary – so long as you are ready to react, strike or cover, anything you are comfortable with will do.

Typically, an assailant will begin his actions at a distance he chooses, but he will base this distance on the nearest part of your body. If you are standing with your hands down, this is your nose. You really do not want to have someone who means you harm that close to you. If your hands are up, then a typical attacker will take his distance from the nearest hand. That gives you a little more time to react, and also creates a barrier (your hands) to protect you.

Most people fight left side forward (in left lead). Left-handed fighters and some people who choose to train the other way around fight southpaw or right lead. There are merits in this, but we will assume a normal left lead, since this is best for most people (including many left-handers). To assume a ready stance:

- Stand square on to your opponent.
- Take a short step back with your right foot.
- Move the back foot out to the right so that your feet are shoulder-width apart.
- Turn your feet a little so that your left shoulder is forward and your toes point off to the right somewhat. Your rear (right) foot will be more sideways than the front one.
- Flex your knees a little.
- Now bring up your hands (open hands or fists). The left hand is forward of and a little lower than the right, which guards your chin.
- Be ready to move.

Practise flowing smoothly into your ready stance so that you can assume it in an instant. You are now ready to evade, strike or to move in any direction. It is a point of law that if you were threatened and stepped *away* from your opponent (even slightly) as you came up on guard, you are considered to have reacted defensively. If you move forward into a ready stance, you can be considered to have reacted aggressively. Most times this will simply not matter, but stepping away a little also gives you some room to work with, so it's not a bad idea.

Movement and Evasion

Movement is vital. A great military thinker once wrote: 'Above all, avoid immobility. That which is static invites attack at a time and in a manner of the enemy's choosing.' This roughly translates as 'move or get clobbered!'

Movement makes you harder to hit. It also disguises your intentions somewhat, since the brain picks out a static object that begins to move far more readily than one it is used to seeing move. In this way, movement can be part of your deception as discussed above – it disguises your location and your intentions.

- Move and keep on moving!

You can also use movement directly against your opponent by getting out of the way of an attack. In its simplest form, this can be stepping back out of range of a punch. You can also duck or move to the side. Sometimes you will actually want an opponent to come to you, so you suddenly stop backing off, let him close and strike!

The basic form of movement you should use resembles a boxer's push-shuffle. This involves taking small steps by pushing yourself forward with the rear foot, or backwards with the front one. Don't take normal steps as this telegraphs your movement and slows it down.

To shuffle forward, drive with your back foot and push yourself forward, keeping your guard up. To move back, drive with your front foot and push yourself backwards. That's all there is to it!

Aikido and some styles of ju-jitsu use a system of evasive movements called tai sabaki (which simply means 'body movement' or 'evasion'). It is an effective way of not being in the way of an attack, yet remaining close enough to be able to counter-attack. Every martial art or combat sport has a system of evasion designed to help the fighter avoid being hit.

It doesn't matter how you evade an attack as long as you do. The best option is to make fast, light movements rather than panicky ducking motions or overblown acrobatics. If you can, try to evade by a small margin rather than a desperate leap; it does not matter if an attack misses by a centimetre or a metre, so long as it misses. By evading, yet remaining close in, you are well positioned for a counter-attack.

Many street attacks involve huge, overcommitted punches like this one. Instead of trying to block, the defender moves back and allows the attacker to stagger off-balance. The time is now perfect for a precise counter-attack.

Situational Awareness and Tactical Mobility

Always, always, *always* be aware of your surroundings. Most unprovoked attacks take place on people who are Code White, not paying attention to the danger they are in. Being aware of potential threats not only allows you to pre-empt or avoid them in many cases, but it also cuts down the mental response time if you must defend yourself.

By being constantly Code Yellow (aware of and habitually evaluating all threats around you) you make yourself a harder target and thus may not be attacked at all. But situational awareness does not end when the punches start.

Be aware of the conditions around you. Particularly, take note of hazards such as slippery footing, confined spaces you can be backed into and additional opponents. As the situation develops, manoeuvre to give yourself a clear escape route or to place obstacles in your assailant's path. Take note of improvised weapons that you or your attacker could grab at need.

- Remain aware of your surroundings at all times.

Always move in a fight; a few random steps or a bit of back-pedalling to keep the distance open can make you a much harder target. Against more than one opponent, you can manoeuvre to make them get in one another's way. You can also strike or throw attackers so that they impede one another. Drop one so that his friend has to step over his body to get to you. Not only is that rather intimidating, but as he takes the big step he'll be distracted and off-balance. That's when to run or attack. Above all, always, *always* keep moving and *stay aware* of what's happening around you.

Distance and Entries

All weapons have an effective range. You can't hit what you can't reach. Many martial arts teach that there are three combat ranges: long, striking and close.

Long range is where someone can hit you, but only by reaching with a weapon or moving in a couple of steps. The big kicks favoured by some martial arts are only useful at long range, but most fights start closer than this. Even those fights that do start at long range don't stay there for long.

- In a fight situation, distance vanishes and you will end up nose-to-nose in seconds.

Striking range is where striking is most effective (!). Punches and other hand strikes are the weapons of choice, with some close-range kicks if you can get or make a good opportunity to use them.

At close range, normal kicking and punching are difficult, and fights become a scruffy mess of grabbing and grappling, interspersed with nasty close-in techniques such as headbutts and elbow and knee strikes. Technique makes up for a lot, but big, strong fighters have a considerable advantage in close. Most fights start at striking range and close rapidly, ending up as a grappling match on the floor.

Where possible, manoeuvre and try to keep your opponent(s) from getting close enough to grapple. However, they may succeed anyway, so be prepared for it. It is a good idea to open the distance whenever possible, forcing your assailant to close with you if he wants to continue the encounter. One reason for this is that an attacker will not break off if he is in a clinch with you, no matter how badly you are hurting him (he can't!). If you allow him some room, he may decide that you are too dangerous (or simply too much trouble) to deal with and depart.

Opening the distance also allows you to break off and to watch for new attackers. It also has the big advantage that your attacker can't drag you to the floor if you're ten feet away.

- If you can, keep some distance between you and the attacker.

Most techniques require what is termed an 'entry' – getting in to actually use the technique. For kicks and punches, this is simply a matter of getting into range with a step or two and having an open line of attack to strike into. For grappling and throwing techniques, you have to be closer. Don't worry about getting in to use your technique in the latter case – the attacker will come to you, and he'll be offering handy arms and legs stuck out for you to grab and use. And if he doesn't come to you? Why then the fight is over, and you can break off. You got what you wanted.

Some attackers, particularly fans of 'real' fighting competitions, may attempt a manoeuvre known as a 'shoot', where they suddenly rush in to take you to the ground. This involves a tackle around waist height and an attempt to grab you around the back of the thighs as the attacker body-slams you backwards. It is possible to stop a shoot by evading, back-pedalling, assuming a strong stance or kneeing the attacker in the face as he comes in, but all of these things require quick reactions and a degree of preparedness. Fortunately, 'shooting' is more committed than most attackers want to be, and thus it is quite rare on the street. Your best defence against someone who wants to do this is to move out of the way and keep the distance open or to be so close that the manoeuvre cannot work (though that means being in grappling range already …)

As a general rule, you can expect things to happen at close or striking range in a street fight. These are the ranges that your skills should concentrate on. Remember this when you are selecting a martial arts or self-defence class. Anyone who wants to get in close will manage it. Be ready.

Covers and Parries versus Blocks

Forget any ideas you may have about hard, heavy blocking actions made with your forearms or hands. While trained martial artists can learn how to make these techniques work for them, you should not try. The powerful karate moves and other 'hard' blocks you see in the movies will not be any use to you on the street. To put that another way:

- Someone who really means to hit you will do so, and placing your left forearm in the way will not stop him!
- Do you really think you can put your arm in the way of a kick and still be able to use it afterwards?

There are other disadvantages to blocking too. If you block hard, your opponent tenses up and usually hurls an even harder punch with the other arm. He knows he's got a fight on his hands and will move up a gear to be sure of winning it.

Forearm blocks work well in films, but a determined attacker will just smash right through and hit you anyway. Pre-empt, evade, parry or cover, but don't meet force with force.

So how do you avoid being hit? One way is to land a good pre-emptive strike as soon as the attacker commits himself. If you can end the matter before he hits you, you don't need to stop his attack. However, this is not always an option.

The secret of not being hit is to move – to be where the punch is not. Boxers, karate practitioners, ultimate fighting contestants and everyone else who knows what fighting is about does this, whatever formal blocking techniques they may study. Moving away from an attack, ducking, circling and other movements keep the attacker's blows from landing and allow you to stay out of his reach unless you move in to strike him.

There are two things you can do to assist your evasion: covering and parrying. Covering is a matter of keeping a good guard up and allowing strikes to land on your forearms rather than your head or body. This is different to blocking, since moving away from the attack robs it of much of its force even if it does land, and covering absorbs what little remains of the attack, if it lands at all. Being hit on a covering arm is painful, but is better than being smashed on the side of the head.

If you can't get out of the way of an attack, you can hunch up and take it on your forearms like this. It's not a great option: it hurts, and you can't see while you're doing it, but it's better than getting a punch in the face.

Parries are relatively subtle attempts to deflect an attack, and they are usually combined with movement. Rather than blocking hard, you push the attack to the side or deflect it past you using a minimum of effort. This has two advantages. Firstly, you are not opposing strength with strength, and secondly a light touch does not warn an attacker what you are doing, or make him likely to increase the fury of his attacks.

As the attacker moves in, deflect his arm (this is not the same as blocking as it involves no power or hard contact) and dart past him to escape. You may be able to pull him off-balance, gaining you more time and possibly making him fall.

As the attacker initiates his strike, move diagonally forward past it, pushing it aside with your hand. This is not a block – the most important thing is to evade and escape, or to turn faster than your attacker so that he runs into your counter-attack if he turns to have another go at you.

The difference between blocks and parries or covers is actually quite simple. A block is a hard motion that goes out and meets the attack. This results in a slamming-together of your limb and the attacker's. Karate practitioners can learn how to do this effectively, but for the rest of us it's a bad idea. Your forearm will not stop a heavy punch or kick and may well be injured.

A parry, on the other hand, is a deflecting motion that pushes the attack away from you. Rather than placing your forearm directly in the way of a blow, you push it away. This requires little force and has no impact involved – the force of the punch is heading towards you, and you push the arm sideways. You don't at any point meet the force of the attack head-on.

Covering is more passive. It is a last resort if you can't parry, or it is done as insurance in case your evasion fails. You don't go to meet the attack at all, but just cover the vulnerable body parts (head, ribs, etc) with your arms to absorb the impact. Not a great option, but better than nothing.

- A block meets the attack head-on with force and attempts to stop it.
- A parry meets the attack and redirects it.
- Covering replaces the target with something less vulnerable.

Summary

- Stun or disable the attacker, then escape. Do not prolong an encounter for any reason.
- Never meet strength with strength.
- Never wrestle or grapple if you can avoid it.
- Always try to remain aware of your surroundings and additional attackers.
- A good ready stance is vital.
- Move! Deliberately evade attacks, but also keep moving a little, even when you're not being attacked.
- Don't try to make hard blocking movements. Evade and cover!
- Maintain distance between you and the attacker if you can.

Chapter 2: Striking Techniques

Most people can punch. However, most of them cannot do it very well. The fact is that while power and size are of course useful, a light person who lands a well-executed strike at a vulnerable point is more likely to win a fight than a big swinger. And, of course, a punch that is not thrown – out of fear or hesitation – cannot hurt anyone.

If matters have deteriorated to the point where you actually have to hit someone, then you must do it wholeheartedly. Nothing is more likely to get you injured or killed than thumping someone hard enough to cause pain and anger, but not to deter them.

- If you have to hit someone, hit them hard!

If you have a good striking technique and get a clear (usually pre-emptive) opportunity, then a fight can often (but not certainly) be ended with a single blow. However, it is far more likely that a scuffle will develop in which you may have to throw several punches, some of which will not connect with any real effect.

At some point, you will land a door-opener, a blow that creates an opportunity by momentarily stunning an opponent or physically knocking him backwards. At this moment, you have an opportunity to end the matter, but if you hesitate, your assailant will come back full of murderous fury and you'll be in more trouble than ever.

You may be best served by flight at this moment, since you have created an opportunity to get a bit of a head start. However, unless your door-opener was a very good one, you are likely to have an angry and hurting assailant in pursuit.

An alternative, once the door is open, is to leap through it with both feet. If you have the skills, you can close in for a takedown. With your assailant on the floor (and you still standing – *never* join him on the deck) you have a far better opportunity to escape, since he has to collect his wits *and* get up, then decide whether he really wants to give chase. You can be long gone by then.

But most likely, upon hitting someone, you will find that the door is open for just a moment, but the fight is not over. You can keep the door open by landing more blows. This is the principle behind the boxer's combination, the 'straight blast' of jeet kune do and many other combination striking techniques. One quick shot opens the door, and while the opponent is physically and mentally off-balance, more powerful blows reduce him to an irrelevance. It is much easier to get a good hit in on someone who is reeling back than an attacker who is advancing with his fists up. Take the opportunity for all it is worth. You have this one chance to end the matter without being hurt. *Take it!*

• Most importantly, do not strike then pause to think 'Look what I just did!'

Take the opportunity and make sure you finish the matter. You must judge for yourself when it's over, but a fleeing opponent or one crumpling to the pavement provides a strong clue. If he goes down and tries to get up, you may be justified in kicking him if you feel that he is still a threat. If he's getting up to attack you some more, you have to prevent him. If, on the other hand, he goes down and stays down, it's over. Job done. Leave.

Principles of Striking

The human body is very tough, but also surprisingly vulnerable in some ways. Anyone, no matter how light or small they may be, can strike effectively enough to put someone down. Doing so is a combination of resolve, technique and the ability to remain calm and just get the job done instead of indulging in panicky flailing. Some people say you should not strike with your fist or arm but with your whole body. This is not true. You should punch with your whole body, *and* with your heart, soul and all your aspirations for the future behind it. If you must hit someone, make it count.

Without delving deeply into applied mathematics or biomechanics, it is still possible to understand how strikes work. Strikes can be categorised into two types: impact techniques and force techniques. There is some crossover between the two, but the distinction between them is important.

Impact techniques may hit the target hard, moving quickly, but they deliver little force. They will cause pain and damage vulnerable areas such as the lips and nose, but they are basically painful nuisance techniques that can cause a distraction but will not put someone down. The backfist, some jabs, slaps and punches thrown too short fall into this category. They can cover an advance or retreat, open a door by causing momentary pain, but basically impact techniques will not stop someone who is full of adrenaline – pain will annoy rather than deter. Don't use impact strikes except as a distraction.

- Impact techniques will hurt your assailant, but they won't stop him.

Done properly, strikes deliver force to the target (in the physics sense, not brute force). How fast this force arrives determines the effect. If the force you deliver arrives relatively slowly, your strike will be a push, driving your opponent's entire body away from you. This can be a good thing. If you deliver your force quickly, his entire body will not have time to move away. Only nearby tissue and body parts will move. This is what causes cheekbones to snap, organs to be shocked, or 'brain shake'.

In all cases, your strike must be driven *into* or even *through* the target. It is rather unlikely that your fist will actually come out of the back of your opponent, but try all the same. This ensures that maximum force is delivered and thus maximum effect.

- Force techniques won't just hurt an assailant – they'll defeat him.

Strikes must be delivered from a firm base, either while you are well balanced and firmly planted on the floor or while you are moving forward. In that case, your fist has your body weight moving behind it, and even if you weigh six stone, that is still a great deal to put behind a punch!

If you choose to study a martial art, you will learn the striking style of that art and how to make it work. What we are presenting here is a basic idea of how to thump someone effectively. There is plenty more to learn, and we could write a whole book on punching alone!

Practise shadow-boxing or use a punchbag (most gyms have them; punching a bag is a great form of exercise) if you can't get to a dojo. You can really unload into a punchbag, which is also a real stress-buster. If you aren't hitting something, make sure you don't overextend your strikes or you'll hurt your joints.

Using your Hands

Your hands are your main weapons in a self-defence situation. Most fights are won by the first person to land a decent blow on the head, and your hands are ideally positioned to launch such a strike or to be in the way of it. Hands can be used to strike in many ways and are normally used to strike in the 'high line' (to the head) or the 'mid line' (abdomen and chest). Punches can be hooked around a guard or driven straight into the target if an opening exists.

There are many ways to strike with the hand: eye jabs, spearhands, tiger claw strikes, hammerfist or knifehand strikes and many more. If you want to learn about these – and they all have their uses – then you may want to take a class. We will concern ourselves with two strikes – punches and palm-heel strikes.

A punch drives the first two (major) knuckles into the target. It is important that you make a good fist if you are going to punch, since a loose hand or bad position can cause you injury. Also, make sure that your knuckles are lined up along the line of the forearm. This delivers more power and reduces the chance of injury to your hand or arm.

How to make a good fist:

- Let your open hand naturally assume a comfortable position. It should be slightly cupped, with the fingers partially curved and the thumb sticking out and forward.
- Turn your hand so that the thumb is on top.
- Curl your fingers into the palm, leaving the thumb out. Don't crunch your fingers in too tight, but make sure they bend at all the joints. Your fingertips will be in a line, down the middle of your palm. (Alternatively, give an imaginary friend a big thumbs-up. You'll get the same finger position.)
- Now fold your thumb down, so that it rests on the outside of your fingers.
- DON'T tuck your thumb inside the fist, leave it sticking up or lie it on the top. This will break your thumb if you hit something.
- Seen from the top, your thumb and first finger should make a sort of spiral.
- Don't clench your fist super-tight, but don't let it rattle loose either.
- Strike with the top two knuckles (the biggest ones, at the thumb end).

Remember that you should not just strike with your arms. You may or may not have a fair set of muscles in your arms, but a strike that comes from the arm alone is weak. Power is generated by twisting the body, dropping or rising a little, or by moving forward with a blow. Strikes launched when you are retreating are by definition weak. The techniques listed below include hints on how to get the most from them.

A good fist. The thumb is well tucked in down the side. Aim to strike with the top two knuckles.

Punches

Punches are the staples of self-defence. There are several styles of punching, each with its own merits and idiosyncrasies. Karate, boxing and kung fu all use different methods – but they get the same result! Here are some of the basics:

Straight Punches: the Jab and the Cross

A jab is fired out, fast, from the front hand. It is not an amazingly powerful strike, but it can open the door for something more powerful, disrupt an opponent's attack or cover you as you move in or out. The jab can be used to probe for an opening. If it lands, a heavy cross from the back hand follows in the classic boxer's combination.

Both jab and cross are aimed at the head. As the cross is launched, pull the jabbing hand back to guard your head. Allow your body to turn as you throw the cross to deliver maximum power. This isn't too hard. Imagine your body is a hinge and allow it to pivot forward. Your right foot (assuming you're throwing the cross with your right hand) will pivot on its toes and the heel will want to come up. Let it. Both the jab and the cross are all about pushing your fist into a target hard and fast.

A good jab is fast and straight, launched from the front hand. Note the good stance and rear hand covering the jaw.

The cross, launched from the rear hand (usually the right) is a powerful weapon. To make the most of it, let the hip come through and pivot on the back foot. Bring the front hand back to cover.

Hooked Punches: the Hook and the Shovel Hook

Big swinging hook punches are typically used by idiots intent on giving someone a beating. They are the most natural of techniques, and done properly they can be very effective, slipping around a guard and causing 'brain shake' that can lead to unconsciousness.

A hook punch travels in an arc rather than straight to the target. To see how it works, hold your arm (fist clenched) straight out in front of you. Now draw your elbow back so that your upper arm is straight out to the side, level with your shoulder, and the fist is still pointing forwards. If you keep the arm bent and swing it forwards from the shoulder, it'll travel in an arc. An actual hook punch will follow that motion, but you should allow your elbow to bend as much or as little as you need, and let the shoulder come round with the punch. This is a basic hook. Play around with the motion until it becomes natural, remembering that you are aiming at an imaginary opponent's head directly in front of you.

The typical 'street' hook is a large and uncontrolled version of the basic hook. To see what one looks like, take your fist back and down to about the level of your hip, as far back as you can get the arm (which should be curved). Now let the arm swing out, up and across in front of you as if you were trying to get it to travel right round and strike your other shoulder. This is a highly inefficient way to punch, but untrained people often do it instinctively.

Hooks can be launched from the lead hand, but this requires practice so they are more usually thrown from the rear, 'power' hand. Make sure your elbow is up and the forearm is in line or the hook will bounce off as your arm crumples. Targets include the side of the jaw, the temple or low into the kidneys.

The shovel hook (or body punch) is made with a shovelling action, driving a fist low into the abdomen or groin. It slips nicely under a guard but requires you to be pretty close. Street thugs will sometimes use a similar body punch, so it is worth being aware of this one for defensive purposes if nothing else. Hooks are thrown with a pivoting action similar to a cross.

The Uppercut

A boxer's favourite knockout punch, the uppercut is a pistoning action up under the chin. Done from in close, uppercuts require both skill and opportunity, but if you have those then the fight is pretty much over.

Palm-Heel Strikes, Backfists and Hammerfists

Punching with the knuckles risks breaking them on bony parts of your opponent, especially in the case of young women whose bones are light and not yet hardened. Striking with the heel of the palm and the bottom of the fist reduce this risk, since there is some fleshy padding there. These strikes have some other advantages too.

Palm-heel strikes are executed in the same manner as punches, but the striking surface is the fleshy heel of the hand with the wrist angled sharply back. This has the advantage of protecting your hand from damage and also lining up the forearm nicely. Palm-heel strikes are concussive – they deliver force deeply into the target – and do not risk damage to the knuckles or wrist. Good targets include the shoulder, the head or ribs. A solid strike, shot out from the shoulders with your weight behind it, will also drive the opponent back, away from you and create an opportunity for escape. Palm-heel strikes are particularly suitable for young people (especially women) and older people whose bones are susceptible to damage.

As an alternative to punching, drive the heel of your palm into the target. Here, a palm-heel strike is used to deter an attacker from grabbing at the defender's lapel.

A backfist strike is carried out by simply straightening a bent arm and swinging the back of your fist into the target. It is a light impact strike that is primarily useful to cover you as you move from an awkward position, or to open the door for something more substantial. If you tense your arm as you hit, you can deliver a fair amount of power with a backfist, but really it's just a weight (the hand) swung out on a string (your arm). No matter how much muscle you have in that arm, backfists cannot be driven 'through' a target. They bounce off and deliver impact rather than force.

The backfist is a painful but not damaging blow. It is best used to create an opening or a distraction.

The hammerfist is similar to a backfist, but is delivered with the fleshy base of the hand. The impact is greater than a backfist, since the arm delivers more power in that direction. Hammerfists can be 'dropped' onto someone in front of you (opportunities arise during vertical or ground grappling) or can be used like a sort of inside hook punch to the nose. This is good against someone who has hold of you.

Striking with the bottom of the fist like this can be a powerful strike, and like the palm heel, it does not risk breaking the knuckles if bone is hit.

Kicking Techniques

A good solid kick can be devastating and can end the fight there and then. However, trying to kick in the street will usually get you into more trouble than you were in before. Kicking really has little place in street self-defence. You will rarely have the room to deliver a good martial arts kick, since fights happen at such close ranges. That said, if you have trained in a martial art that favours kicks and have become very good at them, then you might spot an opening for a sophisticated kicking technique. However, the only really useful kicks on the street are low, short and not very exciting. If you do kick, don't try to be clever, and whatever you do, don't try to do those high movie kicks – not even if you have practised them in training!

Kicking on the Street

The following kicking techniques are useful on the street. They give you some extra options without creating much risk. Against an opponent who has grabbed you or you don't feel able to defeat any other way, a hard kick at the knee can cause enough pain and impair movement to such a degree (even if you don't damage the knee significantly) that you may be able to escape. It's hard to chase someone on a knee that's just been kicked. This is particularly important for small, light people like women and children. If it comes down to it, make sure that the attacker's attention is on your hands (maybe fake a punch), then kick. It's risky but better than nothing. If it works you'll be able to escape.

Foot Stamp

A foot stamp can be surprisingly effective, and it is something anyone can do. It pretty much does what it says on the tin: lift your foot and stamp on his instep (not the toes). It hurts, and if you hit the instep nerve bundle just right, it can floor someone without doing them any actual harm.

Front Snap Kick

This is a martial arts kicking technique. Aim to hit with the ball of your foot (or the toes if you have fairly heavy shoes on; you won't hurt yourself). Lift the knee and 'snap' the foot out; don't swing it as if you were kicking a football. The height you raise the knee to dictates where the kick will go. Good targets are the knee or maybe the groin. Don't bother going any higher.

A downward stamping kick to the leg can disable an attacker, or at least make him (or her!) reluctant to get close to you.

Kicks can be a powerful weapon. In this case, the knee is lifted and the leg straightened to drive the ball of the foot into the attacker's groin. It works well on men and women. The groin is about as high as you should ever try to kick on the street, and only then if you've trained for it.

A front kick can also be launched with the back foot. The principle is much the same. In both cases, get your foot back on the ground as fast as possible, and keep your hands up and guarding while you execute the technique.

Side Stamp Kick

Primarily used to stamp down on the knee (and break it by hyper-extending it backwards or to the side), the threat of this kick is also good for making people keep their distance. Lift your knee, turn the foot sideways and stamp down and out at the knee. You can lean back for balance and to keep your head out of the way of retaliation. But keep that guard up!

Even if it does not disable your attacker, this kick should bring him to a sudden stop. It causes immense pain that will severely limit his ability to chase you. Even if you fail to connect, an attacker who knows he is risking having his knees destroyed will often become rather less keen to tangle with you.

Thrust Kick from the Ground

A close cousin to the stamp kick, this one is for protecting yourself when downed. Turn on your side, draw the top leg back and thrust it out at the knee.

A kick like this, driving your heel into the attacker's knee, will stop him in his tracks. You could also hook his ankle with your other (bottom) foot to ensure he falls; this would also increase the amount of damage caused to his knee by preventing him from moving away.

You can also thrust backwards or with a stamping motion while on your back. There is really nothing to it, just a matter of timing it right and aiming straight. But this technique might be the only thing between you and being kicked around the floor like a football.

It is also possible that you might be faced with an attacker you can't escape from and can't really hurt, for instance, if you are a child under attack by a large man. You do have one (desperately risky but better than nothing) option. This is the one and only time you should even consider going to the ground.

If absolutely everything else fails, drop onto your side or back and launch a stamping kick at the knees of anyone coming close to you. This is about the most powerful strike you will be able to muster, and it'll attack the knees, which are vulnerable. You should *only* go to the ground like this if you have absolutely no chance otherwise, because it makes you very vulnerable to being kicked, and you can't flee. If you're immensely overmatched, this might offer you a chance.

Elbow Strikes

Elbows are deadly, especially in close. There are basically two ways to use the elbow: thrust it or swing it. Swinging elbows are a staple of muay Thai (Thai boxing), and are deadly but require some practice to get right. Tuck your arm in with the hand close to your chest and swing the arm as if doing a hook punch. Aim at the head or ribs.

Thrusting or driving elbows are primarily used to the side or backwards. Aimed at the head or the solar plexus, the effect of driving the point of your elbow into someone can be pretty spectacular. The movement is natural too, Push your elbow back or to the side in the direction of an imaginary opponent. That's all there is to it.

Someone who has grabbed you from behind can be dealt with by driving your elbow straight back into his body. Elbows are powerful, and don't require any real training to use.

As with the cross, allow your body to pivot with the strike and follow through for maximum effect.

Headbutts

Your head can be used as a weapon. This may seem brutal – it is! – but when your safety is at stake you must act decisively. Never butt brow to brow. Instead drive the front corner of your head or your forehead into an opponent's cheek or nose. If you can, set up a whipping action by moving your body forward, then the head. A headbutt can be made more powerful by grabbing an opponent and dragging them in towards you – and an attacker may try to do this to you. You can also drive your head backward into someone who has hold of you from behind. This can be highly effective in gaining release.

Headbutting someone is a little barbaric, but it's certainly effective! Drive your brow hard into the attacker's face, striking him on the nose or cheekbones if you can.

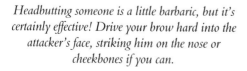

A rear headbutt into the face may convince an attacker to let go of you, and anyone who has grabbed you from behind is ideally placed to be butted. Jerk your head sharply backwards and hit whatever you can.

Knees

Knees are the nuclear weapons of self-defence. Very few people can withstand a knee driven into their body. Lifting the knee is a natural movement that requires only gross motor control, and anyone can do it, even under the most awful stress. There are clever techniques for long-range kneeing, but here we are concerned with close-in situations. Your leg muscles are designed to raise the knee, and they are very powerful! Knee the thigh (front or side) or the abdomen or groin. Don't worry about what you hit – whatever you contact, you'll get a result!

Knee attacks are ideal for close-in grappling situations. A straight driving knee like this one will go in deep and bring most incidents to a rapid close.

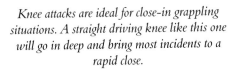

Kneeing is easy. Grab the attacker any way you can and lift your knee, driving it into the thigh, groin or body. You can also swing the knee in an arc, out and back in, aiming under the ribs. This is a devastating, fight-winning technique. In fact, be very careful when practising this with a partner. Quite light contact with the knee (well, everything is relative!) will demolish your partner, especially if you land a strike in the floating ribs/kidneys region.

A knee in the leg will usually result in a dead leg of epic proportions. One in the abdomen will wind someone spectacularly and a hit to the groin (even if you miss the genitals) will considerably diminish an attacker's ability to hurt or chase you, or stand up, for that matter.

A roundhouse knee swings out and then back into the target in a curve. Whether you knee straight or round depends upon the situation – choose whichever one seems to have the best chance of hitting the target.

Summary

- If you are downed, get up as quickly as possible.
- Kick low, punch high.
- Never try to kick high.
- Unless you are skilled, don't kick at all.
- Don't strike bone with your knuckles if you can help it.
- A precise strike is far more effective than a powerful but random blow.

Chapter 3: Defensive Techniques

Self-defence cannot be purely passive or defensive. Unless you can wriggle free and run for it (always an option and not one to be underestimated!), you will have to do something to hurt an attacker to make him back off or to end the attack. Unpleasant as it may sound, it is usually preferable to use a pre-emptive attack. This is quite legal as long as you are *sure* that you are under attack. It isn't always possible, however.

Once an attack has begun, you will need to defend against it before you can begin to carry out your 'bash and dash' escape plan. Frankly, your chances are poorer if you're defending than if you can pre-empt, but with the right techniques you can defeat an attack and cause the assailant some harm in the process. The most important thing is to keep your head and act coherently rather than flailing about in a panic.

Defending Yourself Against Grabs and Chokes

People who mean you harm will often open proceedings by grabbing you, and if you can't deal with it, then it's all over. A fight situation often becomes an exercise in grabbing too. Pretty much any part of your body or clothing can be grabbed and used to immobilise or drag you. Some assailants will try to choke you (deliberately or otherwise). Typical grabs include:

- One or both wrists.
- Shirt front or lapel.
- Bear hug from front or rear, over or under the arms.
- Around the neck from behind.
- Throat from in front.

It is best to break a grab before your attacker has a decent grip on you or to move and prevent him from getting hold in the first place. Once a grab is 'on', it can be difficult to escape. If a large, powerful person has a good bear hug on you, it can be impossible.

Many street attacks begin with a simple wrist grab. Twist your wrist sharply and jerk the arm back or up to break the grab.

A bear hug that immobilises your arms can render you helpless, or even stop you from breathing. Escaping once the attacker has a good hold is very difficult.

As soon as someone tries to get hold of you – even if you aren't sure they mean you harm – react! Move sharply away, push their hands aside and make yourself a hard target. It is especially important to react quickly to a strangle or choke, or when someone gets hold of you from behind.

• React INSTANTLY to anyone grabbing you.

In the case of a strangle or choke, you have seconds to do something about it. The oxygen level in your brain drops, then unconsciousness follows. It is very rare for this to take longer than 10 seconds. If you spoil the choke by moving or dropping your chin then you have a little longer, but escape is imperative all the same.

Defences Against Front Grabs and Chokes

The best defence against grabs is to be out of reach. The next best is to break the grab before it is on properly. The absolute worst is to end up wrestling with someone!

If someone tries to grab your wrist, move away while sharply twisting your wrist and pulling that hand back. If your other hand is free, use it as a distraction. You might shoot it towards his eyes in the hope he'll flinch, flick him in the face with the back of your hand or punch him soundly on the nose. Most important is the sudden movement of the wrist and the twisting action that makes it hard to get or to keep hold of you.

• Move sharply and twist to break a wrist grab.

A wrist grab can immobilise you for a follow-up punch. Be ready to escape instantly if someone gets hold of you.

It is harder to dislodge a solid hold on your clothing. Many garments will tear, which may or may not be a good thing. If this does not happen then you will have a hard time dislodging someone's grip. Strength and wrestling are unlikely to succeed. On the plus side there is a wide range of locks and throwing techniques that could be applied, but you will need to have learned and practised them to have any chance of success. The time to consider doing this is well before someone grabs you!

To dislodge a grab on your clothing or a strangle, your best chance is to hurt your assailant and make him flinch away. A backhanded flick to the eyes or bridge of the nose, coupled with a sharp movement away from him, is an option if you think he is not too serious. If he is determined to hurt you then he will almost certainly punch with his other hand or knee or headbutt you. Your best option is to pre-empt his attack – you have plenty of justification – by moving in with a headbutt, knee or other strike of your own, or grab his chin and the back of his head, and twist him away.

Alternatively, you can jam your forearm across his throat (an arm bar) and push. Make sure you jam his knee by moving your leg forward, but don't strike the throat unless you are willing to risk causing death. Pressure on the throat should change the focus of his attention from grabbing you to getting away from you, allowing you to escape.

- Chokes *must* be broken instantly. *Never* try to counter-choke or you will die.

Do whatever you must to escape. Someone who tries to strangle you means to kill you. You cannot afford to have any doubt about that. If you can relieve the pressure by turning your body away or twisting one hand off then this may help, but do not rely upon wrestling. Instead, make him pull or flinch away. Strike his throat or eyes. Even if you blind or kill him, you're justified. He was in the process of murdering you, and you have the right to prevent that at any cost (to your assailant!).

As the confrontation develops, the defender moves into a fence. Note how the fingers of the right hand are pointed at the assailant's eyes. Simply by straightening his left arm, the defender can launch a devastating eye strike.

Defences Against Rear Grabs and Chokes

Being grabbed from behind is usually a complete surprise – otherwise you would have turned round! An attacker might try to spin you round to hit you in the face, may bear-hug you or may just grab you around the throat to choke or control you. A forearm across the throat can be very difficult to dislodge and can choke you unconscious very quickly. You must act fast, ideally before the grip is properly on.

As in the case of front grabs, there is a plethora of beautiful throwing techniques you could use to make a rear-grabbing assailant wish he'd stayed at home. But these require training and practice, so here we will stick to the simplest of measures.

A choke from the rear will usually be done from close in. If someone tries to put their hands round your neck, you can sometimes slip out of their grasp by moving sharply forward. Forearm chokes (a forearm across your throat rather than hands around your neck) are harder to break unless you can move away as you feel the grab begin.

- Move away or turn if you think someone is close behind you. Don't let them get a choke on you from behind if you can help it.

To escape from a bear hug or similar rear grab, your best bet is, as always, to move as soon as you feel someone grabbing you. Once the grab is on, your chances are slimmer. You have four primary weapons, all of which should be used along with kicking and struggling like a wet cat. It can be hard to keep hold of someone who is thrashing about and yelling, and an attacker may well decide that he does not want to! Your four weapons, in addition to this general wildcat behaviour, are:

- Drive your elbow backward into the solar plexus (pit of the stomach) or up and back at the head.
- Slam your head back, or sideways and back, in a rear headbutt, and keep doing it!
- Stamp down on the instep (not the toes; there is a nerve bundle on the instep that is less well protected than the toes) or scrape your shoe down his shin.
- Bring your heel up by bending the knee sharply. Aim for the groin.

When grabbed from the rear you can also push backwards suddenly and sharply, hopefully sending both of you reeling. This can be a bit of a lottery as to whether he lets go, or one or both of you fall, but it is better than nothing.

 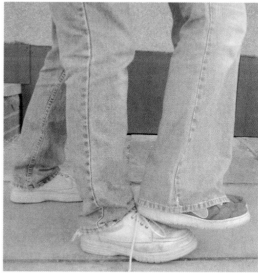

An attacker who is behind you can be discouraged by stamping down hard on his instep (this hurts much *more than the toes) with your heel. Be ready to take advantage of any flinch on the attacker's part.*

As an extreme one-shot defence, you can drop sharply and suddenly forward and to your knees. Don't rely on gravity, lean forward, dig your feet in and lunge forward and down. If you can, twist your body to one side as you go. If this fails and you're on the ground and still held, things are bad. But it may spring you free or turn into a spectacular throw.

Defending Yourself Against Punches

Most assailants will punch you or grapple with you when standing, or kick you if you're down and they are still standing. Few will kick if you're upright, though someone with a little training or who has seen too many movies may try it. The special (but all too common) case where you are both on the ground is dealt with separately.

Remember that all defence against strikes is based around not being hit rather than hard, powerful blocks. Your basic options are to evade while staying in reach, move out of reach or close in and smother the blow before it develops any real power.

A body punch can be defeated by moving back and dropping your hand onto the punch to cover. Pull the attacker off-balance as you strike with your other hand. The most important thing is to move back so that the punch does not strike you.

An effective defence against a punch is to move inside it while pushing the arm away. Grab the attacker's arm to pull him off-balance, then deliver a counter-strike.

Most attackers will throw a series of punches, often in a manner referred to as 'head down and swim', or will grab at you and try to strike you. Turning to flee is not an option since you'll be hit as you try to escape, so getting a strike of your own in is a necessity if you are to create any space to escape. It is very, very difficult to get a decent blow in on someone who is constantly attacking, so you only have a few options:

- Pre-empt the attack.
- Evade and counter.
- Let the attacker come to you and use a throw or takedown.
- Launch a counter-attack.

The last option is feasible if you can time it right – and if you have what it takes to walk into someone and start punching despite their best efforts to knock you off your feet. If you do this, the best option is to try to turn yourself into what the authors call the 'Unstoppable Karate Machine'. Storm into your opponent, throwing out a series of straight punches (they get there quicker than hooks and will force the attacker onto the defensive, protecting you as well as hopefully disabling him).

For most people, though, counter-attacking like this is not an option. Your best bet is to move and keep moving, seeking an opening. If the assailant uses big, slow attacks you may be able to get a fast jab in between them, creating an opening, or you may be able to evade and strike him as he withdraws his hand after he has missed. Either way, if you land a hit you will create an opening to do something else. He may go down dazed or back off in pain. He may flinch and give you time to dart away. Even if your first blow does not end the matter, you can press the attack and he'll find it very difficult to hit you as long as you keep coming forward and attacking. Just be sure not to run into a sucker-punch.

Do remember that you're not fighting with him, you're creating an opportunity to escape the situation. Keep that in mind, and once the chance appears, take it! If you can evade his attack and hit him with a strike, you may end the matter then and there. If not, you might manage to stun him long enough to escape or to hit him again.

There is nothing sophisticated about this; it's simply a matter of applying the evasions and strikes already discussed. However, there is another option. One of the best ways to create an escape opportunity is to get the assailant to fall – or to throw him.

Getting Hit

I've been knocked out exactly once. If it happens then there's nothing you can do about it. But most of the time a blow causes a great deal of pain (and often injury) but only momentary incapacity. I've been hit by blows that threw me back and made the attacker run after me, and by short, sharp blows that simply stunned me. I clearly remember receiving a succession of fairly light (i.e. non-knockout) blows on one occasion. Between each and the next it was as if a little inner voice was yelling at me to act, but I couldn't. By the time my brain was back in gear the next one slammed home. It stopped only when I was on the floor listening to the words, 'you see?'

But this was a very skilled, very fast puncher. Someone less skilled or more angry would have left gaps between the blows. And in that moment as my brain rebooted, and before the next one landed to again take away my conscious volition, I would have had a choice to make: the instinctive (fold up and go down), or the hard but necessary option (stay up, move, cover, and fight back).

That's how it is if you get hit by any significant blow. There will be a second or two where you can't do anything at all, then the 'fold or fight' moment. Panic, fear, anger, pride, training, determination or a desperate need to survive and/or protect your loved ones will be factors in deciding whether you keep your feet or become a football. If you find yourself in a position to make that choice, there is only one possible option – and it's not surrender!

Throws and Takedowns

Many martial arts, especially judo, aikido and ju-jitsu, use a lot of throwing techniques and often get heavily into grappling too. Throws and takedowns are very similar; both aim to get someone on the ground. As a rule, throws are intended to cause injury, while takedowns are less complex and are mainly aimed at just getting the opponent down, either for grappling or to allow an escape.

It is not really possible to deal with effective throwing techniques in the space we have available. Throws can be very effective, especially if someone grabs you, but they require training and practice (with a partner) if they are to become very useful. If you can get to a self-defence class or study an appropriate martial art, then you will learn some useful throwing techniques. Takedowns are mainly used by people who want to grapple, which we are trying our best to avoid.

For these reasons our coverage of throws and takedowns is limited to these highly useful (and simple) techniques. We have grouped them together for clarity; do remember that these techniques can be applied any time someone attacks or grabs you, whenever they seem appropriate.

The Ground is Very Hard!

Gravity and concrete can be great allies, especially for small, light people who feel that they can't deal with a given attacker using strikes. Not only will it take time for an attacker to get up to pursue you, but the fall may cause injury (and, if it's absolutely necessary, you can kick or stamp on your assailant to prevent him getting up quickly).

One tiny, lightweight woman that I had the pleasure of training with had this down to a fine art. She just liked to make people fall. She'd wait until you launched an attack, then dodge, pull your arm and trip you up. Or kick one of your feet away as you took a step. On the hard wooden floor where we trained, this was unpleasant. On the street, it would be very nasty indeed.

She was tiny; I could have punched her into orbit. Yet it was me that limped away from our training. And you know what? She hardly ever hit me. I was soundly beaten up by the ground.

Outside Hock/Trip Takedown

This technique is useful when you find yourself in close, for example, when you have closed in to smother a punch. Keep moving forward, hooking your arm around the attacker's neck and get one foot behind one of his. Then push him backward to make him fall and accelerate away out of danger. The key is that arm around his neck. Pushing back on his throat will make him recoil and remove any need to rely on raw strength. This takedown works even better if you can break the attacker's posture by reaching down his back, bending him backwards and making it difficult for him to keep his balance.

Evasion and Sweep Throw

This makes use of an attacker's momentum as he surges in with a big right hook or cross. He will be moving forward with a lot of momentum. Evading the strike by taking a step forward and to your right (assuming he's attacking with his right hand), reach out and grab the attacker's arm at the biceps with your left hand. Pulling the attacker forward and down with your left hand, keep moving out of the way to the right, sending the attacker stumbling past and gaining time for an escape.

Alternatively, you can turn this into a throw by pushing up under his left armpit with your right hand while sweeping his left foot away. His momentum will make him flip over with stunning force, allowing you to escape.

Dropping Full Shoulder Throw from Rear Grab

This technique is an excellent way to escape from a rear choke if you are standing up. You must act immediately, or you will be choked or dragged backwards. As you feel an arm go around your neck, drop your chin to protect your throat (you may not be quick enough, but try) and get a hand into the crook of the elbow to relieve the pressure.

Pull down and forward with this hand, while dropping to one knee and twisting round. An attacker will normally choke with his right arm, so you should drop to the right knee and twist left. The attacker should fall over you and land in front of you where you can strike him to gain time to get up and escape. Be careful if you try this one out with a partner; the throw happens very suddenly and your partner will hit the floor extremely hard.

If someone gets a good grip on you from behind, especially around the neck like this, you are in serious trouble. You must act immediately to get rid of them. Grab their arm and turn away from it, dropping to one knee. The attacker will crash to the ground in front of you.

Defending Yourself on the Ground

You should never choose to go to the ground, but if you end up there, your goal must be to get up again as quickly as possible. However, sometimes it is necessary to defend or even fight while on the ground.

Many martial arts – especially those intended to prepare practitioners for competitions like Ultimate Fighting Championship and Shoot Wrestling tournaments – do a lot of ground fighting. For the ring, this is an excellent choice – most fights are won on the ground. But on the street you are liable to be kicked while you wrestle someone into submission. Besides, street thugs are unlikely to 'tap out', accept defeat honourably and then leave, are they?

It is very useful to have some training in ground fighting, just in case you end up on the floor with someone. You are far less likely to panic if the situation is familiar, and you'll be better able to break out if you have the skills. Groundwork is also incredibly good for building stamina. However, do not become obsessed with ground fighting. Your goal is to stay up or get back up, not to roll around on the pavement among the broken glass and dog excrement.

Going to the Floor

I have an aversion to going to the floor that borders on phobia. I'm also really, really good at staying upright no matter what (fifteen years of fencing has something to do with that!). And yet, despite all the years of training and practice, I end up on the deck all the time.

I've been dragged down by a big guy who kept hold of me, taken down by experts who can bring buildings down if they want to, thrown by people of all sizes, run into and knocked down by a 16-stone sparring partner with more determination than common sense (and this despite the fact that I thumped him *hard* on the way in), had my feet swept out from under me, been tripped ...

But most of the time, it just happens. The fight closes in and vertical grappling begins. Somebody loses their balance and the floor beckons. The bottom line is that if a fight gets close in, it stays there. After that it's a matter of time before you end up on the ground. Keep your distance and break off as soon as you can.

Defences Against Kicks

If you are downed, it is likely that you will be kicked. You must protect your head, no matter what. Curling into a ball with your arms around your head will delay the inevitable, but you will be kicked unconscious after a while, and your head will be used as a football. Believe it. It happens. So, your defence must not be passive covering – you must fight back!

The first option is to keep your feet towards your attacker and kick out at his knees as he closes. This does not work very well against groups, but against a single attacker it is effective. Alternatively, you can use a side thrust kick (as described in the previous chapter) to strike out at your attacker.

You are very vulnerable on the ground. One option is to pivot so your feet are pointing at the attacker, and kick him if he approaches. Sooner or later, though, you have to get back up!

If you are caught on the ground and are about to receive a kick (it will almost certainly be aimed at your head), you will have to absorb it on your arms. Do *not* attempt to block a kick at its strongest point. Either close in and smother the kick before it gains power, or move away and grab the leg when the force is largely spent.

Now, either kick at the knee or thread your leg through the attacker's and hook it behind one knee, toppling him over you. As he falls forward, get up and run. Give him a disabling kick if you think this is necessary to ensure your escape.

Defences Against Strangles

On the ground you are even more vulnerable to chokes and strangles. You must break the hold on your throat as quickly as possible. Striking upwards is very difficult, so you will have to grapple. Grab your assailant by the chin and back of the head and twist hard. His body will follow his head around and roll off you. Don't worry about damaging his neck; he will move voluntarily before you can do any real damage, and besides, even if you did break his neck – he was in the middle of killing you! The same technique can be used to get a rapist or anyone else off you.

Other techniques for getting someone off you include striking the kidneys, shoving the face or jabbing a hard object like a key or pen into the side of his head or neck.

Getting Up

Getting up is the most important thing you can do in a ground fight. If you are both on the floor then all that matters is speed. However, if you are likely to be attacked as you get up, it is important that you cover yourself. Don't worry about gymnastic manoeuvres you may have seen in films. Instead use this simple procedure:

- Face your opponent; don't turn away.
- Support yourself on one arm. Keep the other ready to guard.
- Get one leg under yourself and stand up.
- Keep a guard up.
- Pull away from the attacker rather than moving your head towards him as you stand.
- Go to a ready stance and be ready to move.

Defending Yourself Against Weapons

Armed attacks are less common than most people think, but all the same it is wise to assume that any attacker may be armed. Don't ever be drawn into a confrontation with someone you 'think you can take'. Not only is it pointless and stupid, but if he has a hidden weapon then the first you may know about it is when it enters your body.

The stereotypical downward stabbing attack is actually very rare.
Most attackers will slash horizontally or thrust straight forward.

Common Sense and Weapons

The only time you should try to fight someone who has a weapon is if he attacks you with it, or if not resisting now will place you in a more dangerous position later.

In the face of a knife, stick, bat or (heaven forbid!) a firearm, you are wisest to hand over valuables and cooperate, as long as the motive only seems to be robbery. On no account should you try to foil an armed robbery – it is only money being stolen, and it's probably not even yours!

If the armed assailant tries to abduct you or cause you harm, then resistance may be the best option. This is a decision you will have to make on the spot. As a rule, if someone with a knife tries to get you into a car, you are best to resist. Wherever you may be, the place he wants to take you is likely to be far worse. You may only have this one chance to save your life.

If you must defend yourself against a weapon, forget any formal, stylised moves that you may have been shown. All weapon defences are a frantic scramble, no matter how skilled the defender. The basic principle is always:

- Immobilise the weapon hand.
- Demolish the attacker.

Do not try to grapple with someone who has a knife other than to immobilise the knife hand. It is just too easy to be cut or impaled when in close. If you can grab the knife hand, try to control the thumb and turn the weapon away from you.

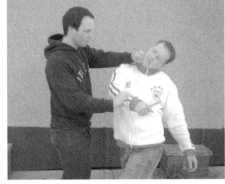

Most knife users will thrust forwards with the weapon. Move to the side, then lunge in and pin the weapon arm as you strike. Remember that any knife defence will be messy. You must take whatever opportunities you can.

You cannot hold back in the face of a lethal attack. You will have a brief moment at best in which to act. You must hit and hit again, doing as much damage as you possibly can, until the attacker collapses. Any less and you will die.

The Reality of Knife Attacks

Nobody ever attacks with an overhead stabbing action. If someone really means to use a knife on you, he will try to keep it concealed and stab or slash you from up close, then walk away as you collapse, bleeding. The most likely knife attacks are either during a robbery where the robber becomes nervous or impatient, or an impromptu attack where an angry person seizes a sharp implement. Another possible scenario occurs if someone tries to abduct you at knife point and you resist.

Whatever happens, it is likely that you will be cut. Keep fighting! To give up is to die. There is no alternative. It's really better not to tackle knives unless you absolutely have to. The best defence against any weapon is to run away. If at any point you get the chance to flee – then run for it!

Knife Defence: Slashing Attack

A slashing attack is very difficult to defend against. You will not be able to kick the knife out of the attacker's hand, so don't try. Your best chance (other than a rapid departure) is to move back out of range and let the slash go past, then move in and pin the knife to the attacker's body. Push his weapon hand against him (if he stabs himself, he stabs himself. You cannot be blamed) and hit him as hard as you possibly can until he goes down. A really hard kick at the knee can also work. Little else will, especially not intricate kata-like defences. Attackers are rarely compliant with formal techniques.

Knife Defence: Stabbing Attack

A stabbing attack is very likely to be fatal. A penetration of two inches at most places on the torso (and that is easy to achieve!) will kill you or disable you so you bleed to death. It is slightly easier to avoid a stab than a slash, but the consequences are even more serious if you fail. Allow the knife hand to reach full extension (move out of the way, obviously) and grab the hand around the thumb. Push it back against the attacker's body or off to the side, and close in. Kick him hard on the knee as a distraction if you get the chance, then hit him again and again until you are sure the attack is over.

Bottle Defence: Overhead Swing

The best defence against an overhead swing is to step to the side and let it go past. Cover yourself, just in case. The attacker will be wide open for a moment. Elbow him in the head or deliver a similarly devastating strike.

Stick and Bat Defence: Body Swing

A more or less flat swing at the body will resemble a slash with a knife. It is difficult to stop such an attack, and it is very likely to connect if you remain within range. The best answer is to move back and let the weapon go past, then close in and, again, pin the weapon hand against the attacker's body as you deliver a series of determined strikes.

Here the defender dodges back and lets the swing go past. He then lunges in to pin the weapon arm as best he can, and launches an all-or-nothing strike to disable the attacker.

Stick and Bat Defence: Overhead Swing

An overhead swing with a heavy implement will break your collarbone and could kill you if it strikes your skull. The previous bottle defence can be used against a stick (and vice versa), or you can close in before the attack gains any power and grab the attacking arm, halting the swing. Immediately attack with your knee or elbow. Do not attempt to block the attack with your forearm. You will merely get a broken arm for your trouble.

An overhead swing like this could kill you outright. You must do something about it. Hesitate and it's all over!

An untrained person will throw up an arm to protect their head – not very effective!

Instead, the defender moves to the side and deflects the swing, pulling the attacker off-balance. A vigorous counter-attack should follow.

Firearms

Firearms are readily obtainable in some countries, and even in Britain the ban on private ownership has done little to alter the number of weapons in criminal hands. However, even in places where guns are legal, you are far more likely to face a punch than a bullet.

If someone produces a firearm of any sort, assume that it is real, that it is loaded, and that your assailant is willing to use it. You may be lucky; it may be a defective weapon, a replica or an air pistol. If it looks real, don't gamble your life on it being a fake.

- Assume that any weapon that looks real *is* real, is loaded and has a hair trigger.
- Assume that a person holding a weapon is willing – eager, even – to use it.

You must tackle a gunman *only* if you have absolutely no alternative. If this is the case, then grab the weapon and twist it to point away from you. Keep hold even if it goes off and becomes hot. If you let go the next shot will hit you. Once the weapon is not aimed at you, attack the gunman and don't stop until you are sure he is no longer a threat.

If you flee a weapon, it is worth knowing that most people (especially if they learned to shoot by watching films) have no real idea what they are doing and will be wholly unable to hit a moving target, even at quite short ranges. Change direction as you run and get as far away as you can.

If you are shot and you are still upright, then you can still fight or flee. A very serious gunshot wound will render you helpless, but anything that does not is not immediately life-threatening, however shocking and painful it may be. You can still win if you haven't been downed. Escape if you can, and if not then fight on and disable your attacker.

Seek medical help for any injury as soon as possible. Most people who are shot do not die immediately, but many bleed to death or collapse from wound shock.

Final Note on Weapons

If you are facing a weapon then you should only fight if you have no alternative. If you do win, make sure you get control of the weapon. Don't leave it lying around where someone could pick it up and attack you again.

- Control the weapon during the fight.
- Secure the weapon afterwards.

Remember that if a weapon is used against you, then the attacker is trying to kill you. You must do anything you can to prevent that. You will get one chance only; make it count.

In Extremis

Some situations are less serious than others, though in this day and age it is wise to assume that any assailant or potential assailant is armed and has several similarly equipped friends with him, even if he seems to be alone. Treat any situation as potentially life-threatening, and be aware that it can all go badly wrong in seconds.

Some situations are obviously potentially lethal from the outset. If an assailant or group of assailants is attempting to use lethal force against you or someone around you – or you have good reason to fear that they will – then you have every legal and moral right to fight back with any and all means at your disposal.

- In a lethal situation, do whatever you must to survive.

In a life-threatening situation you must not hold back. Nor must you flinch from distasteful and downright unpleasant actions. Some of these are oddments that could be used anytime (if you feel the need) but which don't really fit elsewhere. The rest are very nasty things to do to someone and really should be reserved for horrific threats like attempted rape or murder, or else are included for reference because a street thug may choose to use them on *you!*

The important thing when using these dirty fighting tricks is to be inventive and vicious. Some of these tricks are mainly psychological in effect, in that they are just so unpleasant that the person you use them on, though not badly hurt, will usually recoil in shock.

- **Biting**: unpleasant, and bearing some slight health risks, biting is a matter of personal taste (!). It is hard to cause serious injury with a bite, but the pain and psychological effect can be considerable. Anything that you can get your teeth into can be bitten. Whether to hang on or to let go is up to you. It really depends upon the circumstances. To cause the most pain, nip some flesh rather than biting deep.

- **Headbutting**: there is really nothing to a headbutt. Drive the forehead, corner or back of your head into your opponent's face, side of the head or other body parts. It is possible to deliver a dead arm or leg with a powerful butt, and a headbutt under the shoulder blade is painful too. If your limbs are entangled, butt anything within reach. Never meet brow to brow, though, unless you happen to be a Neanderthal.

- **Eye-poking and gouging**: a nasty business, but if it is the only way to prevent your untimely death then it is justified. Eye jabs can be made with fingers or thumbs. It's really not very difficult if you are willing or desperate enough. Even if you fail, you will make the attacker recoil and gain time to do something else.

- **Throat strikes**: crushing the windpipe or other parts of the throat can be fatal. A good firm squeeze or a light jab will usually cause an attacker to recoil, coughing.

- **Face attacks**: as well as the eyes, there are plenty of facial features to scratch at, pull, grab or squash. Pull and twist the lips, crush the nose, grab ears and pull hard. Swing on his hair or any facial piercings. Alternatively, grab the chin and the back of the head and twist hard. This will give you control of your attacker's body and make him thoroughly defensive.

- **Grabbing genitals**: grab and twist, squeeze or yank hard. The results are surprisingly similar. Most people become very defensive when you grab their gonads, which may give you an opening to do something else. However, note that it is actually quite hard to get a useful grip since clothing and legs get in the way.

Targets and How to Exploit Them

The human body is an amazing thing. It can survive 100-mph car crashes almost undamaged, yet be disabled by a few pounds of pressure on a bone. If you must attack a human body, then it is vitally important that you attack it effectively. That means exploiting its weaknesses with precise attacks rather than flailing away at the body in general.

Striking

If aiming at the head from in front, try to strike right on the tip of the chin (many experts call this the 'button' since if you hit it right, the jawbone presses on nerve centres and causes instant unconsciousness). Alternatively, punch the nose. This causes severe pain and makes the target's eyes fill up with tears. Do not hit the mouth. Teeth can severely damage your hand.

From the side (say with a hook punch), a blow on the side of the jaw or the temple will cause 'brain shake' which can result in unconsciousness or disorientation. Hitting the cheekbone will cause the commonest of fight-related injuries – black eyes and possibly a cracked cheekbone – but it is not likely to stop an attacker.

Striking the throat quite lightly will cause the target to cough and lose his breath. A little harder will kill him. Be aware of this. Similarly, a blow to the side of the neck can stun, cause unconsciousness or kill.

The shoulders are good targets for a palm-heel strike intended to crack the collarbone. This will disable the attacker's arm without being life-threatening. Hit both at once to send him staggering away. A straight punch into the shoulder joint is also highly effective and makes it difficult for the attacker to use his arm.

The chest is quite well protected by the rib cage. Even a blow hard enough to crack a rib may not stop an attacker. However, there are some useful targets. A blow over the heart can be very serious since it shocks this vital muscle. The ribs at the sides, about at sternum level, can be struck for good effect. There is a large nerve bundle there, as well as intercostal muscles, which, if struck, will make the target's breathing somewhat painful.

Lower down at the sides, a blow can be hooked into the kidneys, which is very effective. Striking the corner of the rib cage where it curves up at the front to meet the sternum (breastbone) will shock the diaphragm and cause a great deal of pain. Between these two points is the solar plexus. Hitting this requires relatively little force to produce a folding-up effect on the target.

From the rear, strikes to the kidney area are effective. It is also possible to strike the spine, back of the neck or the rear of the skull, though this can cause paralysis or death so should only be done in extreme circumstances. An opponent who is doubled up in front of you can be best attacked by driving an elbow down into his back under the shoulder blades. This causes winding and muscle trauma, but is unlikely to inflict permanent harm.

The groin is a good target. This is about as high as you should kick and is a bit lower than you would normally punch. Obviously, hitting the genitals will floor most attackers, but it is actually quite difficult to do. However, a strike that shocks the hip or pubic bone can also be intensely painful and may limit an attacker's mobility.

Striking at the arms is not normally useful, though a blow to the inner or outer side of the biceps, about halfway up, can cause a dead arm.

The legs can be more usefully struck, usually by kicks. The knee can be kicked from in front or from the side. Kicking the knee from behind will crumple the leg and may make the attacker fall, but it won't cause much damage. You can also kick or knee the front or side of the quadriceps (the big thigh muscle) to cause a dead leg and thus facilitate your escape. A 'pushing' kick to the knee from the side will not cause much damage but will buckle the knee and may make the attacker fall.

Kicks to the shin are very painful, as is stamping down hard on the instep (not the toes). This works even better if you can scrape down the shin on the way.

Attacking Joints

There are many locking techniques available. Most are designed to allow effective restraint, but since they work by moving a joint in a direction it is not supposed to go in, it is obvious that a good lock can be used to damage the joint. Some martial arts teach devastating lock-and-throw techniques that can utterly destroy a joint; however, it is unlikely that you will be in a position where locking techniques are useful to you. If the assailant poses a significant threat to you, you should rely on striking and escaping rather than locking and restraint techniques – for your own safety.

The fingers have particularly vulnerable joints. Grab and bend fingers back to break them or cause pain and make someone let go of you.

Other Attacks

At need you can make a variety of other attacks. The eyes are vulnerable to a poke, jab or push. This need not be a deep, blinding attack. It is possible to push on the face (especially the eyes and nose) to make someone recoil from you without causing any lasting damage.

Other facial features can be grabbed and twisted, pulled, bitten or nipped. The lip, nose and ears are obvious targets. Do *not* attempt to hook a finger into someone's mouth and pull. While effective, it exposes you to a grave risk of being bitten.

The throat is another area that merits special mention. Obviously, you can strike the throat hard to kill if you have no alternative. Under self-defence conditions, it is unlikely that you will have sufficient control to hit the throat lightly, so a throat attack is an attempted kill. However, there are other ways to use the throat. Firstly, pressure on the neck or throat will force compliance on almost anyone – in other words, if you push on someone's throat, the rest of him will move in the same direction. Secondly, you could attempt a choke or strangle.

The word 'could' is used here rather than 'can'. This is because you should not attempt to choke in a self-defence situation unless you have no alternative. It is too easy to cause death by choking someone, and it requires a good hold and a (rather short) period of time to take effect. If you slip or are attacked from elsewhere during that time or if the attacker breaks your hold, then you are no better off than before. Choke holds should be reserved for two occasions: when you have absolutely no other options (say when you are on the ground under someone and can't escape) or as a tool to subdue someone or to ensure compliance with a restraint – and only then if you are trained and know what you are doing.

Nerve-point attacks, as taught in many martial arts, can and do work. However, you have to hit the right spot, which is not always in exactly the same place on different people. Some nerve-point work is valuable as a self-defence tool, for example, knowing where the major nerve bundles are so that you can deliver a blow to them. Subtle use of nerve and pressure points requires long training and is not always effective even then. If you want to attack nerve points (and do understand that this is a useful tool that can be used by anyone – if they know how to do it!) then you will have to undertake a long period of training. Unless you are going to do that, forget about nerve or pressure points.

Summary

- Purely defensive measures will not be enough; defeat the attack then counter-attack!
- Avoid grappling, but be willing to trip or throw an assailant as long as you stay upright.
- Do not tackle weapons unless you have absolutely no option.
- No half-measures in the face of an armed attack. Immobilise the weapon and destroy the attacker.
- Unless you are trained, you will not be able to apply an effective joint lock.
- Facial features can be pushed, pulled, poked or bitten to cause pain.
- Leave the throat alone unless you need to kill someone.
- Do not bother with nerve points unless you are very skilled.
- Do whatever you must to end the attack, especially if your life is in danger, but remember that you must not lose control and become a raging animal.

Afterword

If you've got this far, you have probably had a couple of good scares, disagreed violently with at least one thing we've said and nodded to yourself in a couple of places, thinking 'I already knew that'. However good or bad your experience with this book has been, thanks for reading so far.

If you disagree with us about something (or even everything), that's fine – we respect you and your opinions, and we're sure your reasons for holding them are as valid as our reasons for holding ours. If you do disagree with us, please think about why you hold that opinion; is it for a good reason or is it just complacency and conventional wisdom? Our ideas about what happens out on the street are drawn from experience and research; we believe in our conclusions.

That does not mean that your opinions are wrong, of course. But our advice is to be very sure that you hold those opinions for a good reason; one based on real-world experience rather than films and news reports.

And having got this far, we have something rather unpleasant to tell you. You see, by reading this book, you have achieved very little. The intrinsic worth of all the information in this volume is … nothing at all. You are no safer having read these pages and looked at the pictures than you were yesterday, *unless* you act upon what we have told you. If you think about the contents of this book, implement the measures and maybe get some training or improve your fitness a little – and most of all *begin to practise habitual awareness* – then you will make yourself many times safer without really changing your lifestyle. You owe it to yourself to do this.

You may be a little annoyed at reading this. Sorry about that. But all you've done is spend some money on a book and invested a little time in reading it. Little effort and no gain. In the harsh environment of street survival, safety cannot be bought with money.

If you want to be safe, you will have to practise self-protection. We've shown you how, now it's up to you. There is only one person you can definitely rely on – you! Just remember what we told you many, many pages ago:

- Self-protection begins with the self.

We'd offer blessings and good luck, but self-protection isn't a matter of luck. Instead we'll just part with some advice:

- On the street there are no second chances – so don't take any!

You don't have to be paranoid, and you don't have to be a victim. Don't be afraid; be ready.

Look after yourself!

GEOFF THOMPSON

DEAD
OR ALIVE

THE CHOICE IS YOURS

THE DEFINITIVE SELF-PROTECTION HANDBOOK

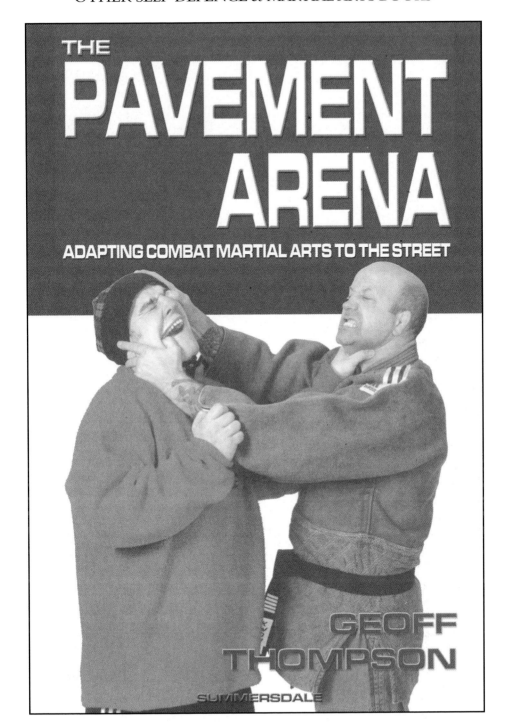

THE
PAVEMENT
ARENA

ADAPTING COMBAT MARTIAL ARTS TO THE STREET

GEOFF
THOMPSON

SUMMERSDALE

Foil Fencing

The techniques and tactics of modern foil fencing

Prof. John 'Jes' Smith

Foreword by
Keith A. Smith
President of the British Fencing Association

summersdale *sports*

KICK BOXING

A FRAMEWORK FOR SUCCESS

Pat O'Keeffe

SUMMERSDALE SPORT

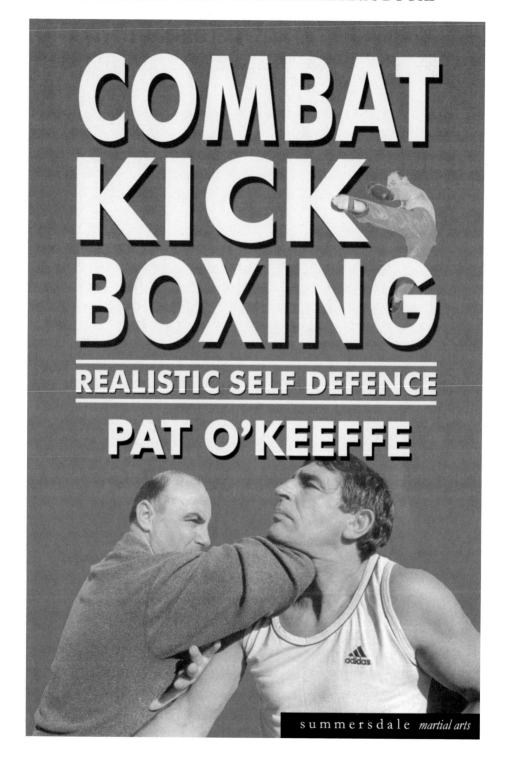

COMBAT KICK BOXING

REALISTIC SELF DEFENCE

PAT O'KEEFFE

summersdale *martial arts*

ADVANCED KICK BOXING

A FRAMEWORK FOR SUCCESS

PAT O'KEEFFE

summersdale *martial arts*

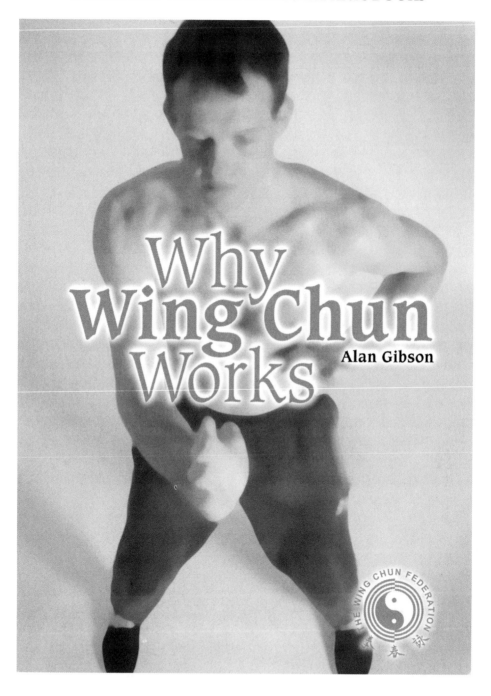

Why
Wing Chun
Works

Alan Gibson

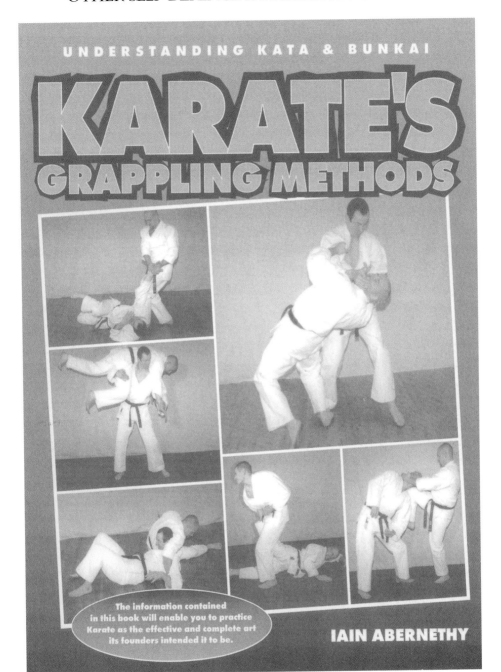

UNDERSTANDING KATA & BUNKAI

KARATE'S
GRAPPLING METHODS

The information contained in this book will enable you to practice Karate as the effective and complete art its founders intended it to be.

IAIN ABERNETHY

WWW.SUMMERSDALE.COM